Teach Yourself VISUALLY™

MacBook® Pro

W9-ATY-239

Visual™

Brad Miser

WILEY

John Wiley & Sons, Inc.

Teach Yourself VISUALLY™ MacBook® Pro

Published by
John Wiley & Sons, Inc.
10475 Crosspoint Boulevard
Indianapolis, IN 46256

www.wiley.com

Published simultaneously in Canada

Wiley publishes in a variety of print and electronic formats and by print-on-demand. Some material included with standard print versions of this book may not be included in e-books or in print-on-demand. If this book refers to media such as a CD or DVD that is not included in the version you purchased, you may download this material at http://booksupport.wiley.com. For more information about Wiley products, visit www.wiley.com.

Library of Congress Control Number: 2012949506

ISBN: 978-1-118-38327-8

Manufactured in the United States of America

10 9 8 7 6 5 4 3 2 1

Trademark Acknowledgments

Wiley, the Wiley logo, Visual, the Visual logo, Teach Yourself VISUALLY, Read Less - Learn More and related trade dress are trademarks or registered trademarks of John Wiley & Sons, Inc. and/or its affiliates. MacBook® is a registered trademark of Apple, Inc. All other trademarks are the property of their respective owners. John Wiley & Sons, Inc. is not associated with any product or vendor mentioned in this book. Teach Yourself VISUALLY™ MacBook® Pro is an independent publication and has not been authorized, sponsored, or otherwise approved by Apple, Inc.

Contact Us

For general information on our other products and services please contact our Customer Care Department within the U.S. at 877-762-2974, outside the U.S. at 317-572-3993 or fax 317-572-4002.

For technical support please visit www.wiley.com/techsupport.

WILEY   **Sales** | Contact Wiley at (877) 762-2974 or fax (317) 572-4002.

Credits

Acquisitions Editor
Aaron Black

Project Editor
Jade L. Williams

Technical Editor
Dennis Cohen

Copy Editor
Scott Tullis

Editorial Director
Robyn Siesky

Business Manager
Amy Knies

Senior Marketing Manager
Sandy Smith

**Vice President and Executive
Group Publisher**
Richard Swadley

**Vice President and Executive
Publisher**
Barry Pruett

Project Coordinator
Kristie Rees

Graphics and Production Specialists
Ana Carrillo
Carrie A. Cesavice
Ronda David-Burroughs
Jennifer Henry
Andrea Hornberger
Jennifer Mayberry

Quality Control Technician
Melissa Cossell

Proofreading
Sossity R. Smith

Indexing
BIM Indexing & Proofreading Services

About the Author

Brad Miser has written more than 50 books, with his favorite topics being anything related to Macintosh computers. In addition to *Teach Yourself VISUALLY MacBook Pro*, Brad has written *MacBook Pro Portable Genius*, and *iPhoto '11 Portable Genius*. He has also been a co-author, development editor, or technical editor on more than 50 other titles.

In addition to his passion for silicon-based technology, Brad enjoys steel-based technology, riding his motorcycle whenever and wherever possible. A native of California, Brad now lives in Indiana with his wife Amy; their three daughters, Jill, Emily, and Grace; a rabbit named Bun-Bun; and a sometimes-inside cat.

Brad would love to hear about your experiences with this book (the good, the bad, and the ugly). You can write to him at bradmiser@me.com.

Author's Acknowledgments

While my name is on the cover, it takes many people to build a book like this one. Thanks to Stephanie McComb who made this project possible and allowed me to be involved. Jade Williams deserves extra credit for leading me through the details; I'm sure working with me was a challenge at times. Dennis Cohen did a great job of keeping me on my toes to make sure this book contains fewer technical gaffes than it would have without his help. Scott Tullis transformed my stumbling text into something people can read and understand. And to the rest of the many great Wiley people involved in the production and sales of this book, I say thanks!

On my personal team, I'd like to thank my wife Amy for her tolerance of the author lifestyle, which can be both odd and challenging. My delightful daughters Jill, Emily, and Grace are always a source of joy and inspiration for all that I do, for which I'm ever grateful.

How to Use This Book

Who This Book Is For

This book is for the reader who has never used this particular technology or software application. It is also for readers who want to expand their knowledge.

The Conventions in This Book

① Steps

This book uses a step-by-step format to guide you easily through each task. **Numbered steps** are actions you must do; **bulleted steps** clarify a point, step, or optional feature; and **indented steps** give you the result.

② Notes

Notes give additional information — special conditions that may occur during an operation, a situation that you want to avoid, or a cross-reference to a related area of the book.

③ Icons and Buttons

Icons and buttons show you exactly what you need to click to perform a step.

④ Tips

Tips offer additional information, including warnings and shortcuts.

⑤ Bold

Bold type shows command names or options that you must click or text or numbers you must type.

⑥ Italics

Italic type introduces and defines a new term.

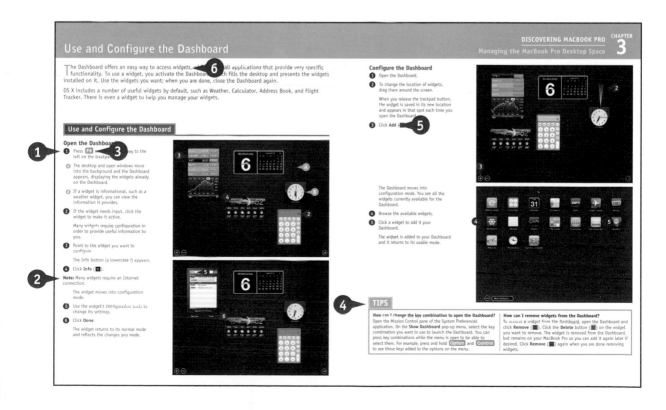

Table of Contents

Part I Discovering MacBook Pro

Chapter 1 Exploring MacBook Pro

Tour MacBook Pro 4

Start Up and Log In 8

Explore the OS X Desktop 10

Point and Click, Double-Click, or Secondary Click 14

Understand Disks, Volumes, Optical Discs, Folders,
  and Files 16

Configure the Keyboard 18

Configure the Trackpad 20

Sleep, Log Out, Restart, or Shut Down 22

Chapter 2 Looking Through the OS X Finder Windows

Understand Finder, Application, and Document
  Windows 24

View Finder Windows in Icon View 26

View Finder Windows in List View 28

View Finder Windows in Column View 30

View Finder Windows in Cover Flow View 32

Configure the Sidebar 33

Use the Action Pop-up Menu and Quick Look 34

Configure the Finder Window Toolbar 35

Chapter 3   Managing the MacBook Pro Desktop Space

Understand Desktop Management Tools...................... 36

Use and Configure the Dock..................................... 38

Manage the Desktop with Mission Control.................. 40

Configure and Use Mission Control and Desktops 42

Manage Open Windows with Mission Control 46

Use and Configure the Dashboard............................. 48

Work with Notifications and the Notification Center.... 52

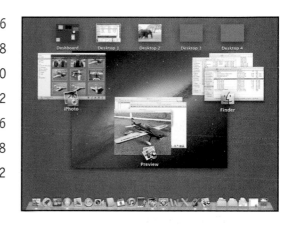

Chapter 4   Working on the Mac Desktop

Move to Locations on the Desktop............................. 56

Rename Files and Folders 58

Compress Files and Folders 59

Find Files, Folders, and Other Information 60

Create Smart Folders... 64

Get Information About Files and Folders..................... 66

Store Files and Folders on CDs or DVDs 68

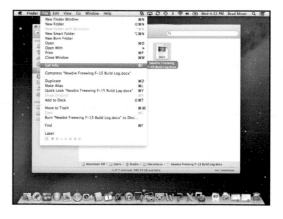

Table of Contents

| Chapter 5 | Working with Mac Applications |

Understand Applications and Documents 72

Install Applications with the App Store Application 74

Install Applications from the Desktop 76

Launch Applications with the Launchpad................... 78

Launch Applications from the Desktop 80

Control Applications... 82

Save Documents 84

Work with Versions of Documents........................... 86

Expand an Application to Full Screen Mode 88

Working with Multiple Application Windows.............. 89

| Chapter 6 | Personalizing MacBook Pro |

Set Finder Preferences 90

Explore the System Preferences Application 92

Change General Preferences................................... 94

Set a Desktop Picture 96

Choose a Screen Saver 98

Set and Configure the Clock................................... 100

Save Energy 102

Configure the Display 104

Control Sound 106

Create and Configure User Accounts........................ 108

Protect Users with Parental Controls 112

Set Login Options 114

Create Mail, Contacts, and Calendar Accounts............ 116

Part II Getting Connected

Chapter 7 Connecting to a Network and the Internet

Understanding Networking Concepts 120

Obtain an Internet Account 124

Set Up a Local Network 126

Protect MacBook Pro from Internet Attacks 130

Connect to the Internet with Wi-Fi 132

Connect to the Internet with Ethernet 134

Use AirDrop to Share Files 136

Share Files on a Local Network 138

Share Screens on a Local Network 142

Troubleshoot an Internet Connection 144

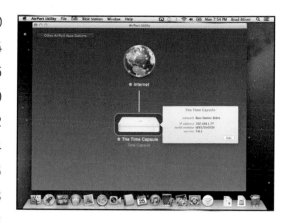

Chapter 8 Connecting MacBook Pro to Other Devices

Expand Storage Space with an External Hard Drive 146

Connect and Use an External Display 150

Use an Apple TV to Display on an HDTV 152

Connect and Use a Bluetooth Mouse 154

Connect and Use a Bluetooth Keyboard 156

Connect and Use External Speakers 158

Connect To and Use a USB Hub 160

Connect To and Use Ethernet Devices 161

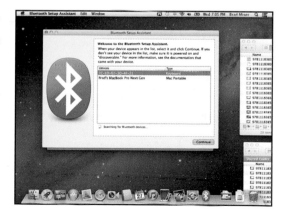

Table of Contents

| Chapter 9 | Traveling with MacBook Pro |

Connect to the Internet with Wi-Fi 162

Connect to the Internet with an AirPort Express
Base Station 164

Connect to the Internet with a Broadband
Wireless Modem 166

Manage Your MacBook Pro's Power 168

Protect Your Data with FileVault 170

Protect MacBook Pro with General Security 172

Protect Your MacBook Pro with Its Firewall 173

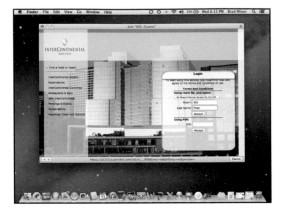

| Part III | Using the Internet |

| Chapter 10 | Using iCloud Online Services |

Explore iCloud 176

Obtain and Configure an iCloud Account 178

Work with Your iCloud Website 180

Synchronize Information Among Multiple Devices 182

Use iCloud Photo Stream 184

Use iCloud to Store Documents Online 186

Chapter 11   Surfing the Web

Explore Safari...188

Navigate to Websites..190

Search the Web 194

Download Files..196

Browse the Web with Tabs.................................198

Set and Organize Bookmarks.............................200

Use and Set Top Sites.......................................204

Open Several Web Pages at the Same Time................206

Watch Movies on the Web 208

Use AutoFill to Quickly Complete Web Forms 209

Save or Share Web Pages...................................210

Use the Reading List 212

Set Safari Preferences.......................................214

Chapter 12   E-Mailing with Mail

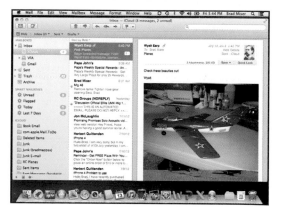

Explore Mail..216

Set Up E-Mail Accounts....................................218

Read and Reply to E-Mail 220

Send E-Mail...222

Work with Files Attached to E-Mail 224

Attach Files to E-Mail.......................................225

Organize E-Mail 226

Search E-Mail 228

Avoid Spam...230

Create and Use E-Mail Signatures 232

Create E-Mail Rules 234

Set Mail Preferences...236

Table of Contents

| Chapter 13 | Communicating in Real Time |

Chat with FaceTime 238
Explore Messages 240
Configure Messages Accounts...........................242
Chat with Text...244
Chat with Audio...246
Chat with Video...248
Add Effects and Backgrounds to Video Chats............250
Present Documents with Theater 251
Share Desktops with Others...............................252
Communicate with Twitter.................................254

Part IV Going Further with MacBook Pro

| Chapter 14 | Printing on Paper or Electronically |

Understanding Printers 258
Install and Configure a USB Printer 260
Install and Configure a Network Printer...................262
Print to Paper 264
Print to PDF..266

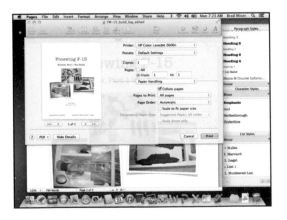

Chapter 15	Managing Contacts

Explore the Contacts Window 268

Add a Contact Manually 270

Work with vCards 272

Find Contact Information 274

Create an Address Group 276

Use Address Cards and Groups................................278

Change or Delete Address Cards or Groups.............280

Print Envelopes and Contact Lists...........................282

Chapter 16	Managing Calendars

Explore Calendar...284

Create a Calendar..285

Add an Event to a Calendar 286

Schedule and Manage Events with Other People.......288

Share Calendars 290

Working with Shared Calendars 292

Configure Calendar Preferences 294

Print Calendars..296

Explore Reminders...298

Create a Reminder...299

Table of Contents

Chapter 17	Maintaining a MacBook Pro and Solving Problems

Keep App Store Software Current 300

Maintain and Update Applications Not from the
App Store 302

Profile Your MacBook Pro 303

Monitor Your MacBook Pro Activity 304

Maintain or Repair the Drive on Your MacBook Pro 306

Back Up with Time Machine and an External
Hard Drive 308

Back Up Wirelessly with a Time Capsule 312

Restore Files with Time Machine 314

Troubleshoot and Solve MacBook Pro Problems 316

Capture a Screenshot 320

Get Help with MacBook Pro Problems 321

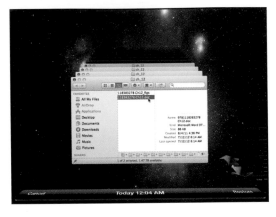

Chapter 18	Enjoying Music and Video with iTunes

Explore iTunes 322

Explore the iTunes Store 324

Obtain an iTunes Store Account 325

Understanding the iTunes Library 326

Browse or Search for iTunes Content 328

Browse the Library with Cover Flow View 330

Browse the Library with Grid View 331

Listen to Audio Content 332

Watch Movies and TV Shows 333

Add Audio CD Content to the iTunes Library 334

Buy Music, TV, Movies, and More from the
   iTunes Store 336

Subscribe and Listen to Podcasts............................ 342

Copy iTunes Content from Other Computers onto
   Your MacBook Pro 344

Create a Genius Playlist 346

Create a Standard Playlist 348

Create a Smart Playlist.. 350

| Chapter 19 | Using a MacBook Pro with iPhones, iPods, and iPads |

Understanding How iOS Devices Work with a
   MacBook Pro.. 352

Use iTunes to Move Music onto an iPhone, iPod,
   or iPad 354

Use iTunes to Manage Apps and Home Screens on
   an iOS Device 356

Use Photo Stream to Synchronize Photos on
   iOS Devices 358

Use iCloud to Synchronize Documents on
   iOS Devices 359

Index... 360

PART I

Discovering MacBook Pro

The MacBook Pro might be one of the best laptops ever. It combines outstanding capabilities with well-conceived design, creating a computer that is powerful, reliable, and distinctive. Your MacBook Pro is capable and intuitive, and its compact size makes it an ideal companion. In this part, you learn fundamentals to guide you on your journey of discovery toward MacBook Pro mastery.

Chapter 1: Exploring MacBook Pro. 4

Chapter 2: Looking Through the OS X Finder Windows . . . 24

Chapter 3: Managing the MacBook Pro Desktop Space . . . 36

Chapter 4: Working on the Mac Desktop. 56

Chapter 5: Working with Mac Applications. 72

Chapter 6: Personalizing MacBook Pro. 90

Tour MacBook Pro

MacBook Pros are elegantly designed and are relatively simple and easy to use. But do not let that fool you: They are also very powerful and extremely capable computers that can do just about anything you want them to. Here you can learn about the MacBook Pro's major features from the outside, including its controls, ports, and other areas that you use to control your MacBook Pro and to connect it to other devices. The various models of MacBook Pros have slightly different features; for example, the Retina versions do not have a built-in DVD drive.

MacBook Pro

A Display

The MacBook's display provides a sharp, bright, and colorful view into all that you do.

B Camera

Use the built-in camera to video-conference, take photos, and more.

C Keyboard

Along with the standard letter and number keys, you have function keys to control your MacBook.

D Trackpad

Enables you to manipulate objects on the screen using finger gestures. The entire trackpad is also the button that you click or double-click.

E Ports

Connect MacBook to other devices, such as hard drives, external displays, iPods, and so on.

F Sleep Indicator Light

Pulses when MacBook is asleep, glows solid when MacBook is on but its display is dimmed.

G Disc Drive

Use or burn CDs and DVDs.

MacBook Pro Keyboard

Ⓐ Brightness

Press **F1** to decrease your screen's brightness or **F2** to increase it.

Ⓑ Mission Control

Press **F3** to open Mission Control so you can quickly move between working spaces.

Ⓒ Launchpad

Press **F4** to open or close the Launchpad.

Ⓓ Keyboard Backlight Brightness

Press **F5** to decrease the brightness of the keyboard backlighting, or press **F6** to increase it.

Ⓔ Previous/Rewind

Press **F7** to move to the previous item or rewind in iTunes and other applications.

Ⓕ Play/Pause

Press **F8** to play or pause iTunes and other applications.

Ⓖ Next/Fast Forward

Press **F9** to move to the next item or fast-forward in iTunes and other applications.

Ⓗ Volume

F10 mutes the MacBook Pro, **F11** turns the volume down, and **F12** turns it up.

Ⓘ Eject (Non-Retina Models)

Press to eject a CD, DVD, iPod, or other mounted device.

Ⓙ Power Button (Retina Models)

Press to turn MacBook Pro on; press and hold to force MacBook Pro to turn off. (On non-Retina models, the Power button is located toward the display and to the right of the Eject button.)

Ⓚ Alternate Function Key

Hold down while pressing a function key to perform the alternate task.

Ⓛ Modifier Keys

Press to invoke keyboard shortcuts.

Ⓜ Scroll Keys

Press to move around the screen.

continued ▶

A MacBook Pro includes the ports you need to connect to other devices, such as external displays, speakers, iPhones, iPads, iPods, disk drives, and more. The specific port you use for any task depends on the devices to which you are connecting your MacBook Pro. And some devices have options; for example, you can use USB or Thunderbolt depending on the kind of drive you are connecting.

The Retina and non-Retina models have different types and numbers of ports, but you can identify the ports on either type using the illustrations in this section.

MacBook Pro Ports Retina Models

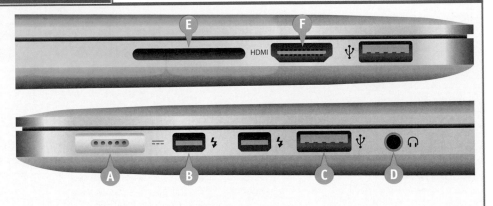

Ⓐ Power Adapter

Connect the MacBook Pro to power.

Ⓑ Thunderbolt

Use these high-speed ports to connect to Thunderbolt hard drives and Apple external displays.

Ⓒ USB

Connect USB devices, such as iPods, iPhones, iPads, and disk drives. The ports support USB 1.1, 2, and 3 versions.

Ⓓ Analog/Digital Audio In/Out

Connect headphones or analog speakers or use a TOSLINK adapter to connect for digital audio, such as with surround-sound speakers. Connect microphones or other sound input devices to use the audio they provide.

Ⓔ SDXC Card

You can insert SDXC (Secure Digital eXtended Capacity) and other types of SD cards here so you can store files.

Ⓕ HDMI

Use this port to connect your MacBook Pro to displays or projectors that use the HDMI (High-Definition Multimedia Interface) interface.

MacBook Pro Ports Non-Retina Models

Ⓐ Power Adapter

Connect the MacBook Pro to power.

Ⓑ Ethernet

Connect the MacBook Pro to an Ethernet network.

Ⓒ FireWire 800

Use these high-speed ports to connect to external hard drives and other devices.

Ⓓ Thunderbolt

Use these high-speed ports to connect to Thunderbolt hard drives and Apple external displays.

Ⓔ USB

Connect USB devices, such as iPods, iPhones, iPads, and disk drives. The ports support USB 1.1, 2, and 3 standards.

Ⓕ SDXC Card

You can insert SDXC (Secure Digital eXtended Capacity) and other types of SD cards here so you can store files.

Ⓖ Analog/Digital Audio In/ Out (13-Inch)

Connect headphones or analog speakers or use a TOSLINK adapter to connect for digital audio, such as with surround-sound speakers. Connect microphones or other sound input devices to use the audio they provide.

Ⓗ Analog/Digital Audio In

Connect microphones or other sound input devices to use the audio they provide.

Ⓘ Analog/Digital Audio Out

Connect headphones or analog speakers or use a TOSLINK adapter to connect for digital audio, such as with surround-sound speakers.

Ⓙ Battery Status Lights

Press the button to see lights corresponding to the status of your battery (more lights equals a higher charge in the battery).

Start Up and Log In

Starting a MacBook Pro is not much of a challenge. After you turn it on, you might also need to log in to start using it. That is because OS X supports multiple user accounts so that each person who uses the computer can have his or her own resources. You created at least one user account when you first turned on your MacBook Pro. The automatic login feature bypasses the login process. If it is not turned on, you need to know a username and password to be able to log in to a user account.

Start Up and Log In

Start Up

1 Open MacBook Pro by lifting its lid.

2 Press the **Power** button.

The MacBook Pro turns on and starts the boot process and you see the Apple logo and the processing "spinning" wheel on-screen. When the startup process is complete, you see the Login window if automatic login is turned off or the OS X desktop if automatic login is turned on.

If the Login window appears, it has either a list of user accounts or empty username and password fields. Each option requires slightly different steps to log in.

Log In with the User List

1 Start up the MacBook Pro.

The Login window appears, showing a list of user accounts on the MacBook Pro.

2 Slide your finger over the trackpad until the pointer is over the appropriate user account.

3 Press the trackpad.

Note: To click the trackpad button, just press down once on the trackpad; the whole trackpad is a button.

The Password field appears.

4 Type the password for the user account.

5 Press **Return**.

You log in to the user account and the OS X desktop appears.

Log In with a Username

1 Start up the MacBook Pro.

The Login window appears, showing the Name and Password fields.

2 Type the name of the user account in the Name field.

3 Type the password for the account in the Password field.

4 Press **Return**.

You log in to the user account and the OS X desktop appears.

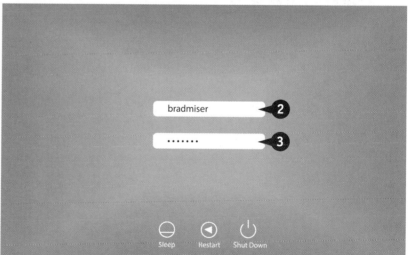

TIPS

What if I forget my password?

If you enter a password incorrectly, the Login screen shudders when you try to log in. This lets you know that the password you provided does not work. Try entering it again. If that does not help, click **Forgot Password** and a password hint appears on the screen if a hint was configured for your account. If you still cannot log in, try a different user account.

What kind of user accounts are there?

OS X supports several types of user accounts. An Administrator account enables you to configure the system; the first user account you created during the first time you started your MacBook Pro is an Administrator account. Standard accounts cannot access very many of the configuration tools and can be limited even further to specific applications or documents. Guest accounts also have limited access to the system.

Explore the OS X Desktop

Your MacBook Pro operates through the OS X operating system, which is currently in version 10.8 Mountain Lion. The Macintosh operating system has long been known for being very intuitive and is also pleasing to look at. It was the first major system interface to focus on graphical elements, such as icons.

The OS X desktop is the overall window through which you view all that happens on MacBook Pro, such as looking at the contents of folders, working on documents, and surfing the web.

OS X Desktop

A Menu Bar

A menu bar usually appears at the top of the screen so that you can access the commands it contains. (This is sometimes hidden in certain situations.)

B Drives

The MacBook Pro stores its data, including the software it needs to work, on hard drives or on a flash drive. It includes one internal drive, but you can also connect external drives.

C SuperDrive

On a non-Retina model, you can read from and write to DVDs or CDs using the SuperDrive. For a Retina model, you can connect to an external SuperDrive or use Remote Disc.

D Folders

Containers that you use to organize files and other folders stored on MacBook Pro.

E Files

Documents (such as text, graphics, movies, and songs), applications, or other sources of data.

F Finder Windows

You view the contents of drives, folders, and other objects in Finder windows.

G Application and Document Windows

When you use applications, you use the windows that those applications present, for documents, web pages, games, and so on.

Finder Menu Bar and Menus

Ⓐ Apple Menu

This menu is always visible so that you can access special commands, such as Shut Down and Log Out.

Ⓑ Finder Menu

This is where you control the Finder application itself, such as to empty the Trash or set preferences.

Ⓒ File Menu

Use commands on this menu to work with files and Finder windows.

Ⓓ Edit Menu

This menu is not as useful in the Finder as it is in other applications, but here you can undo what you have done or copy and paste information.

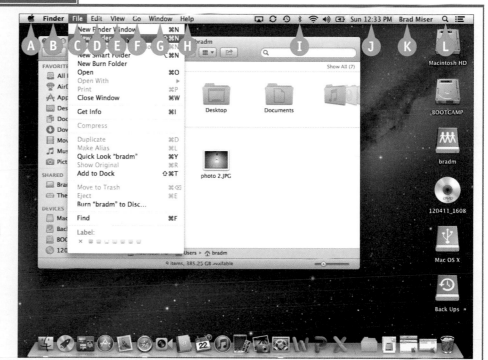

Ⓔ View Menu

Enables you to determine how you view the desktop; it is especially useful for choosing Finder window views.

Ⓕ Go Menu

Takes you to various places, such as specific folders.

Ⓖ Window Menu

Enables you to work with open Finder windows.

Ⓗ Help Menu

Use when you need help with OS X or the other applications.

Ⓘ Configurable Menus

You can configure the menu bar to include specific menus, such as AirPlay, Volume, Wi-Fi, Battery, and many more.

Ⓙ Clock

Here you see the current time and day.

Ⓚ Fast User Switching

Enables you to change user accounts and open the Login window.

Ⓛ Spotlight Menu

Enables you to search for information on the MacBook Pro.

continued ▶

The Finder application controls the OS X desktop, and so you see its menu bar whenever you work with this application. When you view the contents of a folder, you do so through a Finder window. There are many ways to view the contents of a Finder window, such as the Icon or List view. The Sidebar enables you to quickly navigate around the desktop and to open files and folders with a single click. The Dock and Sidebar on the desktop enable you to access items quickly and easily.

Finder Windows

A Close Button

Click to close a window.

B Minimize Button

Click to shrink a window and move it onto the Dock.

C Zoom Button

Click to expand a Finder window to the maximum size needed or possible; click it again to return to the previous size.

D Window Title

The name of the location whose contents you see in the window.

E Toolbar

Contains tools you use to work with files and folders.

F Search Bar

Use this tool to find files, folders, and other information.

G Sidebar

Enables you to quickly access devices, folders, and files, as well as searches you have saved.

H Files and Folders

Within a window, the contents of a location are shown; this example shows the Icon view.

I Status Bar

Shows information about the current location, such as the amount of free space when you are viewing the MacBook Pro's drive.

J Resize Handle

Drag this corner to change the size of a window.

K Path Bar

Shows the path to the location of the folder being displayed in the window.

Dock and Sidebar

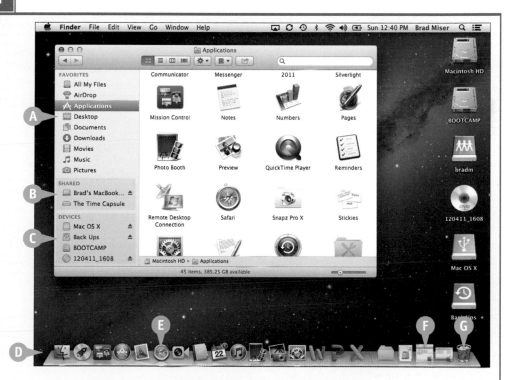

Ⓐ Favorites

Files, folders, searches, and other items that you can open by clicking them.

Ⓑ Shared

Computers and other resources being shared on a network.

Ⓒ Devices

Contains your internal drive, a DVD or CD, external hard drives, and other devices that your MacBook Pro can access.

Ⓓ Dock

Shows applications, files, and folders you can access with a single click along with applications currently running.

Ⓔ Applications

Icons on the left side of the Dock are for applications; open applications have a glowing dot under their icon with that preference set.

Ⓕ Files, Folders, and Minimized Windows

Icons on the right side of the Dock are for files, folders, and minimized windows (the default Dock includes the Downloads folder for files you download from the Internet along with your Documents folder).

Ⓖ Trash/Eject

Items you delete go here (to get rid of them, empty the Trash); when you select an ejectable device, such as a DVD, this becomes the Eject icon.

Point and Click, Double-Click, or Secondary Click

If you logged in using the earlier steps, you know the basics of using the trackpad. This is a fundamental skill and bears repeating here. To tell the MacBook Pro what you want to do, point the on-screen pointer to the object that you want to work with by sliding a finger over the trackpad.

After you point to something, you tell the computer what you want to do with it. You do this by pressing the trackpad down to click it. This is referred to as clicking the trackpad. The number of times and how you click it determine what happens to what you are pointing at.

Point and Click, Double-Click, or Secondary Click

Point and Click

① Slide your finger on the trackpad until the pointer points at something you want to work with, such as the icon of a file or folder.

② Press the trackpad once to click the trackpad, which is a single click.

The object is highlighted to indicate that it is now selected.

Double-Click

① Slide your finger on the trackpad until the pointer points at something you want to work with, such as a file's or folder's icon.

② Click the trackpad twice.

Your selection opens.

Point, Click, and Drag

① Slide your finger on the trackpad until the pointer points at something you want to move, such as a file's or folder's icon.

② Press down the trackpad and hold it.

The object at which you were pointing becomes attached to the arrow and remains so until you release the trackpad.

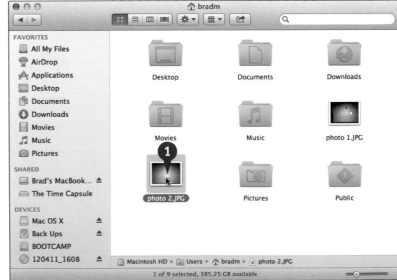

③ Drag your finger on the trackpad to move the object.

④ When you get to the object's new position, release the trackpad.

The object is moved or copied to the new location.

Note: Dragging something to a different hard drive, flash drive, or disk volume copies it there. Changing its location on the same disk moves it instead.

Secondary Click

① Point to an object on the desktop or even the desktop itself.

Note: To select more than one item at the same time, press and hold ⌘ while you click each item you want to select.

② Press and hold **Control**.

③ Click the trackpad.

A contextual menu appears. It is called a contextual menu because the commands appearing on it depend on what you are pointing to.

④ Choose a command on the resulting menu by pointing to it and clicking the trackpad once.

 TIP

Why do things I click stick to the arrow?
You can configure the trackpad so you can drag things without having to hold down the trackpad. When this setting is on and you click something, it gets attached to the pointer. When you move the pointer, the object moves too. To configure this setting, see "Configure the Trackpad."

15

Understand Disks, Volumes, Optical Discs, Folders, and Files

As you use your MacBook Pro, you work with data. Underlying all this data is the need to store and organize it. The major items that MacBook Pro uses for storing and organizing data are described in this section.

These items include disks, volumes, discs, folders, and files. The Finder manages these items, and you access them directly from the desktop or from within applications. You can use different types of devices for different purposes. For example, you can use an external hard drive to back up the data stored on your MacBook Pro.

Drive

A drive is one type of physical device that you use to store data. Drives come in different types. The MacBook Pro has one internal drive that contains the software it needs to work, applications you install, and documents you create. You can connect external disk drives to expand the available storage room. Disks are represented on MacBook Pro with icons that look different to represent different kinds of drives (internal versus external, for example).

Volume

A volume is an area of a disk created using software rather than a physical space. A drive can be partitioned into multiple volumes, where each volume acts like a separate drive. A volume performs the same task as a drive, which is to store data. You can access volumes being shared with you over a network. Volumes are used to organize data in different ways and to represent various resources you work with.

Optical Discs

CDs and DVDs serve many purposes. Examples abound, including listening to audio CDs, watching DVD movies and TV shows, and installing applications stored on a CD or DVD. You can also put your own data on CD or DVD, such as burning audio CDs with iTunes and backing up your data on DVD. Some MacBook Pros have a slot-loading disc drive located on their right side; if yours does not have an internal drive, you can connect an external one.

Folders

Like manila folders in the physical world, folders on a MacBook Pro are a means to organize things, such as files and even other folders. OS X includes many folders by default, including Music, Pictures, Documents, and so on. You can create, name, delete, and organize folders in any way you see fit (mostly any way — some folders you cannot or should not change). You open a folder in a Finder window to view its contents.

Files

A file is a container for data. Files can contain many different kinds of data. For example, some files are documents, such as text documents you create with a word processor. Files can also be images, songs, movies, and other kinds of content. Files also make up the operating system that runs MacBook Pro; you typically do not interact with system files directly. Files have names that include filename extensions, such as .jpg and .doc, and are represented by icons in Finder windows and e-mail attachments. Icons show a preview of what the file contains in their thumbnail image.

meteor.jpg

Configure the Keyboard

Obviously, using a MacBook Pro is a hands-on experience. One of your primary inputs is the keyboard, through which you issue commands, add content to documents, send and receive e-mail, and so on. You can configure the keyboard to work the way you want it to.

You use the Keyboard pane of the System Preferences application to configure your keyboard. For example, you can set keyboard shortcuts for commands so you can activate the command by pressing a combination of keys.

Configure the Keyboard

Configure Keyboard Settings

1. Click **Apple** (🍎) and select **System Preferences** from the menu.

2. Click **Keyboard**.

3. Click the **Keyboard** tab.

4. Drag the **Key Repeat** slider to the right to increase the number of times a character repeats when you press and hold a key.

5. Drag the **Delay Until Repeat** slider to the right to increase the amount of time you have to press and hold a key for its letter or number to repeat.

6. If you want the built-in functions to act as normal function keys, click the **Use all F1, F2, etc. keys as standard function keys** check box.

7. To have the backlight dim or brighten automatically, click the **Adjust keyboard brightness in low light** check box.

8. Drag the slider to set how long the backlight remains on when you are not using the computer.

9. Click the **Show Keyboard & Character Viewers in menu bar** check box to show the Keyboard and Character Viewers through the Input menu.

10. Click **Modifier Keys**.

11. In the Modifier Keys dialog, click the pop-up menus to select the key presses associated with the various modifier keys.

12. Click **OK** for your changes to take effect and the sheet to close.

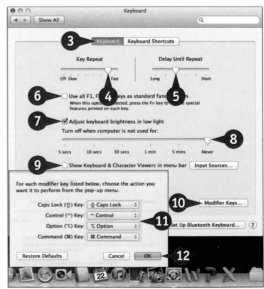

Configure Keyboard Shortcuts

1. Click the **Keyboard Shortcuts** tab.

2. Click a category.

3. Uncheck a shortcut's check box to disable it.

4. To change the keys used for any shortcut, select the current shortcut and then press the new keyboard combination you want to use.

5. To add a new keyboard shortcut, click the **Application Shortcuts** category and then click **Add** (⊞).

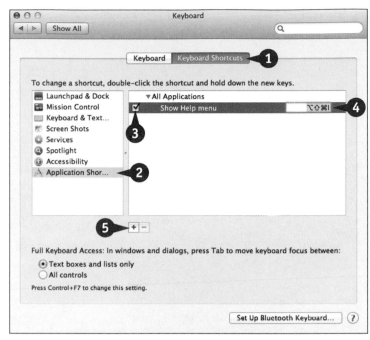

6. On the Application menu on the New Shortcut sheet, choose the application to which the shortcut applies, or choose **All Applications** to have it impact all of them.

7. Type the name of the command in the Menu Title field; you must type the name exactly as it appears on the menu.

8. Click in the **Keyboard Shortcut** field and type a key combination.

9. Click **Add**.

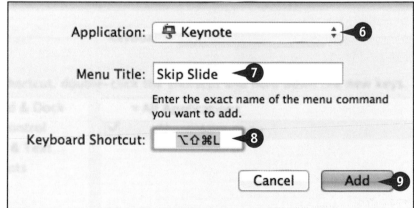

TIPS

How can I see the new keyboard shortcuts I have created?
On the Keyboard Shortcuts tab, select the **Application Shortcuts** section. Then expand the All Applications section to see all application shortcuts, or expand a specific application, such as Microsoft Word, to see the shortcuts created only for that application.

How do I get back to the original shortcuts?
Move to the Keyboard Shortcuts tab, select any category but Application Shortcuts, and click the **Restore Defaults** button to set all keyboard shortcuts as they were when you first started your MacBook Pro. You lose any changes you have made over time, so if you want to reset only a couple of shortcuts, just change those back to what you want them to be.

Configure the Trackpad

The other primary control MacBook Pro has is its trackpad. At its most basic, you can use the trackpad to move the pointer on the screen by dragging your finger around the trackpad. As discussed earlier, you also click the trackpad to perform various actions, such as to select a command on a menu.

However, you can do a lot more with the trackpad than just moving the pointer and clicking. You can also configure it so that you can scroll in windows, rotate objects, and much more with various gestures using up to four fingers.

Configure the Trackpad

① Click **Apple** (🍎) and select **System Preferences**.

② Click **Trackpad**.

③ Click the **Point & Click** tab.

You see the settings for gestures related to pointing and clicking.

④ Point to one of the gestures.

Ⓐ A video demonstrating how the gesture works plays in the Preview pane. You see the gesture in the lower part of the pane and its effect in the upper part of the pane. These videos are very helpful when learning about gestures.

5 To use a gesture, click its check box.

6 If the gesture has a menu associated with it, open the menu and configure the additional options.

7 Repeat steps **5** and **6** until you have configured the point and click gestures you want to use.

Note: OS X is designed to take advantage of gestures on the trackpad so it is worth your time to explore all the options and adjust them over time to make using your MacBook Pro even more efficient.

8 Drag the **Tracking Speed** slider to the right to cause the pointer to move more for the same amount of finger movement, or to the left to cause it to move less for the same finger movement.

9 Click the **Scroll & Zoom** tab.

10 Set the scroll and zoom gestures.

11 Click the **More Gestures** tab.

12 Set the additional gestures you want to use.

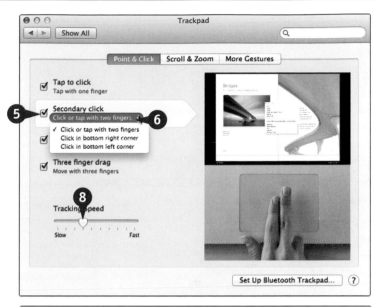

TIPS

How can I use a mouse with MacBook Pro?
You can connect any Mac-compatible USB mouse to your MacBook Pro. You can also use a Bluetooth mouse; see Chapter 8 for the steps to configure and use a Bluetooth mouse. When a mouse is connected, use the Mouse pane of the System Preferences application to configure it.

How do I drag things with a gesture on the trackpad?
You can use the method described earlier, but it is even easier to enable the Three finger drag preference on the Point & Click tab. With this enabled, you can touch the trackpad with three fingers while you are pointing to what you want to move. As you move your fingers on the trackpad, the object moves on the screen. When it is in its new position, lift your fingers off the trackpad.

Sleep, Log Out, Restart, or Shut Down

There are several ways to stop using your MacBook Pro. Most of the time, you either put it to sleep or log out. During sleep, everything you had open remains open, but the MacBook Pro goes into low-power mode; you can wake it up to quickly get back to whatever you were doing. When you log out, all open documents and applications close and you return to the Log In screen. When you want to turn the MacBook Pro off, you shut down. There also may be times when you want to restart the MacBook Pro.

Sleep, Log Out, Restart, or Shut Down

Sleep or Log Out

1. Click **Apple** () to open the menu.

2. Scroll down by dragging on the trackpad until **Sleep** or **Log Out** **Account Name** (where *Account Name* is your user account name) is highlighted.

3. Click the trackpad.

   If you selected Sleep, most activity on the computer stops.

Note: You can put MacBook Pro to sleep even faster by simply closing its lid.

If you selected Log Out, the Log Out confirmation dialog appears.

4. If you want all your open documents, Finder windows, and applications to open again when you log back in, click the **Reopen windows when logging back in** check box.

5. Click **Log Out**.

   All applications and documents close, and the Log In screen appears.

Note: A faster way to log out is to press [Option]+[⌘]+[Shift]+[Q].

Restart or Shut Down

1 Click **Apple** (🍎) to open the menu.

2 Drag down the trackpad until **Restart** or **Shut Down** is highlighted.

3 Click the trackpad.

Depending on which option you chose, the appropriate confirmation dialog appears.

4 If you want all your open documents, Finder windows, and applications to open again when the computer restarts (whether you choose Restart or Shut Down), click the **Reopen windows when logging back in** check box.

5 To restart MacBook Pro, click **Restart**.

MacBook Pro shuts down and then starts up again. If you selected the Reopen option, all the windows you had open are restored.

6 To shut down MacBook Pro, click **Shut Down**.

MacBook Pro turns off.

Note: You can also perform the steps in this section by pressing the Power button. The dialog that appears contains Restart, Sleep, and Shut Down buttons. Click a button to perform that action.

TIPS

How often should I turn my MacBook Pro off?
Just putting it to sleep is usually better than shutting down. When you want to use it again, wake it up and it is ready in just a few seconds. If you will not be using the MacBook Pro for an extended period of time and it is not connected to the power adapter, shutting it down so the battery does not get completely drained is better.

How can I protect my information when I need to step away from the MacBook Pro?
If you leave your MacBook Pro where other people can get to it, log out. Everything you had open closes and you return to the Login screen. When you want to use it again, you can quickly log back in. Later, you can learn how to set MacBook Pro so it automatically locks to protect it when you are not actively using it.

Understand Finder, Application, and Document Windows

Like windows in the physical world, windows on your MacBook Pro enable to you to view objects on-screen, such as folders, files, applications, and documents. If you learn to work with windows efficiently, you can accomplish tasks you want to do more quickly and easily.

In OS X, most windows have common elements no matter what application you are using. In some cases, particularly with games and utilities, you might not see familiar windows when you run those applications. Instead, you see windows specific to their function. Being comfortable with any kind of window you encounter is important.

Finder Windows

A Title

Shows the name of the drive, folder, or other location you are currently viewing.

B Toolbar

Contains tools to control windows, move among them, change views, and perform actions.

C Search Bar

Enables you to search for files or folders.

D Files and Folders

The contents of the drive, folder, or other location you are viewing appear within the main part of Finder windows.

E Sidebar

Contains icons for locations, files, and folders; you can click an icon to view its contents in the Finder window or to open an application or document.

F Status

Displays status information for what you are viewing, such as available disk space on the current drive.

G Scroll Bars

By default, shows you your position in a window while you scroll. The scroll bars appear when you hover over the scroll area.

H Resize Handle

Drag this handle to change the size and shape of a window in both directions at the same time.

I Size Slider (Icon View Only)

Drag to the left to make icons smaller or to the right to make them larger.

Application Windows

A Application Title

The name of the application itself or the name of one of its windows.

B Window Controls

Enable you to close, minimize, or zoom the window.

C Toolbar

Provides buttons and controls for specific actions in the application.

D Content

The main window of the application presents the content you can work with in the application, such as a document or website.

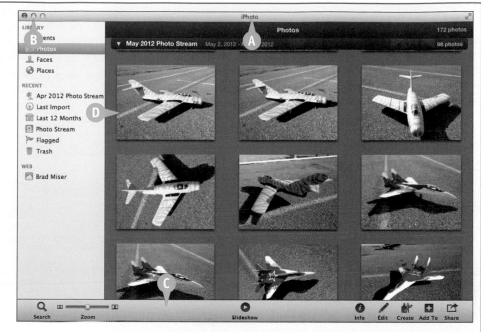

Document Windows

A Document Title

The name of the file being shown in the window.

B Scroll Bars

Enable you to move up, down, left, or right within a window to see all of its contents and show you your relative position in the document.

C Resize Handle

Drag the corner to resize the window in both directions at the same time.

D Application-Specific Tools

Most applications provide tools in their windows specific to the application.

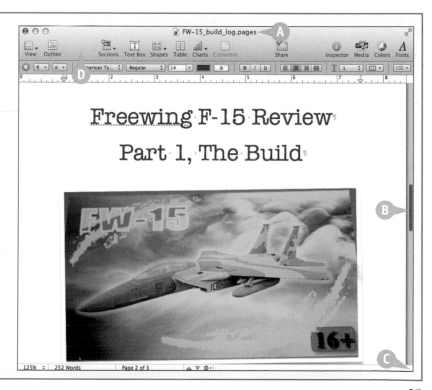

View Finder Windows in Icon View

I con view is the view synonymous with Mac computers. Icons are pleasing to look at and visually indicate the kind of object they represent, such as a file or folder. Although colorful, Icon view is not the most useful one, but it does have a few things to offer. This view is appealing because the icons themselves are pleasing to look at, and some icons are miniature works of art. You also have more control over how a window in Icon view looks because you can set the window's background color or use an image as the background.

View Finder Windows in Icon View

1 Click a folder in the Sidebar to view its content.

2 Click **Icon View** (⊞).

3 Drag the slider to the left or right to change the size of the icons.

4 Click **Arrange** (⊞▾) and select how you want the icons grouped.

The icons are grouped by the category you selected. (The options depend on the contents of specific folder you are viewing.)

5 Click **View** and then click **Show View Options**.

6 Click the **Always open in icon view** check box to have the folder always open in Icon view.

7 Click the **Browse in icon view** check box if you want folders in the current folder to appear in Icon view.

8 Click the **Arrange By** arrows and select an option by which to arrange items in the window.

9 Click the **Sort By** arrows and select an option by which to sort items in the window.

10 Drag the **Icon size** slider to increase or decrease the size of icons.

11 Drag the **Grid spacing** slider to decrease or increase the space between icons.

12 Click the **Text size** arrows and select the size of the text for icon labels.

13 Select a **Label position** option to place text labels on the bottom or right side of the icons.

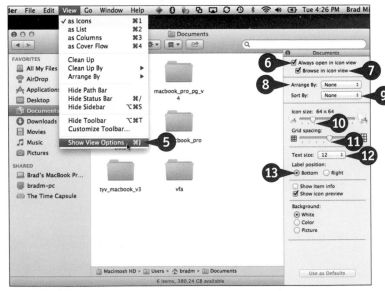

14 Click the **Show item info** check box to show additional information about items.

15 Click the **Show icon preview** check box to show a preview of items within the icon.

Note: Not all types of files support the preview function.

16 Click the **Color** option to use a background color.

17 Click the color button.

Ⓐ The color picker appears.

18 Select the color you want for the background.

19 Click **Close** (⬤).

Ⓑ The color picker closes and you move back to the window, which now has the color you selected as its background.

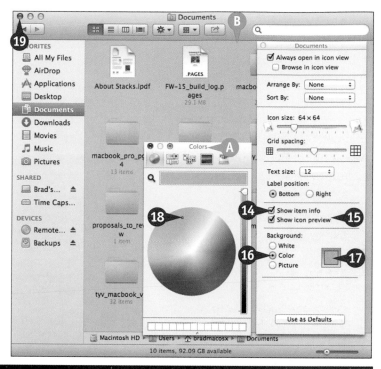

20 Click **Picture** to use an image as a background picture.

21 Drag an image file onto the image well.

Ⓒ The image is applied to the window's background.

22 Click **Use as Defaults** to have every window you open in Icon view use the current settings by default.

23 Click **Close** (⬤) to close the View Options dialog.

Where does a file's icon come from?
OS X automatically creates icons for some documents based on their content, and others get their icons from the associated application. For example, an image file's icon is a thumbnail view of the image, whereas a Word document's icon is a text file with the word "DOC" on it. Application files display the application's icon to make it easy to identify a file type.

How can I browse items when I have grouped them?
Items you group are placed in categories by the criterion you select, such as Size. If a particular group has more items than can be displayed, the remaining items appear in a fan on either side of the displayed items. Click either side to flip through the items.

View Finder Windows in List View

Icon view is visually appealing, but it does not provide a lot of information about the files and folders you see. In addition, even if you make the icons small, they take up a lot of room, making it harder to see all the contents of a Finder window.

List view may not look as nice as Icon view, but it does provide much more information. You can more easily sort the content in windows so that the items appear in the order you want. You can also select items stored in different folders at the same time.

View Finder Windows in List View

① Click a folder in the Sidebar.

② Click **List View** (☰).

③ Click the **View** menu and then click **Show View Options**.

④ Click the **Always open in list view** check box if you want the folder to always open in List view.

⑤ Click **Browse in list view** check box to cause all the folders within to display in List view too.

⑥ Click the **Arrange By** menu and choose how you want the items in the window grouped.

⑦ Click the **Sort By** menu and choose how you want items in the window to be sorted.

⑧ Select an **Icon size** option.

⑨ Click the **Text size** pop-up menu to choose the text size for the List view.

⑩ Click the check box options for each column you want to see.

⑪ Check the **Use relative dates** check box if you want relative dates to be shown, such as Yesterday or Today.

⑫ Click the **Calculate all sizes** check box if you want the sizes of folders to be shown.

Note: Calculating the size of folders can take a lot of processing power, which may slow MacBook's performance somewhat.

⑬ Click the **Show icon preview** check box if you want to see previews in the icons for each item.

⑭ Click **Use as Defaults** if you want other windows in List view to use the current settings by default.

⑮ Click **Close** (●).

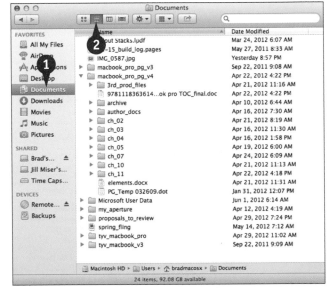

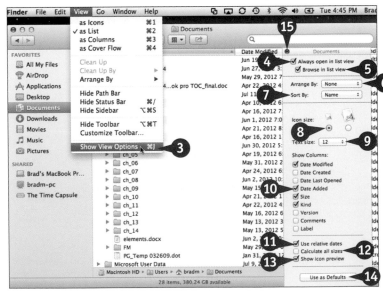

16 Drag a column heading to the left or to the right to change the order in which columns appear in the window.

Note: The Name column always appears on the far left; it cannot be moved.

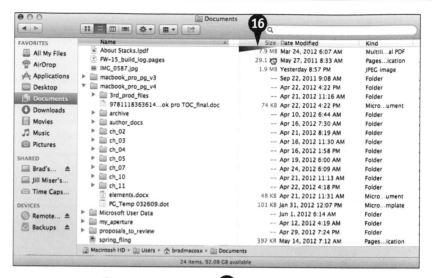

17 Release the trackpad button when the column is in its new position.

18 To change the order in which the items are sorted, click the column heading by which you want to sort the items.

19 To reverse the sort order, click ▲.

20 To reveal the contents of a folder, click ▶.

Ⓐ The folder expands so that you can see the folders and files it contains.

21 Click ▼ to collapse a folder.

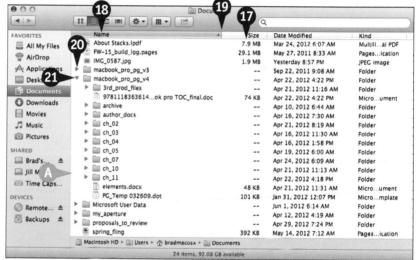

TIPS

How do I expand all the folders within a window at the same time?
Press and hold **Option** while you click a folder's ▶. The folder expands, along with all the folders contained within that folder. Press and hold **Option** and click any folder's ▼ to collapse all the folders in the window again.

How do I tell where a folder is when I view its window?
Click **View** and then click **Show Path Bar**. A bar appears at the bottom of the window that shows you the path from the startup disk to the location of the current folder.

View Finder Windows in Column View

Column view is best for navigating quickly around MacBook Pro. This view allows you to see the contents of folders along with the locations of those folders. You can click any folder's icon to immediately see the contents of that folder in the same window. As you learn to use MacBook Pro, you should become comfortable with the Column view so that you can use it to quickly move to any location.

View Finder Windows in Column View

1 Choose the content you want to see by clicking a folder in the Sidebar.

2 Click **Column View** (▥).

3 Click **View** and then click **Show View Options**.

4 Check the **Always open in column view** check box if you want the folder to always open in Column view.

5 Click **Browse in column view** to have sub-folders display in Column view too.

6 Choose an option on the **Arrange By** pop-up menu to group items in the window.

7 Choose an option on the **Sort By** menu to determine the order in which items are shown.

8 Open the **Text size** pop-up menu to choose a text size for labels.

9 Check the **Show icons** check box to see an icon for each item.

10 Check the **Show icon preview** check box to see a preview of items within their icons.

Note: The icons in this view are very small, so do not be surprised if you have a hard time recognizing them.

11 If you want to see a preview of a file you select, check the **Show preview column** check box.

12 When you are done making changes, click **Close** (●).

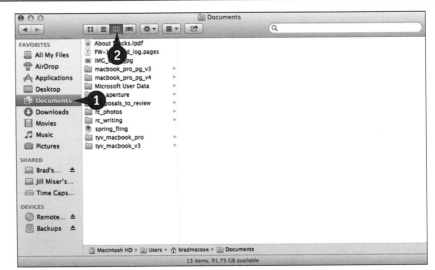

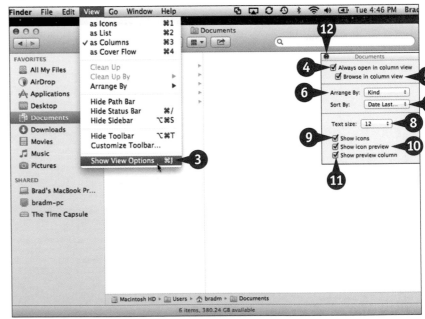

13 Select a location in the Sidebar to view it.

14 Click a folder to see its contents.

A The contents of the folder appear in the column to the right of the one on which you clicked.

Note: As you move through the folder hierarchy, columns shift to the left so that you always see the last column opened toward the right side of the window.

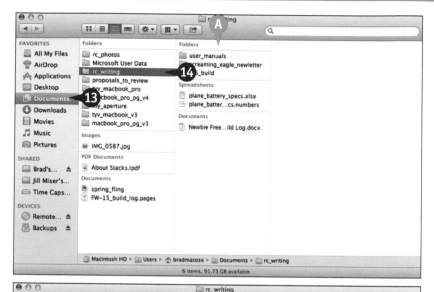

15 Click a file.

B You see information about the file in the far right column, including a preview of the file if that option is enabled. If the file is dynamic, such as audio or video, you can play its content in the preview.

16 To change the width of a column, drag its right edge to the left or right.

17 To group items, click **Arrange** (⊞▾) and choose how you want the window grouped.

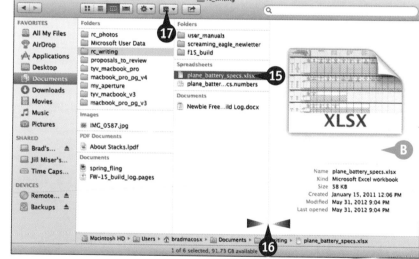

TIPS

How do I resize all the columns at once?

Press and hold **Option** while you drag one column's right edge. All the columns are resized at the same time. If you double-click a column's right edge, the column collapses or expands to show the full file or folder name.

How do I tell the difference between a folder and a file?

In Column view, folders always have a right-facing triangle at the right edge of their column to show that when you select this triangle, the folder's contents appear in a new column to the right. Files do not have this arrow.

View Finder Windows in Cover Flow View

Cover Flow view is a graphical way to quickly scan through contents of a Finder window. In addition to making scrolling through lots of files and folders faster, this view displays thumbnail images of each item you are browsing.

The easiest way to think about the Cover Flow view is to visualize a stack of CDs that you flip through. A Finder window in Cover Flow view behaves similarly. You can flip through the various folders and files to browse them in the top part of the window. In the bottom part of the window, you see the items in the folder you are browsing in List view.

View Finder Windows in Cover Flow View

1 Open a Finder window.

2 Click **Cover Flow View** (▦).

Ⓐ The Cover Flow viewer appears at the top of the window.

Ⓑ The items in the folder you are viewing appear at the bottom of the window in List view.

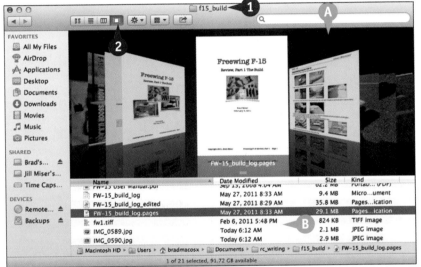

3 To browse the contents of the folder quickly, drag across the "covers" to the left or right.

As you browse, a preview of each item flips by in the Cover Flow viewer at the top of the window.

Ⓒ The item currently selected is the one directly facing you and is highlighted on the list at the bottom of the window.

4 To jump to a specific file or folder, click its icon.

5 To make the Cover Flow part of the window larger or smaller, drag ▦ up or down.

Configure the Sidebar

The Finder's Sidebar makes it easy to get to specific locations, documents, folders, applications, and other items of interest to you. It comes with a number of default locations and folders, but you can add items to or remove them from the Sidebar so that it contains the items you use most frequently.

The Sidebar is organized into sections. Favorites are your favorite items; a number of defaults are stored here. Shared includes disk drives or computers you are accessing over a network. Devices include hard drives and other devices (such as iPods) connected to your MacBook Pro.

Configure the Sidebar

1 To remove an item from the Sidebar, **Control** +click it.

2 Choose **Remove from Sidebar**.

The item is removed from the Sidebar.

Note: When you remove something from the Sidebar, it is not removed from the computer. The item remains in its current location on MacBook Pro; it is just no longer accessible from the Sidebar. You can always add it back again later.

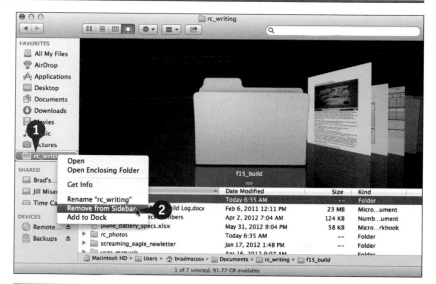

3 To add something to the Sidebar, click its icon, open the **File** menu, and choose **Add to Sidebar**.

4 To change the order of items in the Sidebar, drag them up or down the list.

5 To collapse a section of the Sidebar, point to that section and click **Hide**.

6 To expand a section of the Sidebar, point to that section's title and click **Show**.

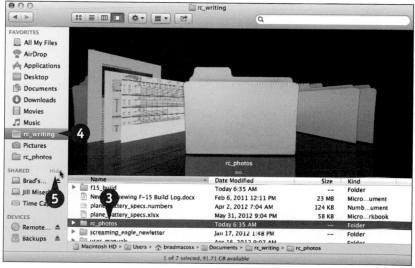

Use the Action Pop-up Menu and Quick Look

The Action pop-up menu is a powerful element of Finder windows, though you might not think so to look at it. This menu contains a list of contextual commands that you can use.

The Finder's Quick Look command enables you to view the contents of a file or group of files without actually opening them. This can save time, especially when you are looking for specific files.

Use the Action Pop-up Menu and Quick Look

Use the Action Pop-up Menu

1. Open a Finder window.

2. Click the **Action** pop-up menu (⚙▾).

3. Choose the command you want to use.

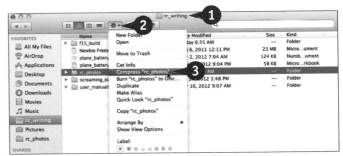

Use Quick Look

1. Open a Finder window containing files.

2. Select the files you want to view.

Note: To select multiple files at the same time, press and hold ⌘ while you click each file.

3. Press Spacebar.

The Quick Look window opens and shows the contents of the files you have selected. Initially, you see the contents of the first file or folder you selected.

4. To move forward and backward through the items you selected, click ◀ or ▶.

5. To see thumbnails of each item you selected, click ⊞.

6. To see Quick Look in full screen, click **Full Screen** (⤢).

7. To open the file in a related application, click the **Open with Preview** button.

8. When you are done with Quick Look, click **Close** (⊗).

Configure the Finder Window Toolbar

The toolbar that appears at the top of the Finder window contains buttons that you can use to access commands quickly and easily. For example, the various View buttons appear there along with the Action menu button.

Although the Finder toolbar includes a number of buttons by default, you can configure the toolbar so that it contains the buttons you use most frequently.

Configure the Finder Window Toolbar

1 Open a Finder window.

2 Click **View** and then click **Customize Toolbar**.

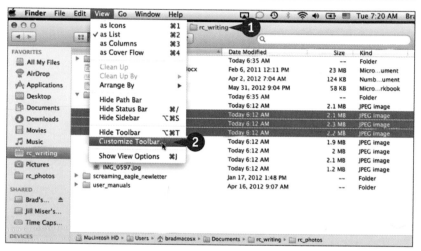

3 To remove a button from the toolbar, drag its icon from the toolbar onto the desktop.

When you release the trackpad, the button disappears in a puff of smoke.

4 To add a button to the toolbar, drag its icon from the sheet and drop it on the toolbar at the location in which you want to place it.

When you release the trackpad, the button is added to the toolbar.

5 To change the locations of buttons on the toolbar, drag their icons from the current location to a new one.

6 When you are finished customizing the toolbar, click **Done**.

The Customization sheet closes and you see your customized toolbar.

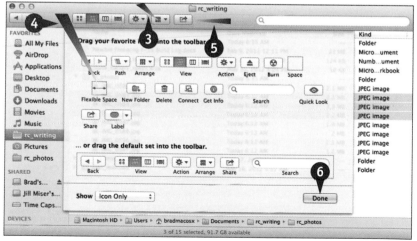

Understand Desktop Management Tools

Your MacBook Pro has a lot going on. You will use multiple applications to work on documents, send e-mails, surf the web, and more. Each task has one or more windows associated with it. This can really clutter up the desktop, making working not as efficient or enjoyable. Fortunately, OS X has a number of tools that help you manage your desktop efficiently.

Dock

The Dock provides you with one-click access to applications, folders, and documents; it is also the home of the Trash/Eject icon. The Dock has a number of applications and folders installed on it by default, but the good news is that you can configure the Dock so it contains the items you find the most

useful. You can also configure many aspects of the Dock, such as its location on the desktop, size, and so on.

Mission Control

Mission Control helps you make even better use of your desktop because with a swipe on the trackpad or press of a button and a swipe, you can quickly cycle through your Dashboard, desktops and spaces, and applications in Full Screen mode. When you see what you want to work with, you can jump right into it.

Window Control

Mission Control also enables you to quickly arrange open windows on the desktop so that you can more easily move between them. For this purpose, Mission Control has three modes. When you open Mission Control, all the open windows are reduced in size and grouped by application. You can click a window to jump into it. It can also shrink all the open windows for an application so you can see them all at the same time; click a window to move into it. In addition, you can use Mission Control to quickly move all open windows off the sides of the screen so you can access the desktop.

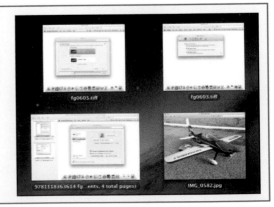

Desktops

Desktops, also called *spaces*, are collections of applications that you can switch between quickly and easily to work with a different space. For example, you might have one desktop with your communication

applications, such as e-mail, chat, and so on. Another desktop might have your work applications, such as Pages and Numbers. Yet another might have entertainment apps in it. With a gesture and a click, you can move from one set to another.

Dashboard

The Dashboard contains "mini applications" called widgets; you can quickly pop open the Dashboard, use your widgets, and close the Dashboard again to move it out of the way. The Dashboard contains quite a few widgets by default, but like other desktop management tools, you can customize its contents to suit your needs.

Launchpad

The Launchpad presents icons for all the applications stored in the Applications folder on your MacBook Pro on multiple screens. The first screen contains OS X's default applications along with other Apple applications, such as the iLife applications. You can drag your fingers across the trackpad to "flip" through the screens to see the other applications you have. When you see an application, you want to use, click its icon. Because the Launchpad is focused on helping you use applications, its section is in Chapter 5.

Use and Configure the Dock

The Dock is very useful OS X, because it provides single-click access to various items, including applications, documents, and folders. The Dock includes a number of default icons, and you can add as many icons to your Dock as you want. You can also customize the way the Dock looks and works to suit your preferences.

Different results occur when you click different kinds of icons. If the icon is a closed application, the application opens and you see its initial window. If the application is already open, you jump into it and see its active windows. If the icon is for a minimized window, the window moves onto the desktop.

Use and Configure the Dock

Use the Dock

1 Point to an icon on the Dock.

The name of the related item appears above the icon.

2 Click the **trackpad** to take action on the item, such as opening an application.

3 To open a Dock icon's contextual menu, perform a secondary click by pressing and holding `Control` and then click.

4 Choose the command you want to use from the menu; you can also jump into one of the application's open windows by selecting it on the menu.

Note: As more icons appear on the Dock, they get smaller and the Dock expands so it can contain all its icons.

Configure the Dock

1 Perform a secondary click on the dashed dividing line just to the right of the last application icon.

The Dock menu appears.

2 Choose **Dock Preferences**.

The Dock pane of the System Preferences application appears.

3 Drag the **Size** slider to the left or right to make the default size of the Dock smaller or larger.

4 To magnify icons when you point to them, click the **Magnification** check box and then drag the slider for more or less magnification.

5 To position the Dock on the left, bottom, or right side of the desktop, click **Left**, **Bottom**, or **Right** option.

6 Click the **Minimize windows using** pop-up menu to choose an effect.

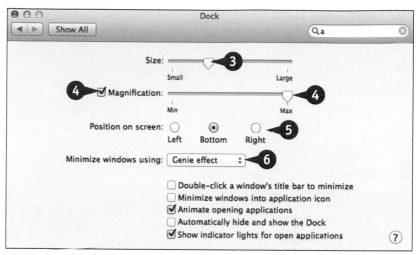

7 Click the **Double-click a window's title bar to minimize** check box to minimize a window by double-clicking its title bar.

8 Click the **Minimize windows into application icon** check box to move minimized windows onto the associated application.

9 Click the **Animate opening applications** check box to have icons bounce while their applications are opening.

10 Click the **Automatically hide and show the Dock** check box to automatically hide the Dock when you are not pointing to it.

11 Click the **Show indicator lights for open applications** check box to mark open applications with a blue dot under their icons.

12 Press ⌘+Q to close the System Preferences application.

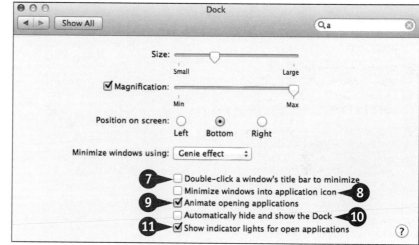

TIPS

How can I add icons to or remove them from the Dock?
To add an icon to the Dock, drag it from a Finder window onto the Dock; an application's icon must be placed on the left side of the dividing line, whereas a document or folder's icon goes on the right side. When the icon is at the desired location, release the trackpad button. To remove an icon, drag it up onto the desktop and release the trackpad button.

What happens when I add folder icons to the Dock?
When you click a folder's icon, a fan or grid showing the folder's contents appears. You can click an icon to work with one of the items, such as a document icon to open it. For example, the Dock contains the Downloads folder, which is the default location for files you download from the web. When you click this icon, the files you have downloaded appear, either in a fan or a grid (which one appears depends on how many items the folder contains).

Manage the Desktop with Mission Control

Mission Control is a quick way to get to any open window on your MacBook Pro. You can also use it to get to the Dashboard, applications running in Full Screen mode, and your desktops (spaces).

When you open Mission Control by using gestures on the trackpad, at the top of the screen you see thumbnails of your desktops, applications in Full Screen mode, and the Dashboard. You see thumbnails of the open applications in the current desktop in the center part of the screen, and you see the Dock. You can quickly get to any window you see.

Manage the Desktop with Mission Control

Configure the Mission Control Gesture

1 Click the **Apple** menu and click **System Preferences**.

2 Click **Trackpad**.

3 Click the **More Gestures** tab.

4 Click the **Mission Control** check box.

5 Click the menu under Mission Control and choose **Swipe up with three fingers** or **Swipe up with four fingers** to suit your preference.

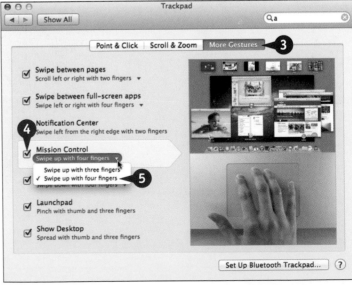

Use Mission Control

1 Using three or four fingers, swipe up the trackpad toward the screen.

Mission Control opens.

A At the top of the screen, you see a thumbnail for the Dashboard on the far left.

B To the right of the Dashboard, you see a thumbnail for each desktop, labeled with Desktop *X*, where *X* is a sequential number for each space.

C In the center of the screen, you see thumbnails for all the open windows in the current desktop. The windows are grouped by the application with which they are associated.

2 Swipe to the left or right to change the focus to the previous or next desktop, or click its thumbnail to bring that desktop into focus.

3 To jump into an application in Full Screen mode, or the Dashboard, click its thumbnail. To jump into a specific window within the space in focus, click in it.

Note: When you point to a window, a blue box outlines it, indicating it will be your destination when you click.

The window you clicked in becomes active and you move onto the desktop with which the window is associated.

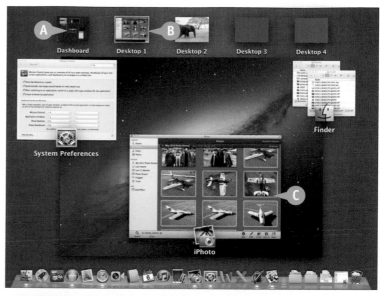

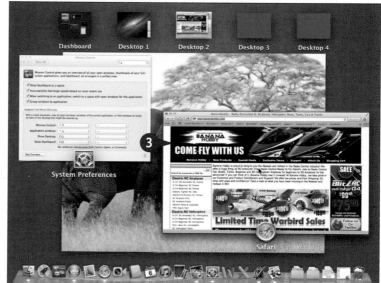

TIPS

Does Mission Control work if I do not set up desktops?
You do not have to configure desktops to work with Mission Control. If you do not set up additional desktops (you learn how in the next section), when you activate Mission Control, you see only the Dashboard, applications in Full Screen mode, and your only desktop's thumbnails, and these work just like they do when you have desktops configured.

Can I have a different desktop picture in each desktop?
Yes. Configure System Preferences to be in either no spaces or all of them — you learn how to do this later in this chapter. Move into each space and set the background picture for that space. When you move into a space, its picture fills the desktop.

Configure and Use Mission Control and Desktops

As described earlier, desktops, also called spaces, are collections of applications and documents that you can use to jump between sets of windows easily and quickly. When you use desktops, you do not have to bother locating individual windows. Instead, you can see the windows in each desktop and quickly jump into the window with which you want to work.

For example, if you have several Internet applications that you use at the same time, you can create an Internet desktop and add your applications to it. To use the Internet, you just open this desktop, and its open applications are ready to use immediately.

Configure and Use Mission Control and Desktops

Configure Mission Control

Note: The steps in these Mission Control sections are performed with the default preferences.

① Open the System Preferences application.

② Click the **Mission Control** icon.

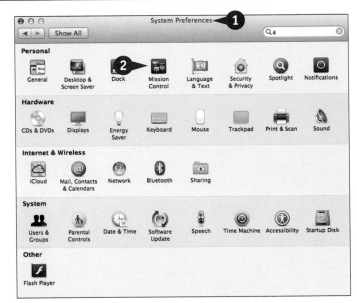

③ Click **Show Dashboard as a space** for the Dashboard to be accessible via Mission Control.

④ Click this check box and Mission Control automatically rearranges spaces based on the ones you have most recently used.

⑤ Click this check box and when you change applications, you move into the desktop in which the application has windows open.

⑥ Click this check box to show open windows grouped by their applications.

⑦ Open these menus and select the keyboard shortcuts you want to use with Mission Control.

⑧ Click **Hot Corners** and make choices on the menus on the resulting sheet to choose a hot corner for each action. (You point to a hot corner to activate the related function.)

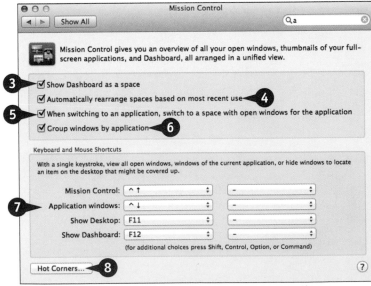

Create Desktops

1 Activate Mission Control, such as by dragging four fingers up on the trackpad.

The Dashboard (if included), current spaces, and applications in Full Screen mode are shown at the top of the screen. The applications and windows open in the current space are shown in the center of the screen.

2 Point to the upper right corner (or the top-left if the Dock is on the right) of the screen until the Add button (■) appears and click it.

A new space called desktop *X*, where *X* is a sequential number, appears and is ready for you to configure.

3 Repeat step **2** until you have created all the desktops you want to be available.

Delete Desktops

1 Activate Mission Control.

2 Point to the desktop you want to delete.

3 Click **Delete** (⊗).

The desktop is removed, but any applications in the desktop are not deleted. They are just no longer associated with the desktop you deleted.

TIP

How many desktops should I use?
You want to keep the number of desktops you use to a manageable number. If you have too many desktops, it can be cumbersome to work with them; too few and each desktop may have too many applications in it. Try a low number (such as three or four) to start and adjust over time as you use desktops.

continued ▶

Desktops can take a bit of getting used to because they are not familiar to many Mac users. It might take some trial and error to configure your desktops in a way that you get the most benefit from them. The most common problem is having too many desktops or too many applications in one desktop.

Use these steps to configure your desktops initially. Over time, you will discover which desktops work for you and which do not. Keep tweaking your desktops until they suit the way you work.

Configure and Use Mission Control and Desktops (continued)

Change Desktops with a Gesture

1 Swipe on the trackpad to the left or right with three or four fingers (depending upon the gesture set; the default is four fingers).

A As you swipe, the current space moves off the screen in the direction you swipe.

B The next space moves onto the screen in the direction you swipe.

Note: A space can be a desktop, the Dashboard, or applications in Full Screen mode.

2 When you get to the space in which you want to work, lift your fingers off the trackpad.

The desktop, application in Full Screen mode, or Dashboard on which you stopped becomes active.

Change Desktops with Mission Control

1 Click **Mission Control** (⊞) on the Dock.

2 Click the space you want to make active.

The desktop, application in Full Screen mode, or Dashboard on which you clicked becomes active.

Configure Desktops

1 Make the desktop you want to configure active.

2 If the icons for applications you want to add to the desktop do not appear on the Dock, launch the applications you want to add to the desktop so their icons do appear on the Dock.

3 To configure the application relative to the desktop, perform a secondary click on its Dock icon.

4 Choose **Options**.

5 Select one of the following options:

C You can choose **All Desktops** to add the application to all desktops so it is available no matter which one is active.

D You can choose **This Desktop** to add the application to the active desktop.

E You can choose **None** to remove the application from all desktops so it behaves independent of the desktop you are using.

Note: If the application is already assigned to a space, you also see Desktop *X*, where *X* is a sequential number on the menu indicating to which space the application is assigned.

6 Repeat steps **2** to **5** until you configure all the applications you want to associate with the active desktop.

TIPS

What happens when I open an application that is not part of the desktop that I am using?
If an application is available in only one desktop, when you open it from any source, such as the Dock or the Finder, you switch into the desktop with which that application is associated (if you have enabled that on the Mission Control pane). If the application is not part of a desktop, it opens in the space you are currently using.

Do I need to add every application I use to a desktop?
No, you do not need to add every application you use to a desktop; just add those that you use most often. In addition, applications you use in Full Screen mode do not need to be in a desktop because they appear in Mission Control just as desktops do, so there is no benefit to adding them to a desktop.

Manage Open Windows with Mission Control

ission Control greatly helps with the inevitable screen clutter as you use MacBook Pro and open window after window for documents and applications. For this purpose, Mission Control has three modes. You can hide all open windows to show the MacBook Pro desktop. You can reduce all open windows to thumbnails so that you can quickly jump into a window you want to use. You can also see thumbnails for just the open windows within a specific application.

Manage Open Windows with Mission Control

Hide All Open Windows with Mission Control

1 Open several windows, including those from the Finder and from applications.

2 Press **Fn** + **F11** .

A All the windows are moved off the MacBook Pro screen, leaving an uncluttered desktop for you to work on.

Note: To return the desktop to its cluttered state, press **Fn** + **F11** again, or click one of the sides of the windows that you see at the edges of the desktop.

Show Thumbnails of All Open Windows with Mission Control

1 Make a desktop with open windows active.

2 Open Mission Control by swiping three or four fingers up the trackpad.

B All windows shrink down so that they fit on the desktop.

3 Point to a window.

C The window is highlighted with a blue line.

4 Click a window to move into it.

The window becomes active and moves to the front so that you can use it. The rest of the windows move into the background.

46

Show All Open Windows for an Application with Mission Control

1 Open multiple windows within the same application.

2 Perform the gesture associated with App Exposé (by default, swipe down with four fingers).

D All windows currently open in the application appear as thumbnails at the top of the screen. You see the title of each window underneath its thumbnail.

E At the bottom of the screen, you see thumbnails for the windows you have worked with but that are closed.

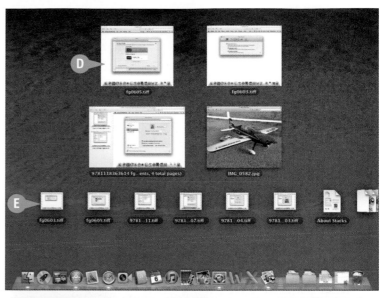

3 Point to a window (it can be open or closed).

F The window is highlighted with a blue box.

4 Click a window to move into it.

Note: You can also press the arrow keys to move to a window and press `Return` to move into it.

The window becomes active and moves to the front so that you can use it.

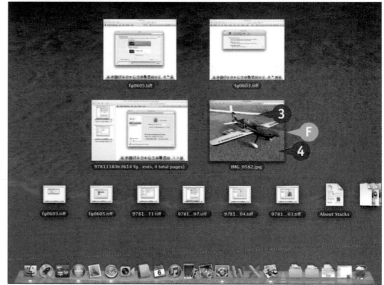

TIPS

How can I get back to a closed window?
To browse the closed windows, swipe to the left or right across the thumbnails along the bottom of the screen. When you see the closed window in which you want to move, click it. The related file opens and you can use it.

How can I change the set of windows that I am viewing?
With the windows for an application showing, press `⌘`+`Tab`. The Application Switcher appears. Continue pressing `⌘`+`Tab` until the application whose windows you want to see is highlighted with a white box. When it is, release the keys. All the windows open in that application appear.

Use and Configure the Dashboard

The Dashboard offers an easy way to access *widgets*, which are small applications that provide very specific functionality. To use a widget, you activate the Dashboard, which fills the desktop and presents the widgets installed on it. Use the widgets you want; when you are done, close the Dashboard again.

OS X includes a number of useful widgets by default, such as Weather, Calculator, Address Book, and Flight Tracker. There is even a widget to help you manage your widgets.

Use and Configure the Dashboard

Open the Dashboard

1 Press **F4** or swipe all the way to the left on the trackpad.

Ⓐ The desktop and open windows move into the background and the Dashboard appears, displaying the widgets already on the Dashboard.

Ⓑ If a widget is informational, such as a weather widget, you can view the information it provides.

2 If the widget needs input, click the widget to make it active.

Many widgets require configuration in order to provide useful information to you.

3 Point to the widget you want to configure.

The Info button (a lowercase *i*) appears.

4 Click **Info** (ⓘ).

Note: Many widgets require an Internet connection.

The widget moves into configuration mode.

5 Use the widget's configuration tools to change its settings.

6 Click **Done**.

The widget returns to its normal mode and reflects the changes you made.

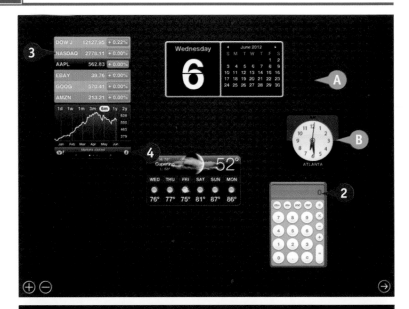

Configure the Dashboard

1 Open the Dashboard.

2 To change the location of widgets, drag them around the screen.

When you release the trackpad button, the widget is saved in its new location and appears in that spot each time you open the Dashboard.

3 Click **Add** (⊕).

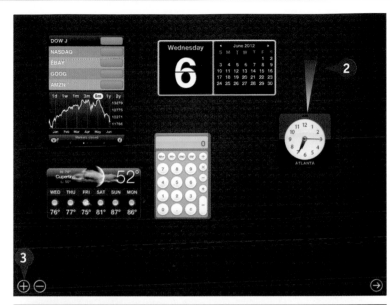

The Dashboard moves into configuration mode. You see all the widgets currently available for the Dashboard.

4 Browse the available widgets.

5 Click a widget to add it your Dashboard.

The widget is added to your Dashboard and it returns to its usable mode.

TIPS

How can I change the key combination to open the Dashboard?
Open the Mission Control pane of the System Preferences application. On the **Show Dashboard** pop-up menu, select the key combination you want to use to launch the Dashboard. You can press key combinations while the menu is open to be able to select them. For example, press and hold **Option** and **Control** to see those keys added to the options on the menu.

How can I remove widgets from the Dashboard?
To remove a widget from the Dashboard, open the Dashboard and click **Remove** (⊖). Click the **Delete** button (⊘) on the widget you want to remove. The widget is removed from the Dashboard, but remains on your MacBook Pro so you can add it again later if desired. Click **Remove** (⊖) again when you are done removing widgets.

continued ▶

Although OS X includes a number of widgets, these are by no means all of the widgets available to you. Thousands of other widgets are on the Internet for you to download, install, and add to your Dashboard to expand its functionality.

Downloading and installing widgets is a snap because OS X recognizes widget files and automatically prompts you to install them as soon as they are downloaded to your MacBook Pro.

Use and Configure the Dashboard (continued)

Find and Install More Widgets on the Dashboard

1 Open the Dashboard and click **Add** (⊕).

2 Click **More Widgets**.

Your web browser opens and takes you to the Dashboard Widgets page on the Apple website.

3 Use the web page to browse or search for widgets.

Note: Details about using Safari to browse the web are provided in Chapter 11.

4 When you find a widget you want to install, click its **Download** button.

The widget is downloaded to your MacBook Pro. When the process is complete, you are prompted to install the widget.

Note: If you see a security warning after the widget downloads, you need to disable the Gatekeeper by opening the General tab of the Security & Privacy pane of the System Preferences application and clicking Anywhere. When you are done installing widgets, click Mac App Store or Mac App Store and identified developers again. See Chapter 9 for more information.

Note: If the widget you downloaded does not install automatically, open your Downloads folder to install it.

⑤ Click **Install**.

The widget becomes available to add to your Dashboard.

⑥ Click the widget to add it to your Dashboard.

TIPS

What if I want widgets to show information for more than one location or situation?
You can have as many copies of the same widget on your Dashboard as you want. For example, if you want to track the weather in five locations, add five copies of the Weather widget to your Dashboard and configure one for each area you want to track.

How can I create my own widget?
Use Safari to move to a web page containing content you want to make available on the Dashboard. Click **File**, **Open in Dashboard**. Select the part of the screen from which you want to make a widget. Click **Add**. The content you selected is added to your Dashboard as a widget.

Work with Notifications and the Notification Center

As you use your MacBook Pro, a lot of activity goes on. You receive e-mail, reminders about appointments and tasks, information updates, and so on. Each application you use can send notifications to keep you informed about what is happening.

You receive individual notifications from applications as events warrant. There are two types of individual notifications. When Alert notifications appear on the screen, you have to take some action to clear them, such as clicking the Dismiss button. Banner notifications are more informational; they appear briefly on the screen and then go away automatically. You can view and work with groups of notifications in the Notification Center.

Work with Notifications and the Notification Center

View Alert Notifications

1 View the information presented in the alert.

Note: You cannot move an alert on your screen. The only action you can take on it is by clicking its buttons.

2 If you want to see the details of what you are being notified about, click the alert.

You move into the application that sent the alert and can work with the item in detail. For example, if you click an event, you move into Calendar and can access all the event's detail.

3 If you want to dismiss the alert, click one of its buttons.

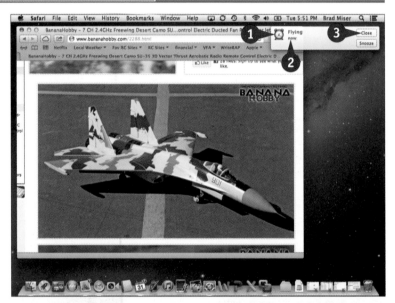

View Banner Notifications

1 View the information presented in the banner.

2 If you want to see the details of what you are being notified about, click the information.

You move into the application that sent the banner and can work with the item in detail. For example, if you click an e-mail banner, you move into Mail and can read the entire message.

If you do not click the banner, after a few seconds, it disappears.

View Notifications in the Notification Center

1 Click the **Notification Center** button (☰).

The Notification Center opens. You see the notifications you have from various applications, organized into groups with the application's name at the top the group.

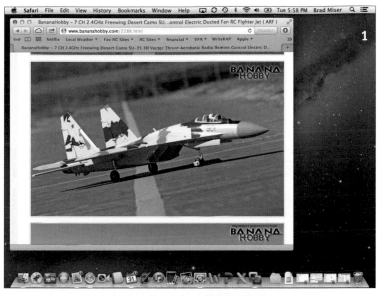

2 Scroll up and down the list to review all the notifications.

3 Click a notification to move into the related application and see all the item's detail. For example, if you click a reminder notification, you move into the Reminders application and can see all the information in that reminder.

4 To close a section, click the **Close** button (✖).

5 To close the Notification Center, click the desktop.

TIPS

How can I change the order in which notifications are listed?
By default, groups of notifications are sorted so that the newest notifications appear at the top of the Notification Center. If you prefer to set the order manually, you can use the Notifications pane of the System Preferences Center, explained in the next section, to allow manual configuration. When that is set, drag sections up or down the list to change their order.

How do I know when there are new notifications in the Notification Center?
The color of the dot at the center of the Notification Center button is blue if you have notifications that you have not seen before. If you do not have any new notifications, the dot is gray.

continued ▶

Notifications are useful, but too many of them can be a nuisance. To set a good balance between keeping informed and being interrupted as you work, you should configure which applications send notifications to you and how those notifications are sent using the Notifications pane of the System Preferences application.

There are two other types of notifications. Badges are numeric counters that appear on an application's icon to let you know how many new "things" the application has. Many applications support badge notifications. Audible notifications are the other type, which are sounds that an application plays for various events.

Work with Notifications and the Notification Center (continued)

Configure Notifications

1 Open the System Preferences application.

2 Click **Notifications**.

The Notifications pane appears.

3 Choose **Manually** on the **Sort Notification Center** menu to be able to drag notifications up and down the list in the Notification Center; choose **By time** if you want notifications always to be sorted based on when you received them.

4 Browse the applications until you see one for which you want to configure notifications.

5 Click here and select the application you want to configure.

The notification configuration controls for that application appear in the right part of the pane.

6 Click **None** to disable alerts, **Banners** to have the application use banner alerts, or **Alerts** to have it use the alert style of notification.

7 Uncheck the **Show in Notification Center** check box if you do not want the application's notifications to appear in the Notification Center.

Note: When you uncheck this option, the application moves from the In Notification Center group to the Not in Notification Center group.

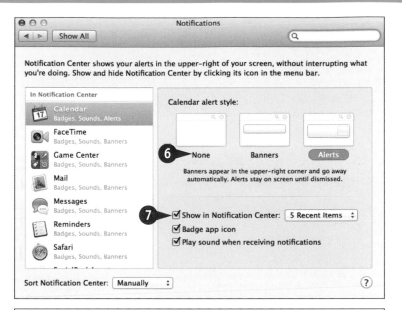

8 Click the **Show in Notifications Center** check box if you want the application's notifications to appear in the Notification Center, and choose how many of the recent notifications you want to see in the Notification Center on the menu.

9 Uncheck the **Badge app icon** check box if you do not want badge notifications to appear on the application's icon.

10 Uncheck the **Play sound when receiving notifications** check box to disable audible alerts when you receive notifications from the application.

11 Repeat steps **5** to **10** until you have configured notifications for all the applications shown.

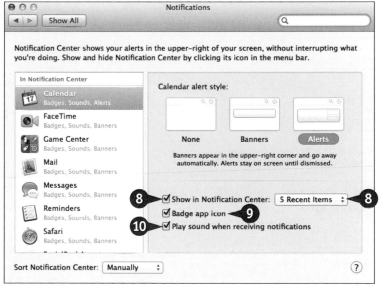

How to I disable all notifications?
If you want to hide all alerts and banners, open the Notification Center and scroll to the top. Set the Do Not Disturb switch to the ON position. All banners and alerts will be hidden. To resume receiving these notifications, set the switch position to OFF again.

How do I get back a notification section that I closed?
When you close a section of notifications by clicking its **Close** button (⊠), it disappears only while the Notification Center remains open. If you close the Notification Center and open it again, the section you closed reappears.

Move to Locations on the Desktop

Moving to specific locations is a critical skill to master because it is involved in just about every task for which you will use your computer. The Mac desktop provides many ways to get to specific folders that you want to view and work with. Two of the most useful of these are the Sidebar and the Go menu.

Starting from the Sidebar and using the Column view, you can quickly get to any location on the desktop. With the Go menu, you can easily jump to many locations that you commonly visit, along with locations typically hidden on the desktop.

Move to Locations on the Desktop

Go Places with Column View

1 Open a new Finder window.

Note: For information about working with Finder windows, see Chapter 2.

2 Click **Column View** (▥).

3 Select a starting point such as your Documents folder or a disk.

4 Click the first folder whose contents you want to view.

Ⓐ The contents of that folder appear in the column immediately to the right of the folder you selected.

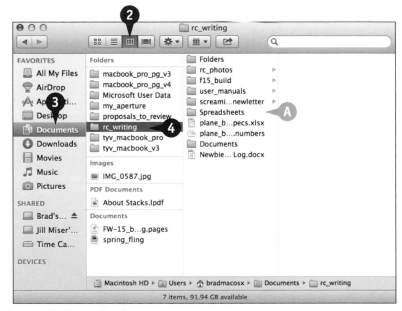

5 Click the next folder you want to move into.

Ⓑ The contents of that folder appear in the column immediately to the right of the folder you selected.

Note: In Column view, folders have a right-facing arrow at the end of the column; files do not.

6 Keep selecting folders until you get to the specific folder or file you want.

Note: You can always select one of the other views (such as Icon or List) after you have moved into a folder if you prefer to see a window in one of those views.

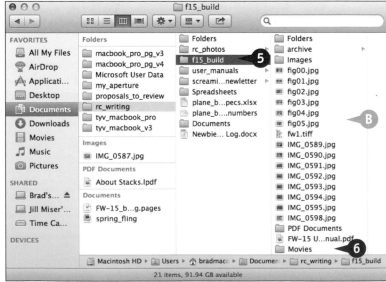

Go Places with the Go Menu

1 With a Finder window active, click the **Go** menu on the Finder menu bar.

2 Select the location you want to move to.

A Finder window opens, showing the location you selected.

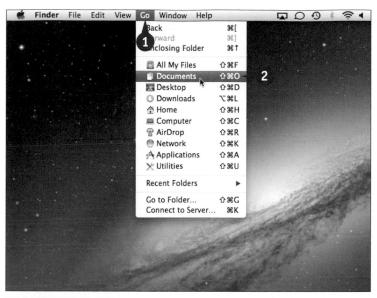

Go Back to a Recent Folder

1 Click the **Go** menu.

2 Point to **Recent Folders**.

3 Click the folder you want to open.

TIPS

How can I go places with the keyboard?
The standard folders on the MacBook Pro desktop all have keyboard combinations that you can press to jump to them. The following list shows some of the more useful locations and keyboard combinations (in parentheses):

All My Files (Shift+⌘+F) Computer (Shift+⌘+C)
Documents (Shift+⌘+O) AirDrop (Shift+⌘+R)
Desktop (Shift+⌘+D) Network folder (Shift+⌘+K)
Downloads (Shift+⌘+L) Applications (Shift+⌘+A)
Home (Shift+⌘+H) Utilities (Shift+⌘+U)

How do I make it even easier to move to a folder I use all the time?
Drag the folder onto the right end of the Dock and drop it anywhere on the right side of the dividing line. The folder is installed on the Dock, and you can easily get to its contents. Or, drag the folder onto the Sidebar so that you can click its icon there to open it in a Finder window.

Rename Files and Folders

Y ou can change the name of files or folders as you need to, although you may be prevented from changing the names of folders you do not create, which you should not do in any case. Just as when you create them, you can change the names to be just about anything you want, using up to 255 characters.

When you change the name of files, you should usually avoid changing the filename extension (everything after the period in the name) because this extension is one important way that OS X associates documents with applications. However, you can change the part of the name before the period.

Rename Files and Folders

1 In a Finder window, select the folder or file whose name you want to change.

2 Press **Return**.

A The name becomes highlighted to indicate that you can change it.

Note: Filename extensions are hidden by a default preference setting. If you do not see them, you have not changed this optional preference.

Note: If your user account does not have write permissions for a folder or file, you cannot change its name.

3 Type the new name of the folder or file.

4 Press **Return**.

The new name is saved.

Note: When you change a file extension, you can change the application with which the file is associated. OS X warns you so that you do not inadvertently change the filename extension.

Compress Files and Folders

Files and folders require disk space to store their contents. You can compress them to reduce the space they consume. This is most useful when you move these files over a network, especially when you e-mail files as attachments. Not only do compressed files move more quickly, but you can also include all the relevant files in one compressed file to make them easier for the recipient to work with. (See Chapter 12 to learn how to attach files to e-mail messages.)

Compress Files and Folders

Compress Files or Folders

1 In a Finder window, select the files and folders you want to include in the compressed file.

Note: Press and hold ⌘ or **Shift** to select multiple items.

2 Perform a secondary click on one of the selected files (**Control**+click) and then select **Compress *X* Items**, where *X* is the number of items selected.

The files and folders are compressed, and a file called Archive.zip is created.

Note: If you compress one file, the Zip file's name is the same as the file you compress.

3 Change the name of the Archive.zip file.

Note: Leave the filename extension as .zip or the file might not expand correctly.

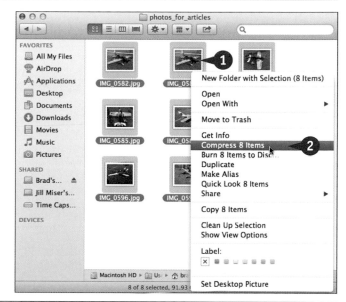

Expand Compressed Files

1 In a Finder window, double-click a compressed file.

A OS X expands the file. It stores the uncompressed files in a folder with the same name as the compressed file.

2 Open the expanded folder to work with the files and folders it contains.

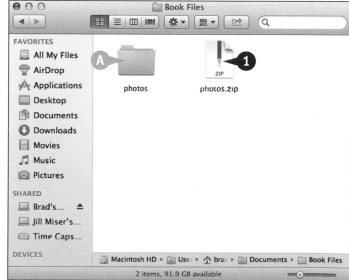

Find Files, Folders, and Other Information

As you use MacBook Pro, you create a lot of data in various documents, images, movies, and other kinds of files. You also interact with e-mail, web pages, and other sources of information. Over time, you might not remember where all this information is. OS X includes tools to help you find the information you need.

You can search for files using the Search bar in Finder windows. You can also use Spotlight on the desktop to search many kinds of information at the same time.

Find Files, Folders, and Other Information

Find Files and Folders with Finder

1 In a Finder window, type the information you want to search for in the Search bar.

A As you type, the Finder suggests options for how you want to search, such as Filename contains or Kinds.

2 Click the option by which you want to search.

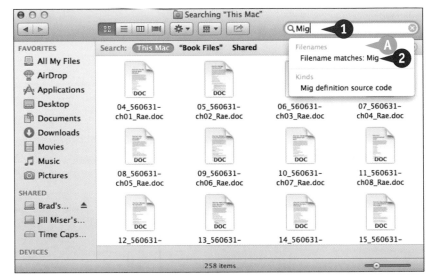

B Files and folders that meet your search appear in the window.

3 To make the search more specific, click the **Add** button (⊕).

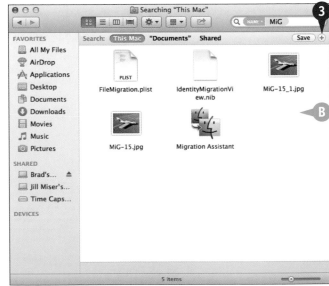

4 Click the arrows to select the criteria by which you want to narrow your search from the pop-up menu.

5 Select the condition from the pop-up menu.

6 Select other conditions on additional menus that appear.

7 Repeat steps **3** to **6** to add more conditions to your search.

As you add more conditions, the search results become more specific and you see only files that meet your search in the Finder window.

Find Information with Spotlight

1 Click the **Spotlight** icon (🔍) located in the upper right corner of the desktop.

The Spotlight bar appears.

2 Type the information for which you want to search.

C As you type, Spotlight searches your computer to locate information that relates to the text or numbers you entered.

3 Point to a result to see more information about it.

D Additional information appears.

4 To open one of the found items, click it.

How can I find information not stored on my MacBook Pro?
Spotlight can search the web for you too. In the search results, look for the Web Searches category. Select one of the results in that category to perform a web search for the term you entered.

How can I use keyboard shortcuts for Spotlight?
You can start a Spotlight search by pressing ⌘+ Spacebar . If you click outside the Spotlight window, it closes, but you can easily open it again by pressing ⌘+ Spacebar .

continued ▶

When you search with Spotlight, you find a variety of content at the same time. This is good because your searches can easily and quickly expose many different kinds of documents that might be of interest to you. However, if you are not specific when you enter a search term, the results might overwhelm you. Use as specific a search term as you can at first, and make it less specific if you do not find what you want. You can also configure the items included in searches and the order in which they appear. You can search for help using the OS X Help system or the help systems provided by third-party applications.

Find Files, Folders, and Other Information (continued)

Ⓐ The item you clicked on opens and you can work with it.

⑤ To return to the search results, click the **Spotlight** icon again (🔍).

The Spotlight results window appears, and you can view other items in the results, or you can change the search criteria.

Note: To clear a Spotlight search, click Clear (🔘).

Configure Spotlight

① On the Spotlight menu, choose **Spotlight Preferences**.

Ⓑ The Spotlight pane of the System Preferences application opens.

② Uncheck the check boxes for any categories of items that you do not want to be included in Spotlight searches.

③ Drag categories up or down the list to change the order in which those categories appear in the Spotlight results window.

④ To change the keyboard combination that activates Spotlight, use the **Spotlight menu keyboard shortcut** menu.

⑤ To change the keyboard combination for the Show All command, use the **Spotlight window keyboard shortcut** menu.

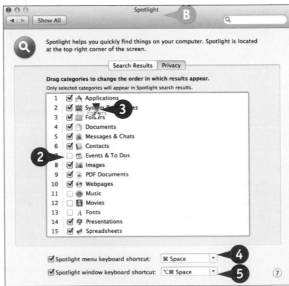

6 Click the **Privacy** tab.

On this pane, you see areas not searched when you perform Spotlight searches. Although it is called the Privacy pane, you can use it to exclude an area for any reason, such as to limit the kind of results that you see.

7 Add folders or volumes to the list using **Add** (⊞) or by dragging them from the desktop onto the list.

8 Click **Close** (⊙) to quit the System Preferences application.

The next time you search with Spotlight, your preferences are used in the search.

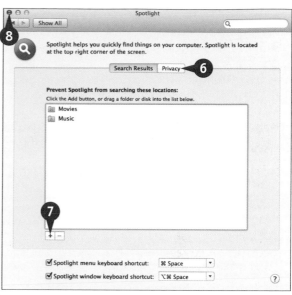

Find Help

1 On the Finder menu, click **Help**.

2 Type the information related to the help you need.

As you type, the Mac Help system is searched.

3 To see where a menu item is, point to it.

Ⓒ The menu opens and a large pointer indicates the menu item.

4 To read a help topic, click it.

Ⓓ The Help window opens and you see the help topic you selected.

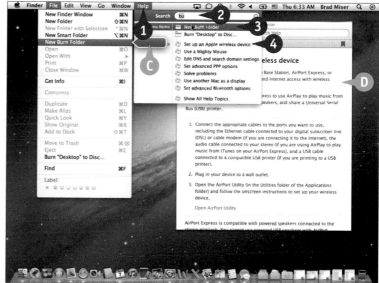

What does the Show All in Finder option in the Spotlight results window do?

When you click **Show All in Finder** in the Spotlight results window, a Finder window appears, configured with the search information you entered in Spotlight, as if you had started the search from the Finder window rather than from Spotlight. Like other Finder searches, you can add search criteria, save the search, and so on.

Do all applications use the Mac Help system?

All applications are supposed to provide a Help menu that you can use to get help. Apple applications use the Help system provided by OS X so that you can use the same tools to find help in any of these applications. Some non-Apple applications also use the OS X Help system, but others implement their own help systems that work a bit differently. No matter what application you happen to be using, start a search for help from its Help menu.

Create Smart Folders

A *Smart Folder* is smart because instead of manually placing items within it, you define a set of search criteria, and the items that meet those search criteria are placed within the folder automatically. For example, you can create a Smart Folder for a specific project that includes a key phrase that is part of all the file and folder names related to that project. Whenever you create a folder or file whose name includes that phrase, an alias to the folder or file is included in the project's folder automatically. Each time you open the Smart Folder, you see all of the files and folders that currently meet its criteria, such as being associated with the project.

Create Smart Folders

1. With the Finder active, click **File** and then click **New Smart Folder**.

2. Type the text or numbers for which you want to search.

Ⓐ As you enter conditions, the Finder suggests options for how you want to search, such as Filename contains.

3. Click the option by which you want to search.

Files and folders that meet your search criteria appear in the window.

4. In the Search field, click where the Finder should search.

For example, click **This Mac** to search all areas; click **All My Files** to search all the files you have saved; or click **Shared** (when you are connected to network resources) to search the network.

5. Click the arrows and select the criteria by which you want to narrow your search and then select the condition from the pop-up menu.

Note: To search for files using the Search bar in Finder windows, see the "Find Files, Folders, and Other Information" task.

6. To make the search even more specific, click **Add** (⊕).

A new condition appears.

7 Click the arrows and select the attribute by which you want to search on the first pop-up menu.

For example, choose **Created date** to search for files that have been created within a specific time period, or choose **Kind** to look for a specific type of file.

8 Click here and select the operator from the pop-up menu.

9 Configure the rest of the parameters for the condition you created, such as how long a time period you want to search if you selected a date in step **7**.

10 Repeat steps **6** to **9** to add more conditions to the search until you find all the content you want to include in the folder.

Note: To remove a condition, click Remove (⊖).

11 Click **Save**.

12 Type the name of the folder in the Save As field.

13 Click the arrows and select a save location from the pop-up menu.

14 Uncheck the **Add To Sidebar** check box if you do not want the folder to appear in the Favorites section of the Sidebar.

15 Click **Save**.

Whenever you open the Smart Folder (such as by clicking its icon on the Sidebar), you see all the files and folders that currently meet its search criteria.

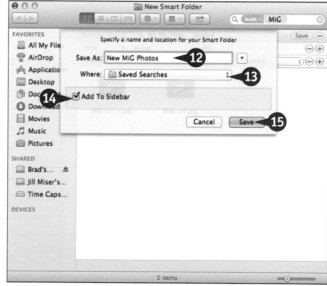

TIPS

Where is the Saved Searches folder?
When you accept the default location in which to store your smart folders, they are saved in your Saved Searches folder. To access this folder, press and hold Option and click the **Go** menu. Click **Library**. You will see the Saved Searches folder in the Library folder. If you do not save your searches on the Sidebar, add the Saved Searches folder to your Dock or to the Sidebar to make moving back there easier.

What determines how many choices are on the recent menus?
You can determine how many items are "remembered" by using the Number of recent items menu on the General pane of the System Preferences application. For example, if you select 10 on this menu, the Finder remembers the most recent 10 items you have accessed.

Get Information About Files and Folders

As discussed in Chapter 2, you can choose the specific information you see in some of the views, such as the List view. However, what you see in Finder windows is just some of the information about files and folders on MacBook Pro.

To see more detail about any file or folder, you can use the Finder's Get Info command. This command opens the Info window, which provides a lot of detailed information about what you have selected. The information in this window depends on the type of item you selected. For example, you see a different set of information when you select an application file than when you select a document.

Get Information About Files and Folders

① In a Finder window, select a file or folder you want to get information about.

② Click **File** and select **Get Info.**

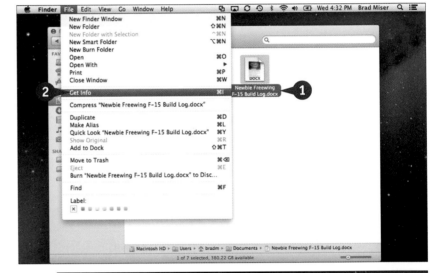

③ Click a section's disclosure triangle to see the information it contains (▶ changes to ▼).

Note: In addition to viewing information about a file or folder, you can also use the Info window to make changes to a file or folder. For example, the following steps show you how to change the application used to open a file. You can do other tasks as well, such as change the permissions for an item or enter comments for Spotlight searches.

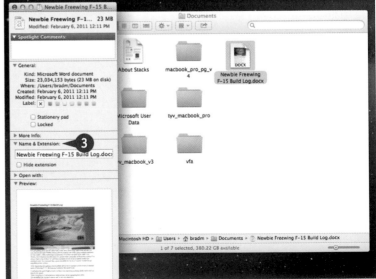

④ Scroll down the window to see all the sections available for the selected item.

⑤ Click the **Open with** arrow to expand the section.

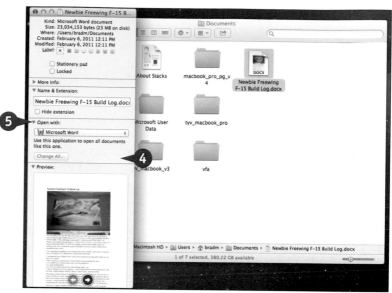

⑥ Click the **Open with** arrows and select the application in which you want the document to open from the pop-up menu.

⑦ Click **Change All** to open all documents of the same type in the application.

⑧ When you are done viewing or changing information, click **Close** (⬤) to close the Info window.

Note: You can leave the Info window open as long as you want, and you can have many Info windows open at the same time, which makes comparing items easy.

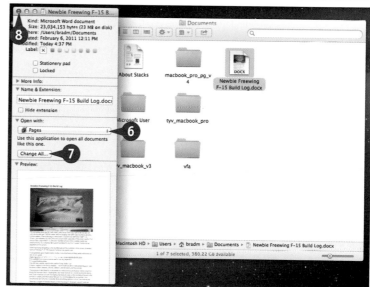

TIPS

What are Spotlight Comments?
The Spotlight Comments section appears at the top of the Info window. You can enter text in this field to associate that text with an item. When you search using Spotlight, this information is included in the search. For example, you could type a keyword for all the files relating to the same project. When you perform search for that keyword, files and folders are found based on the keyword you entered.

What is the Sharing & Permissions section used for?
Here, you see each person or group who has access to the item along with the permissions each has. You can use the controls in this section to change the access people or groups have to the item. First, click the **Lock** icon (🔒) and enter an administrator username and password. Second, use the pop-up menus to change privileges and **Add** or **Remove** (➕ and ➖) to make changes.

Store Files and Folders on CDs or DVDs

All MacBook Pros include a drive that you can use to burn CDs and DVDs. You might want to burn files and folders from the Finder to CDs or DVDs for many reasons, such as to transfer them to someone else or to safeguard copies of important folders and files for future use.

You can burn folders and files onto a CD or DVD in several ways. One of the most useful is by creating a burn folder. You can place and organize folders and files within a burn folder and then burn the folder onto a disc.

Store Files and Folders on CDs or DVDs

Create and Organize a Burn Folder

1. Open a Finder window showing the location in which you want to create a burn folder.

2. Open the **File** menu and choose **New Burn Folder**.

   Ⓐ A new burn folder is created; its name, "Burn Folder," is highlighted and ready for you to edit.

3. Type the name of the burn folder and press **Return**.

4. Open the burn folder in the Finder window.

   Ⓑ The folder's icon indicates it is a burn folder.

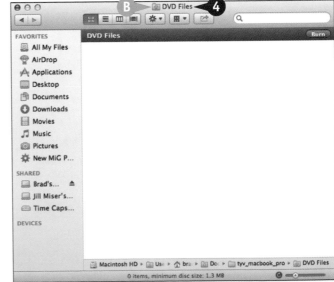

⑤ Open a new Finder window so that you have two windows on the desktop.

⑥ In the second window, move to the first folders or files you want to burn to a disc.

⑦ Drag the folders or files from the second window onto the burn folder's window.

Aliases (which are pointers that tell the Finder where the original file or folder is located) are created in the burn folder for each file or folder that you move there.

⑧ Repeat steps **6** and **7** until you have moved all the folders and files into the burn folder that you want to put on a disc.

⑨ Organize the files and folders in the burn folder as you want them to be organized on the disc. For example, you can create new folders and place the files and folders into them.

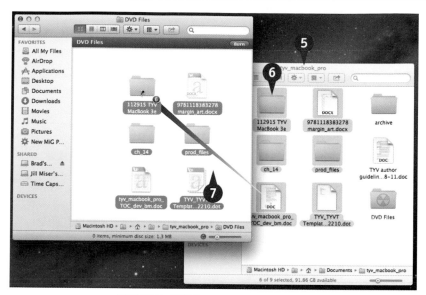

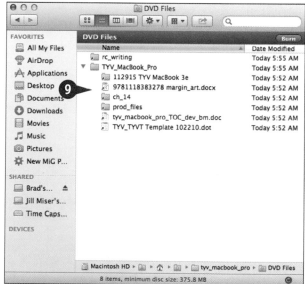

TIPS

How can I use erasable disks?
You can erase and reuse disc media of the type CD RW, DVD-RW, or DVD+RW. To erase a disc, open the Disk Utility application, select the disc you want to erase, click the Erase tab, and use the controls you see to erase the disc. Then, you can place new content onto the disc as if it was new.

How do I know how much data discs hold?
A CD holds about 700MB of data, and a DVD holds approximately 4.7GB of data. A DVD-DL (the DL stands for Dual Layer) disc holds about 8.5GB of data. You can determine how much information you are trying to place on a disc using the application creating the disc. For example, when you burn a disc in iTunes, it shows you how much data you will place on the disc.

continued ▶

Using a burn folder is a great way to store data files onto a disc for backup purposes. If you use a nonerasable disc format, make sure you test out the folder you intend to put on disc; if you burn it to a disc and then find a mistake, you have to start over, which wastes both your time and money.

Organizing your files and folders in a burn folder is the labor-intensive part of the task. The disc-burning process can take a while for lots of data, but you do not need to do anything other than start it; it runs without your interaction until the disc is complete.

Store Files and Folders on CDs or DVDs (continued)

Burn a Disc

1 Open the burn folder you want to place on a disc.

2 Check the minimum disc size for the folder by looking at the status bar at the bottom of its window.

If the size is less than about 700MB, you can burn the folder onto a CD. If it is larger than that, you need to use a DVD (up to 4.7GB for a single-layer DVD or 8.5GB for a dual-layer DVD) or burn the folder to multiple discs.

3 Click the **Burn** button.

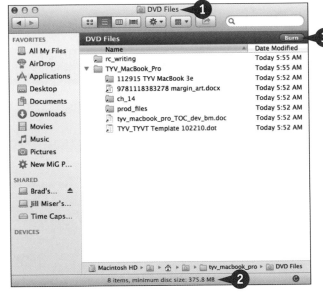

The insert disc prompt appears. The prompt also tells you how much disc space you need to burn the disc.

4 Insert a blank CD or DVD.

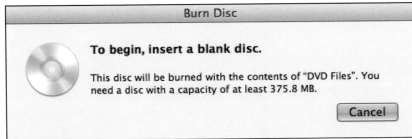

Burn Disc

To begin, insert a blank disc.

This disc will be burned with the contents of "DVD Files". You need a disc with a capacity of at least 375.8 MB.

Cancel

The burn disc dialog appears.

5 Enter the name of the disc you are burning; by default, its name is the same as the burn folder. You can change it or leave the default.

6 On the Burn Speed pop-up menu, choose the speed at which you want the disc to be burned. In most cases, leave the setting as **Maximum Possible**.

Note: If the burn process fails, try a slower burn speed.

7 Click **Burn**.

The burn process starts and you see the Burn progress window. This window remains open until the burn is done. How long the process takes depends on the size of the burn, what else MacBook Pro is doing, and the media you use. You can use MacBook Pro for other tasks while the disc is burning.

When the process is complete, the progress window disappears, a tone plays, and the disc is mounted.

8 Open a Finder window.

9 Select the disc you burned in the Devices section of the Sidebar.

A You see the contents of the disc, which look exactly like the burn folder. You can use the contents of the disc on your MacBook Pro or on most other computers.

10 Click ⏏ to eject the disc.

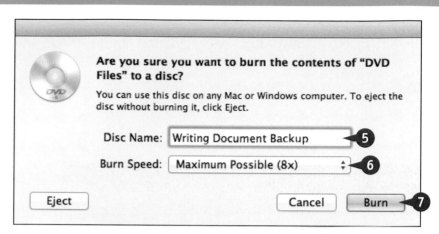

TIPS

What other applications can I use to burn CDs or DVDs?
Many applications enable you to burn discs. For example, you can use iTunes to create audio CDs. From iPhoto, you can burn photos to disc to archive them or make them easy to share. Each of these applications provides its own burn commands, typically located on the File menu or on the application's toolbar.

How can I create my own application installation discs?
Most applications you download from the web are in the disk image format. You can use the Disk Utility application to burn these onto a disc. Launch Disk Utility and select the disk image you have downloaded. Choose the **Burn** command; follow the prompts to burn the disk image on to a disc.

Understand Applications and Documents

The main reason to use a computer is to run applications, which enable you to do all sorts of useful things, such as create text documents, analyze spreadsheets, edit photos and movies, browse the web, create presentations, send and receive e-mail, play games, and so on. There are many types of applications available to you, and each provides specific functionality. There are even different applications that provide similar functionality, such as word processors. However, all applications share fundamental concepts that apply to each of them. Understanding these fundamentals will help you use a wide variety of applications on your MacBook Pro.

Applications

The reason computers work so well is that they are very good at following repetitive instructions that adhere to very specific syntax and logic rules. An *application* is a compilation of programming statements, more commonly called *code*, constructed according to a specific programming language. Applications separate you from the detailed code so that you can control what the application does by interacting with menus and graphical elements of the user interface, instead of having to re-create the lines of code each time you want to do something. Applications are created for many purposes, from running your MacBook Pro (OS X is a very complex collection of applications) to providing the weather at a glance through a simple Dashboard *widget* (a specific kind of application delivered through the Dashboard).

Documents

Most applications, but certainly not all of them, work with documents. A document is much more than just a text file; documents can certainly contain text, but they can also be images, e-mails, and songs. Basically, a *document* is the content an application works with. So, for a text processor such as Microsoft Word, a document can include text and graphics. A graphics application, such as Photoshop, uses images as documents. The songs and video stored within iTunes can also be considered documents. If you open or save something with an application, that something can be called a document.

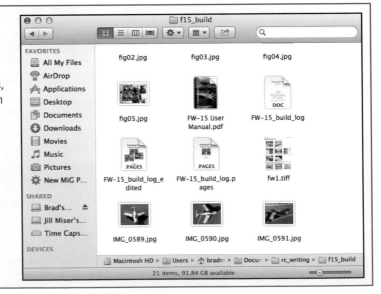

Windows

Chapter 2 talked about the various kinds of windows you see on your MacBook Pro. As that chapter mentioned, applications provide windows through which you view documents, or controls and functions when an application does not work with documents (such as a game). An application's windows are whatever you see when you open and use that application. Most applications allow you to have many documents open at the same time, with each appearing in a separate window.

Standard Menus

Applications contain commands that you use to perform actions. For example, when you want to save changes to a document you are working on, you use the Save, Save As, or Save a Version command. Commands are organized into logical collections on menus. When you open a menu, you can see and choose the commands it contains. OS X applications are supposed to support a set of standard menus that have the same or similar commands; these include the *Application* menu (where *Application* is the name of the application), File, Edit, Window, and Help. These menus also contain sets of standard commands; for example, the application menu always contains the Quit command. Applications can and usually do have more menus than just the standard menus that are part of OS X design specifications. Some applications, mostly games, do not include standard menus at all.

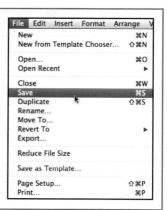

Application Preferences

Not everyone uses applications in the same way; everyone has her own preferences. Because of this, applications include preferences that enable you to configure various aspects of how the application looks and works. You can use preferences to enable or disable functions, change the appearance of the application's windows, and so on. In effect, these commands enable you to tailor the way they work to your preferences, thus the name for this type of command. You can set preferences by opening the application menu and choosing Preferences.

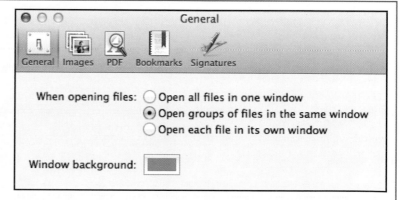

Install Applications with the App Store Application

The App Store application enables you to quickly find, purchase (some are free), download, and install applications from the Mac App Store. The application also enables you to update your applications easily.

To use the Mac App Store, you need an Apple ID; you sign in to the store using your ID. Your Apple ID contains the payment information you use to purchase applications (such as the credit or debit card associated with your Apple ID account). This makes the purchase process fast and convenient.

Install Applications with the App Store Application

Sign In to the Mac App Store

① Launch the App Store application by clicking its icon on the Dock ( ).

② In the Quick Links section, click **Sign In**.

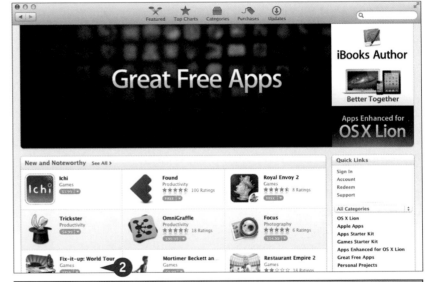

③ Type your Apple ID.

④ Type your password.

⑤ Click **Sign In**.

You sign in to your account and are ready to shop in the App Store.

Browse For and Install Applications from the Mac App Store

① Click one of the three tabs that enable you to browse for applications: **Featured**, **Top Charts**, or **Categories**.

② Browse for applications of interest to you.

Most of the text and graphics you see in the store are links you can click to move around the App Store.

Note: You can search for applications by typing the information for which you want to search in the search box located in the upper right corner of the window.

③ Click an application's icon to get more information about it.

The application's information screen appears.

④ Read the information for the application; this includes a description, screenshots, user reviews, and so on.

⑤ To download and install the application, click the button showing the price if it has a license fee (the amount is shown within the button) or click the **Install** button if the application is free.

⑥ If the application has a license fee, click **Buy** at the prompt; skip this step for free applications.

Note: Depending on when you last purchased an application, you may be prompted to confirm the purchase or enter your account's password.

The application is downloaded to and installed on your MacBook Pro. The application is ready for you to use.

TIPS

How can I install applications I obtain through the App Store on more than one Mac without paying for them again?
To install the same application on a different Mac, launch the App Store application on that Mac. Sign in to the account under which you downloaded the application. Click the **Purchased** tab. Click the **Install** button for the application you want to install. The application downloads and installs.

What should I do when the App Store icon and its Updates tab has a number next to it?
This number indicates how many of the applications you have obtained through the Mac App Store have updates to the version you currently have installed. To update your applications, click the **Update** tab and click the **Update** button for the applications you want to update, or click **Update All** to update all your applications that have updates available.

Install Applications from the Desktop

Although the Mac App Store has many applications, it certainly does not have all the applications that are available. You can add more applications by downloading them from the web and installing them or installing them from a disc. Whether you download them from the web or use a disc, you can install applications from the desktop in two basic ways.

Some applications include an installer program; to install the application, you open the installer and follow the on-screen instructions. Other applications use a drag-and-drop installation method that requires you to drag a folder or file into the Applications folder.

Install Applications from the Desktop

Install Applications with an Installer

Note: By default, only applications you obtain from the App Store can be installed. To install applications from other sources, you need to change the Gatekeeper settings. See Chapter 9 for the details.

1 Download the application's installer from the Internet or insert the CD or DVD it came on.

Note: In most cases, the installer starts automatically; if so, skip step **2**.

2 Double-click the application installer's icon.

3 If prompted to accept the license agreement, click **Agree**.

4 Read the information on the first screen of the installer and click **Continue**.

5 Continue reading the information presented on each screen of the installer and providing the required input.

Eventually, you move to the Install screen.

6 Click **Install**.

You are prompted to authenticate yourself as an administrator.

7 Type your username. If you are logged in under an administrator account, this is filled in automatically.

8 Type your password.

9 Click **Install Software**.

The installer runs and presents progress information in its window. When the process is done, you see the Complete screen and usually hear the Process Complete sound.

10 Click **Close** or **Quit**.

The installer quits and the application is ready for you to use.

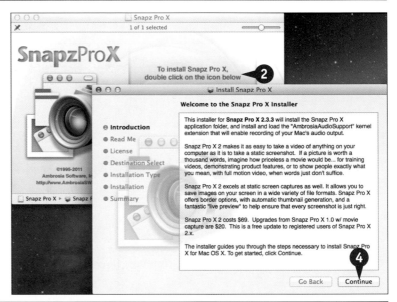

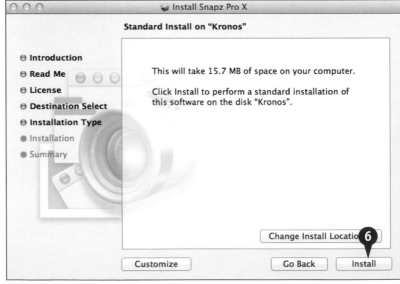

Install Applications with Drag and Drop

1 Download the application from the Internet or get it from the CD or DVD it came on.

Note: In most cases, the files are provided as a disk image, which usually mounts on MacBook Pro automatically. If so, skip step **2.**

2 Double-click the disk image file ending in .dmg.

The disk image is mounted on MacBook Pro.

3 View the files in the disk image, which are typically organized into a folder and explain what you need to do.

4 Click **Go** and then click **Applications**.

A new Finder window appears, showing the Applications folder.

5 Drag the application folder from the disk image window onto the Applications window and release the trackpad button.

The application is copied to and installed in the Applications folder, ready for you to use.

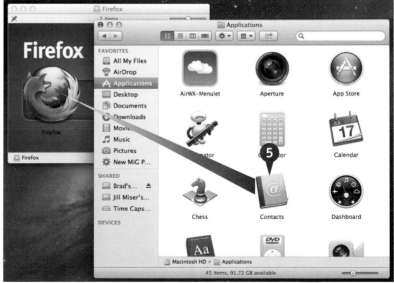

How do I customize an install?

Most installer applications include a Customize button that enables you to customize the application's installation, such as to exclude features or resources you do not need. In most cases, you can ignore this and just perform a standard install. However, if your MacBook Pro is low on disk space, you might want to use the customization options to see if you can skip features or resources you do not need.

Where should I install an application?

In most cases, you should install it in the Applications folder. Most installer applications choose this folder by default, and the instructions with drag-and-drop installations tell you to install there. Keeping your applications in the Applications folder makes them easier for everyone who uses MacBook Pro to find, as well as updaters and other programs that need to know the location of applications to run.

Launch Applications with the Launchpad

The Launchpad provides quick, one-click access to your applications. No matter how you install applications, they are added to your Launchpad automatically. To use an application, you simply pop the Launchpad open and click the application's icon.

On the Launchpad, applications can be organized in folders. Some applications, such as OS X's utilities, are in a folder already. You can create folders for other applications to keep them organized.

Launch Applications with the Launchpad

Open Applications from the Launchpad

① Click **Launchpad** () on the Dock.

Note: You can also perform a three-finger (and thumb) pinch on the desktop to open the Launchpad.

The Launchpad fills the screen. The Launchpad has pages with each page containing a set of applications.

Ⓐ The first page has OS X's default applications.

② To move through the Launchpad's pages, swipe your fingers on the trackpad to the left to move to later pages or to the right to move to earlier pages.

Ⓑ The applications on the page appear.

Ⓒ The page you are currently viewing is indicated by the lighted dot just above the Dock.

Note: You can jump to a specific page by clicking its dot.

③ To use an application, click its icon.

The application opens.

Note: Applications are shown on the Launchpad based upon when you installed the applications. The most recent applications you installed are located in the lower right corner of the last page.

Access Applications in Folders

1 If the application you want to use is in a folder, click the folder's icon.

D The folder opens and you see the applications it contains.

2 Click the application you want to use.

The application launches.

Organize the Launchpad with Folders

1 To create a folder, drag one application's icon on top of another one.

E A new folder is created and named based on the type of applications you put in it.

2 To rename the new folder, click its name.

It becomes highlighted.

3 Type the new name.

4 Press **Return**.

TIPS

How can I remove applications from my MacBook Pro?

When you decide you no longer want an application on your MacBook Pro, you can delete it. You can do this in two basic ways. If the application included an uninstaller application, run the uninstaller application to remove the application from your MacBook Pro. If it does not include an uninstaller, just drag the application's icon into the Trash.

How can I get an application that I have removed back?

To restore an application, you need to reinstall it. If you got it from the App Store, move to the **Purchases** tab and click **Install**. If you installed it from an install application, run the installer again. If you saved a copy of the disk image, use that to reinstall the application.

Launch Applications from the Desktop

The first step in using an application is to open (also called launch) it. You can do this in many ways, and as you use MacBook Pro, you will no doubt develop your preferred method. That may be the Launchpad described in the last section. However, the Launchpad is just one way to open applications.

You should try other ways to launch applications too; some of these you have probably already used. Over time, you will probably find that some methods work better for you than others.

Launch Applications from the Desktop

Open Applications from the Dock

1 Click an application's icon on the Dock.

Note: The first time you open an application you have downloaded from the Internet, you may see a warning dialog. This is intended to prevent you from unintentionally opening applications that might harm your computer, such as viruses. Click Allow to open the application if you are sure of its legitimacy.

The application's icon bounces as it opens, and is marked with a light-blue dot to show that the application is running (assuming those preferences are enabled).

A When complete, the application's windows appear and are ready for you to use.

Open Applications from the Sidebar

1 Select the application you want to add to the Sidebar.

2 Press ⌘+T.

B The application's icon is installed on the Sidebar and is ready to use.

3 Repeat steps **1** and **2** for all the applications you want to be available on the Sidebar.

4 To launch the application, click its icon on the Sidebar.

Open Applications from the Applications Folder

1 Click **Go** and then click **Applications**.

Note: You can also click Applications on the Sidebar to move into that folder.

C The Applications folder appears in a Finder window.

2 Scroll in the window until you see the application you want to open.

3 Double-click the application's icon, or click the icon once to select it and press ⌘+O.

The application opens and is ready for you to use.

Open Applications from Documents

1 Find a document in a Finder window.

2 Double-click the document's icon.

The application that the document is associated with opens, and you see the contents of the document.

Note: Chapter 6 explains how to have applications open automatically when you log in to your user account.

TIPS

Why do some applications disappear from the Dock when I quit them?

Only applications whose icons are installed on the Dock remain there at all times. When you open an application not installed on the Dock, its icon appears toward the dashed dividing line. You can use the application's contextual menu to control it. When you quit the application, its icon disappears from the Dock.

How do I configure the applications on the Dock?

Drag the application's icon onto the Dock in the location where you want to install it; icons already there slide apart to make room for the newcomer. If the Dock is already as wide as it can be, the icons shrink a bit so they all fit. To remove an icon from the Dock, drag it off the Dock and release it. It disappears in a puff of smoke (the application itself is not changed).

Control Applications

N o doubt you will find lots of applications to be very useful. Fortunately, you can have multiple applications running at the same time, such as Mail, Safari, iTunes, and so on. So, you do not have to waste time opening and closing applications; you can leave them running until you do not need them anymore.

Once applications are running, you can control them in a number of ways. You can switch between them, hide them, minimize their windows, and eventually, quit them.

Control Applications

Switch Applications

1 Open several applications.

2 Press ⌘+**Tab**.

A The Application Switcher appears, showing an icon for each currently running application.

B The application you currently selected is highlighted in the white box.

3 Click the application you want to move into, or press **Tab** or **Shift**+**Tab** (while pressing and holding ⌘) until the application you want to use is highlighted, and release the trackpad button.

The application you selected becomes active, and you can use it.

Hide Applications

1 Click *Application* and then click **Hide Application,** where *Application* is the name of the application you want to hide.

All the windows open in the application disappear, as does the application's menu bar. However, the application is still running; you can move back into it by using the Application Switcher, clicking the application's icon on the Dock, and so on.

Minimize Application Windows

1 Click **Minimize** (⊡) to reduce the active window.

The window shrinks down to a thumbnail and moves onto the Dock. You can move back into the window by clicking it. (If you selected the other option, it moves onto the application's icon instead and you can use the application's contextual menu to move back into the window.)

Switch Applications with Mission Control

1 Swipe down on the trackpad with the gesture you configured for Mission Control to activate it.

C Thumbnails of the Dashboard, your spaces, and applications in Full Screen mode appear.

D Thumbnails of the applications that are open on the current desktop appear.

E The windows that are open in an application appear as individual thumbnails.

2 To move into an application, click its icon if it is Full Screen mode, or move onto the desktop on which its windows are shown and click the thumbnail into which you want to move.

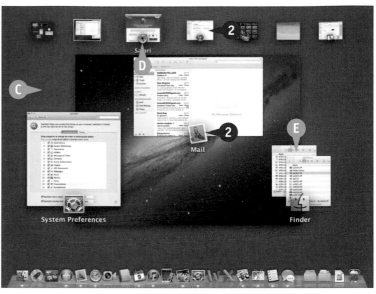

Quit Applications

1 Click *Application* and then click **Quit Application**, where *Application* is the name of the application you want to quit, or press ⌘+Q.

The application stops running. If you have any documents open with unsaved changes, you are prompted to save them before quitting.

How do I handle an application that does not appear to be doing anything and a spinning wheel is on the screen?

Occasionally, an application hangs. Let some time pass to see if the application starts working again. If not, open the **Apple** menu (🍎) and choose **Force Quit**. Select the application having problems and click **Force Quit**. Click **Force Quit** again. You lose any unsaved changes, so do this only as a last resort. Restart your MacBook Pro.

I have opened a lot of applications and do not want to quit all of them one by one. Is there a faster way?

Yes. Log out of your user account by pressing **Shift**+⌘+Q, unchecking the **Reopen windows when logging back in** check box, and clicking **Log Out**. When you log out, all open applications and windows are closed. The next time you log in, no applications are open.

Save Documents

As you make changes to a document, you need to save those changes. This sounds simple, and it is, but many people do not regularly save their work. If an application quits before you save changes, you lose all the work you have done. So, get in the habit of saving documents frequently. OS X supports *versioning* of documents, which means you can save and return multiple versions of documents.

When you save a document for the first time, you use the Save As command. This is important because you name the document and choose the location in which you save it.

Save Documents

Save Existing Documents

Note: This section applies only to applications that do not support OS X's Version feature.

1. Open a document and work with it using its associated application.

2. Click **File**.

3. Click **Save**.

Note: The first time you save a document, you use the Save As command instead.

> The document is saved in its current state, and the new version replaces the previous version you saved.

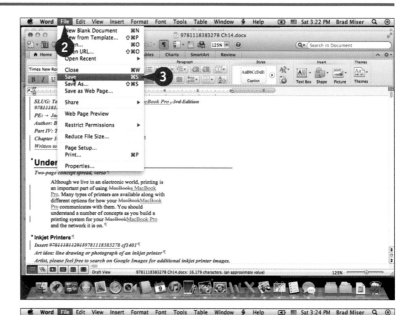

Save New Documents

1. Open the application with which you want to create a new document.

2. Click **File**.

3. Click **Save As**.

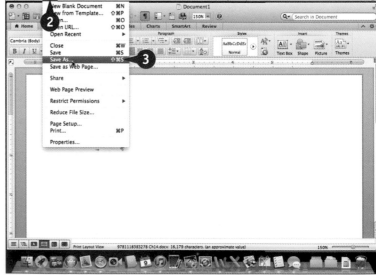

Note: The first time you save a document, you can use the Save or Save As command because it does the same thing. When you want to rename a document or save a new version, you can use the Save As command.

The Save As dialog appears.

4 In the Save As field, type a name for the file; you should leave the filename extension (if it is shown), which is everything after the period, as it is.

5 Click the down arrow (▼).

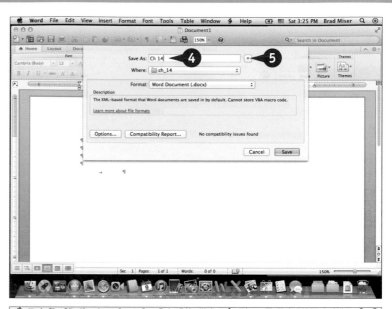

The dialog expands so that you see more details.

6 Select the location in which you want to save the file.

Note: You can choose save locations on the pop-up menu just under the Save As field.

A You can click the Format down arrows to change how the file is created.

B You can show the filename extension by deselecting the **Hide extension** check box.

The filename extension is appended to the filename.

7 Click **Save**.

The document's file is created in the location you set, and you are ready to get to work.

TIPS

Can my documents be saved automatically?

If an application supports OS X's Version feature, it is saved automatically. Many applications have preference settings that you can configure to save your documents periodically. Open the application's Preferences dialog and look for the save preferences. Set them to save frequently. The amount of time that passes without saving your document may be the amount of time you have to spend redoing what you have already done.

My hard drive crashed. Can I recover my saved document?

It depends on what kind of failure your disk had. In some cases, the documents and other data can be restored. In other cases, you are out of luck. You should always keep important documents backed up so you can recover them if needed. Chapter 17 discusses how to use the OS X Time Machine feature to protect your documents.

Work with Versions of Documents

Applications that support OS X's Version feature automatically save documents as you change them. Each time a document is saved, a version is created. Versions are created at least every hour, and more frequently when you are making "significant" changes to the document. You can also save a version at any time. Versions are useful because they enable you to go back to a previous edition of a document.

Hourly versions are saved for 24 hours. Daily revisions are available for a month, after which time weekly versions are available.

Work with Versions of Documents

Save a Version of a Document

1 Click **File**.

2 Click **Save**.

The current version of the document is saved and becomes available in the document's version history.

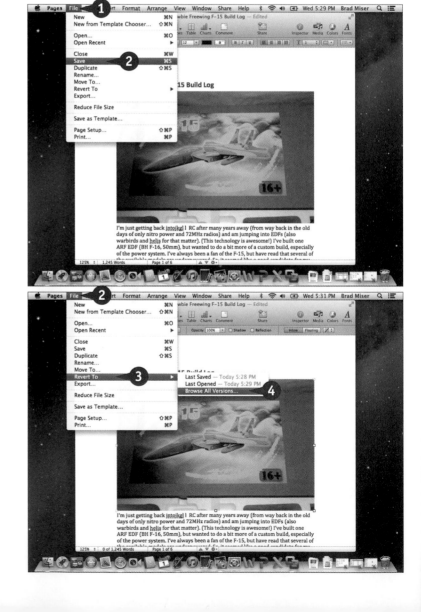

Restore a Previous Version of a Document

1 Open the document for which you want to recover a version.

2 Click **File**.

3 Click **Revert**.

4 Click **Browse All Versions**.

The available versions of the document fill the screen.

Ⓐ On the left, you see the current version of the document.

Ⓑ On the right, you see the saved versions, with the most recent facing you and the older versions behind it. The date and time shown under the document is for the frontmost version.

Ⓒ To the right is the timeline history of the document from the frontmost version back to the oldest version (from bottom to top).

❺ To move back to a previous version, click in the windows behind the current one or click the timeline.

Ⓓ The version you selected comes to the front.

❻ To compare the versions, scroll up and down in each window.

❼ To restore the frontmost version, click **Restore**.

The version you selected replaces the one you were working on.

Note: To return to the version of the document you were working on, click Done.

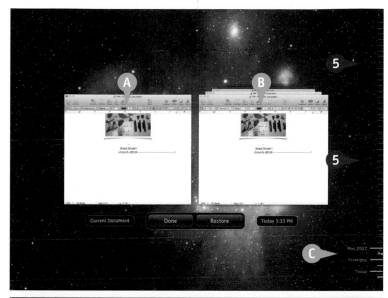

TIPS

How does versioning relate to Time Machine?
Time Machine automatically backs up files every hour. So, the most amount of working time at risk is 1 hour. Versioning also saves documents every hour, and also saves them when a significant amount of changes have been made. So, if a problem occurs with the current version of a document and you made changes over the past hour, try reverting to a previous version instead of restoring from Time Machine.

What happens to versions when I delete a document?
When you delete a document, all of its versions are deleted too. If you have the document backed up via Time Machine, you can retrieve it from your backups (assuming the backup containing the document has not been deleted due to lack of space).

Expand an Application to Full Screen Mode

When it comes to application windows, more room in which to work is always better because you see more of whatever you happen to be working on. This includes word processing documents, photos, and spreadsheets. However, more room makes working with webpages, e-mail, and just about everything else better too.

All Apple applications and some others support OS X's Full Screen mode. In this mode, the application fills the entire desktop, giving you the maximum amount of room. In fact, even the menu bar gets hidden to make as many pixels available for you as possible.

Expand an Application to Full Screen Mode

1 Move to an application.

2 Click **Full Screen** ( ).

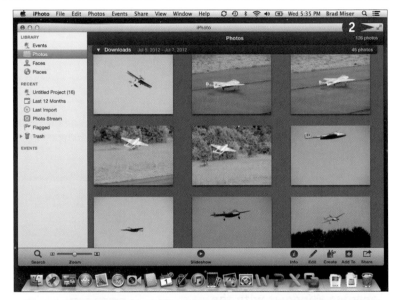

The application fills the screen.

A To access the application's menu bar, point to the top of the screen and the menu bar will appear.

3 To exit Full Screen mode, press Esc.

Working with Multiple Application Windows

In many situations, you will have more than one document open in the same application at the same time. You may need to reference one document while working on the other, or you may be comparing two versions. Many applications allow you to have multiple windows open at the same time.

For this to be effective, you must understand how to easily move between the windows open in the application you are using. Like so many other tasks, there are multiple ways to work with more than one window at a time.

Working with Multiple Application Windows

Managing Windows with App Exposé

1 Swipe three or four fingers (depending your trackpad setting) down the trackpad.

A App Exposé shows you thumbnails of all the open windows in the application at the top of the screen.

B Thumbnails of recently closed windows are shown at the bottom of the screen.

2 Click the window in which you want to work.

The window you clicked moves to the front and you can use it.

Note: If you click the thumbnail of a closed window, the related document opens and moves to the front so you can work within it.

Managing Windows with the Windows Menu

1 Click **Window**.

You see a list of all the windows currently open. The window marked with a check mark is the current window. Windows that are open and minimized are marked with a diamond.

2 Click the window in which you want to move.

That window comes to the front and you can work with it.

Set Finder Preferences

The Finder is the application that controls the OS X desktop, how files and folders are managed, and many other aspects of the way your MacBook Pro operates. Like all the other applications you use, the Finder has a set of preferences you can configure to change the way it looks and works.

You change Finder preferences using its Preferences command. The resulting dialog has several tabs that you use to configure specific aspects of how the Finder looks and behaves.

Set Finder Preferences

1 Open the **Finder** menu and choose **Preferences** to open the Finder Preferences window.

2 Click the **General** tab.

3 Check the **Hard disks**, **External disks**, **CDs, DVDs, and iPods**, or **Connected servers** check boxes if you want any of these to show up as icons on the desktop (they are always available on the Sidebar within Finder windows).

4 Use the **New Finder windows show** pop-up menu to choose the default location for new Finder windows; choose **All My Files** to open a window showing all your files, your account's username to always open your Home folder, **Documents** to open your Documents folder, a volume to go there, or **Other** and select a start location.

5 If you always want folders to open in a new window rather than inside the current one, check the **Always open folders in a new window** check box.

6 If you want folders to spring open when you drag icons onto them, check the **Spring-loaded folders and windows** check box, and drag the slider to the left to shorten the time before a folder springs open or to the right to increase the time.

7 Click the **Labels** tab.

Note: You can associate files and folders with labels to help you identify and organize them more easily on the desktop. To do so, perform a secondary click on a file's or folder's icon and select the color of the label you want to apply.

8 Enter a name for each label in the field next to its color.

Note: When you apply a label to a file or folder, both the color and name are used, but you do not always see both on the desktop.

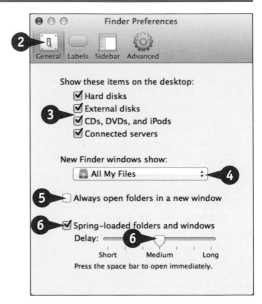

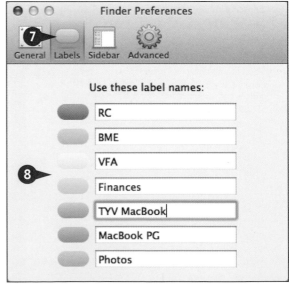

9 Click the **Sidebar** tab.

10 Check the box next to each item you want to appear in the Sidebar, or uncheck the box next to each item you do not want to appear in the Sidebar.

Note: When you uncheck an item's check box, it is still available in Finder windows; you just do not see its icon on the Sidebar.

11 Click the **Advanced** tab.

12 If you always want filename extensions to be shown, check the **Show all filename extensions** check box.

13 To be warned when you change a filename extension, check the **Show warning before changing an extension** check box.

Note: Checking both boxes in steps **12** and **13** is recommended because being aware of filename extensions is important to understanding the application you use for each file.

14 If you want to have to confirm emptying the Trash, check the **Show warning before emptying the Trash** check box.

15 If you want the Trash to be emptied securely, making things you delete harder to recover, check the **Empty Trash securely** check box.

16 Choose the default search scope on the **When performing a search** pop-up menu; choose **Search This Mac** to search your MacBook Pro, **Search the Current Folder** to search the active folder, or **Use the Previous Search Scope** to repeat your last search.

Note: You can change the scope of any search regardless of the default scope setting.

17 Click **Close** (●).

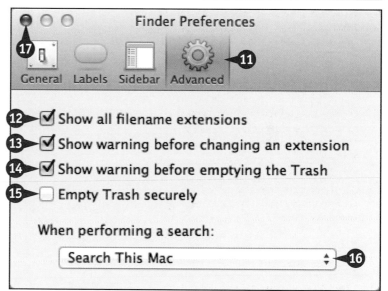

TIPS

Which folders can I use as my start folder for new Finder windows?

The initial location is your All My Files folder, but you can choose any folder you want. For example, if you keep all of your active projects in a folder, you might want that folder to open by default instead. On the **New Finder windows show** pop-up menu, choose **Other**. In the resulting dialog, navigate to and select the folder you want to be the default, and then click **Choose**. Each time you open a new Finder window, you move to that folder automatically.

What is another way to associate labels with folders and files?

Open a Finder window showing the folder or file you want to label. Press ⌘+I . The Info window opens. Expand the General section. Click the label color that you want to apply. The file or folder is marked with that color. You can search for files and folders by their labels; for example, you can create and save a search that automatically finds all folders and files with a specific label!. You can also more easily see which files and folders are related because of the label color visible in Finder windows.

Explore the System Preferences Application

The System Preferences application is used to configure many different aspects of how MacBook Pro looks and works. In fact, most of the personalization you do is through this application.

System Preferences is one application organized in many different panes, with each pane used to configure a specific aspect of MacBook Pro. You open the pane you want to use to configure a specific area. For example, you use the Dock pane to configure the Dock, and the Network pane to specify how MacBook Pro connects to a network.

Explore the System Preferences Application

Open and Use System Preferences

1 Open the **Apple** menu (![]) and choose **System Preferences**.

A The System Preferences application opens and you see all the panes it offers.

2 Click an icon.

B The pane associated with that icon appears.

3 Use the controls on the pane to make changes to the way MacBook Pro works.

4 When you are done with the pane, click **Show All**.

The open pane closes and you see all the icons again.

Show Panes Alphabetically

1 From the **View** menu, choose **Organize Alphabetically**.

C The panes are organized alphabetically instead of by category.

Search for a Pane

1 To search for a pane, type text in the search bar.

D As you type, panes that meet or are related to your search criteria are highlighted.

2 Click the icon you want to use.

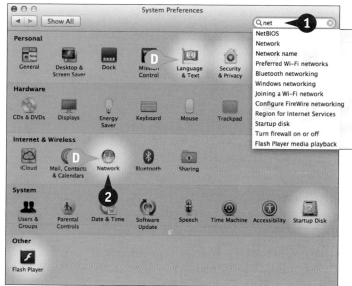

How can I change settings when they are disabled?
In order to make some changes to settings using the System Preferences application, you must verify that you are an administrator. To tell, look at the lock icon located in the lower-left corner of a pane. If you do not see the lock icon, any user can change the pane. If the lock is "closed," click it to verify that you are an administrator by entering your username and password. If the lock is "open," you can make changes.

Why do I see a section called Other in my System Preferences application?
Some software you install, especially when it is associated with a hardware device, includes a pane installed on the System Preferences application that you use to configure that software or hardware. All of these additions to the default panes are placed in the Other category.

Change General Preferences

Using the General pane, you can configure the color of buttons, menus, and windows along with the color used when something is highlighted to show that it is selected. You can also configure how scrolling in windows works.

You also use the Appearance pane to determine how many items are stored on Recent menus. You can also control how font smoothing works. *Font smoothing* makes the edges of large letters and numbers look smoother on the screen — they sometimes can look pixilated or "jaggy."

Change General Preferences

Choose Finder Colors

1 Open the System Preferences application and choose the **General** pane.

2 On the **Appearance** pop-up menu, choose **Blue** to see the default button, menu, and window colors.

Note: For a more subdued color for these items, choose Graphite.

3 On the **Highlight color** pop-up menu, choose the color you want to be used to show when a file or folder is selected on the desktop.

4 To create your own highlight color, choose **Other** on the **Highlight color** pop-up menu.

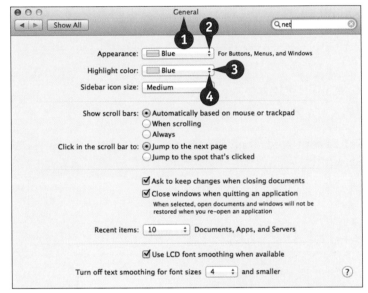

The color picker appears.

5 Click the type of color picker you want to use, such as the **Color Wheel**.

Ⓐ The controls for the color picker you selected fill the window.

6 Use the controls to configure the color you want to use.

7 Click **Close** (⊜).

The color you configured is shown on the Highlight Color menu and is used to highlight items on the desktop.

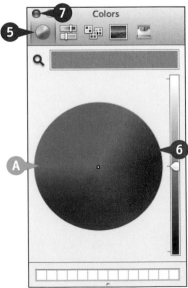

Configure Scroll Tools and Document Behavior

1 Click a **Show scroll bars** option.

2 Click an option to jump to the next page or to jump to the spot that is clicked.

3 Click the **Ask to keep changes when closing documents** check box if you want to be prompted when you close a window without saving.

4 Click the **Close windows when quitting an application** check box if you want all the open windows in an application to close when you quit an application.

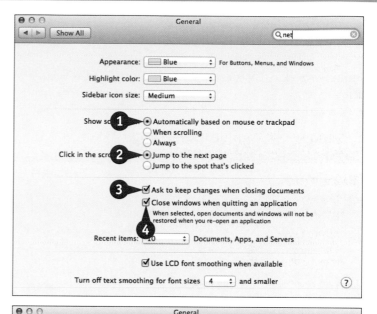

Set Recent Items and Font Smoothing

1 Click the **Recent items** pop-up menu and choose the number of items you want to show on each of the Recent menus.

2 To apply font smoothing, click the **Use LCD font smoothing when available** check box.

3 To determine the point size at which font smoothing is turned off, click the **Turn off text smoothing for font sizes** pop-up menu and select a size.

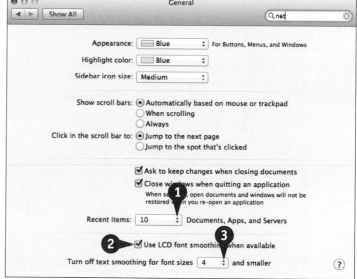

TIP

Which color picker is the best?

The color picker has different pickers that change the way you choose colors. The easiest to use is the crayons picker because you simply choose colors by clicking a crayon. The other pickers offer more control and specificity. For example, you can use the color wheel picker to select any color in the spectrum by dragging the intensity bar up or down and then clicking in the wheel to choose a specific color. Other pickers offer different tools. To add a custom color to a mode's palette, drag it from the sample box at the top of the window to the palette at the bottom; you can choose your custom color again by clicking it on the palette.

Set a Desktop Picture

As you use MacBook Pro, you look at the desktop quite often. So why not look at something you want to see? That is where setting the desktop picture comes in; the desktop picture fills the background on the desktop and you see it behind any open windows.

Although it is called a desktop picture, you are not limited to pictures. You can use just about any kind of graphic file as a desktop picture.

Set a Desktop Picture

Set a Default Image as the Desktop Picture

1 Open the System Preferences application and choose the **Desktop & Screen Saver** pane.

2 Click the **Desktop** tab.

3 Choose a source of images in the left pane of the window, such as the **Desktop Pictures** folder.

Ⓐ The images in that source appear in the right pane of the window.

4 Click the image that you want to apply to the desktop.

That image fills the desktop.

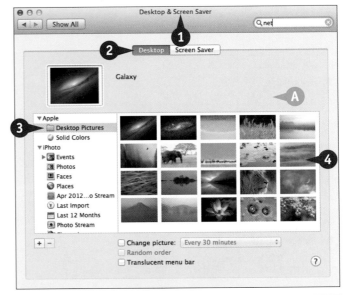

5 To have the image changed automatically, check the **Change picture** check box.

6 On the pop-up menu, choose how often you want the picture to change.

7 If you want images to be selected randomly rather than by the order in which they appear in the source, check the **Random order** check box.

A new image from the selected source is applied to the desktop according to the timing you selected.

8 If you want the menu bar to be solid so that you cannot see the background through it, uncheck the **Translucent menu bar** check box.

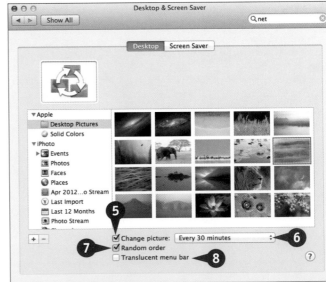

Set a Photo from Your iPhoto Library as the Desktop Picture

① Open the System Preferences application and choose the **Desktop & Screen Saver** pane.

② Click the **Desktop** tab.

③ Scroll down the source list until you see the iPhoto collection; expand it and the sources it contains, such as **Events**.

④ Click the source of photos, such as an event, containing the images you want to use on the desktop.

Ⓑ The images in the selected source appear in the right pane of the window.

⑤ Use the pop-up menu at the top of the window to choose how you want photos to be scaled to the screen; this example chooses the **Fill Screen** option.

⑥ To have the image changed automatically, check the **Change picture** check box.

⑦ On the pop-up menu, choose how often you want the picture to change.

⑧ If you want images to be selected randomly rather than by the order in which they appear in the source, check the **Random order** check box.

Ⓒ A new image from the iPhoto source is applied to the desktop according to the timing you selected.

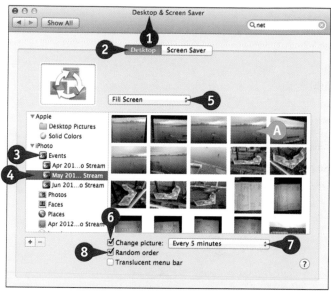

What is the Pictures folder source?
By default, a number of applications store image files in the Pictures folder within your Home folder. If you choose this folder in the source list, you see all the images it contains; you can select images from this source just as you do from one of the other sources.

What if the location of the photos I want to use as the desktop picture does not appear on the source list?
You can choose any folder as a source of desktop pictures by clicking **Add** (⊞) located at the bottom of the source list. Use the resulting dialog to navigate to and select the folder containing the images you want. After you click the **Choose** button, that folder appears as a source in the list.

Choose a Screen Saver

While you do not have to worry about damaging your MacBook Pro's display by leaving it turned on, this can be an issue with some external displays. Probably more important, a screen saver entertains you by displaying images that you choose on the screen. The most functional aspect of a screen saver is that you can require a password to be entered to stop the screen saver, which is a good security measure.

When you are running on battery power, it is better to put MacBook Pro to sleep when you are using it instead of showing the screen saver, see the section "Save Energy."

Choose a Screen Saver

Create a Photo Slideshow Screen Saver

1 Open the System Preferences application and open the **Desktop & Screen Saver** pane.

2 Click the **Screen Saver** tab.

3 Click the slideshow screen saver you want to use from the list in the Slideshows section in the left part of the window.

Ⓐ You see the selected screen saver run in the right pane of the window.

4 Choose the source of images for the screen saver on the **Source** menu.

Note: You can choose images from one of the default collections, any folder containing images, or from your iPhoto library.

5 To display the photos randomly, check **Shuffle slide order**.

6 Open the **Start after** menu to set the amount of idle time that passes before the screen saver activates.

7 If you want the time to appear on the screen saver, click the **Show with clock** check box.

8 Click **Hot Corners**.

The Hot Corners sheet appears.

9 Open the menu located at the corner that you want to set as the hot corner for the screen saver and choose **Start Screen Saver**.

10 Click **OK**.

11 Point to the hot corner you set.

You see the screen saver in action.

12 Press a key or drag on the trackpad to stop the screen saver and go back to the System Preferences application.

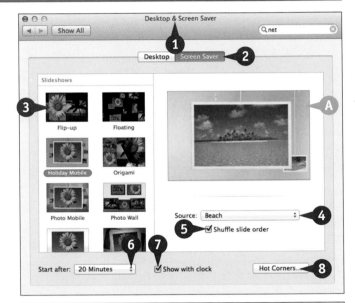

Choose a Default Screen Saver

1 Open the System Preferences application and open the **Desktop & Screen Saver** pane.

2 Click the **Screen Saver** tab.

3 Click the screen saver you want to use from the list in the Screen Savers section in the left part of the window.

Ⓑ You see the selected screen saver run in the right pane of the window.

4 Open the **Start after** menu to set the amount of idle time that passes before the screen saver activates.

5 If you want the time to appear on the screen saver, click the **Show with clock** check box.

6 Click **Screen Saver Options**.

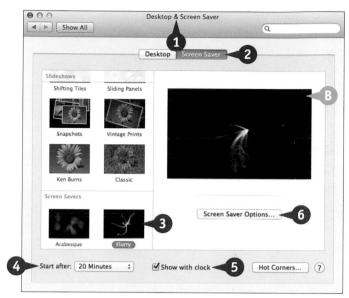

7 Use the tools on the Options sheet to configure the screen saver.

Note: Each screen saver has its own set of options, and so what you see on the Options sheet depends on the screen saver you select.

8 Click **OK**.

9 Set the hot corner for the screen saver (see the previous section).

10 Point to the hot corner.

You see the screen saver in action.

11 Press a key or drag on the trackpad to stop the screen saver and go back to the System Preferences application.

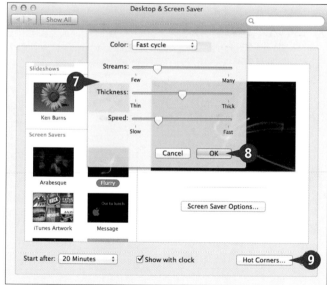

TIPS

Why do I never see my screen saver?
The screen saver interacts with the settings on the Energy Saver pane, one of which is the amount of time that passes before the screen darkens to save energy. If that time is less than the screen saver is set for, then you do not see the screen saver before the screen goes dark. Reduce the time for the screen saver to less than the time for the display to darken.

How can I manually activate the screen saver?
Use the hot corner you set. When you move the pointer to that corner, the screen saver starts. This is especially useful if you have set your MacBook Pro to require a password to stop the screen saver. You can start the screen saver and your MacBook Pro immediately becomes secured because it is protected with a password.

Set and Configure the Clock

Your MacBook Pro can help you by keeping track of the time and date. Obviously, you can use your computer to see what time it is, but time and date are also important because OS X stamps all the files and folders you use with the time and date they were created, when they were changed, or when they were last opened. Likewise, e-mails are also time and date stamped. The time and date applied to these items are those configured on your MacBook Pro. You can set the time and date in two basic ways: automatically using a timeserver, or manually. Having your computer set its clock automatically is a good idea so that you can be sure the current time and date are as accurate as possible.

Set and Configure the Clock

Set the Clock Automatically

1 Open the System Preferences application and click the **Date & Time** icon.

2 Click the **Date & Time** tab.

3 Check the **Set date and time automatically** check box.

4 On the pop-up menu, choose the time server you want to use.

If you live in the United States, choose **Apple Americas/U.S.**

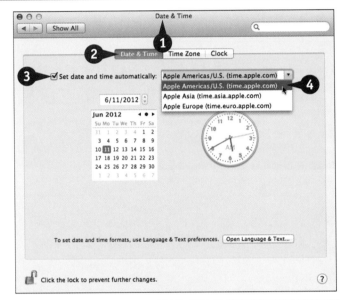

5 Click the **Time Zone** tab.

6 To have the OS X determine your location automatically based on your Wi-Fi connection, click the **Set time zone automatically using current location** check box and skip the rest of these steps. To manually set your location, uncheck the check box and select the time zone you want to set on the Time Zone menu.

Note: If you select the automatic option, the rest of the controls are disabled.

Ⓐ The time zone you select is indicated by the light band on the map and next to the "Time Zone" text.

7 Open the **Closest City** pop-up menu and choose a city in the same time zone as your location.

When MacBook Pro is connected to the Internet, it sets the time and date automatically.

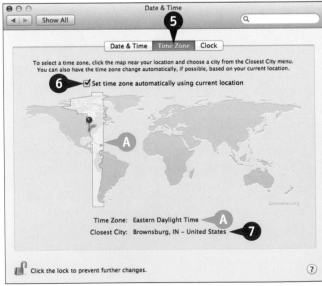

Configure the Clock's Options

1 Open the System Preferences application and click the **Date & Time** icon.

2 Click the **Clock** tab.

3 If you want to see the clock on the menu bar, check the **Show date and time in menu bar** check box.

4 To see the time in the digital format, click **Digital**; to see it in analog format, click **Analog**.

5 If you want to see seconds in the time display, check the **Display the time with seconds** check box.

6 To flash the colon between the hour and minutes at each second, check the **Flash the time separators** check box.

7 To use the 24-hour format, check the **Use a 24-hour clock** check box.

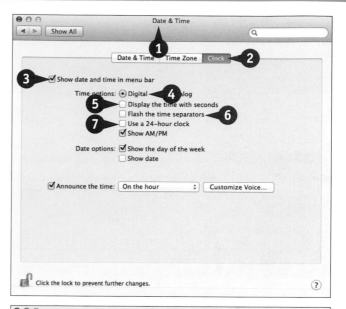

8 To show the AM/PM indicator, check the **Show AM/PM** check box.

Note: This is disabled if you use the 24-hour clock.

9 To show the day of the week, check the **Show the day of the week** check box.

10 To include the date, check the **Show date** check box.

11 To hear an announcement of the time, check the **Announce the time** check box.

12 Use the pop-up menu to choose how often the time should be announced, such as **On the hour**.

13 Click **Customize Voice** and use the resulting sheet to select and configure the voice you want your MacBook Pro to use to announce the time.

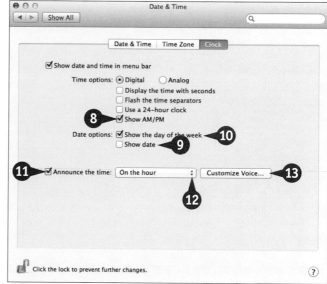

TIPS

What if I take my computer to a different time zone?
When you are in a different time zone than the one configured in OS X, its time will not match the local time. If that bothers you, you can always change the current time zone using the previous steps. If you use the automatic setting, your MacBook Pro updates the time and date based upon the Wi-Fi network to which it is connected.

What if the time and date are not in the right format?
Open the **Language & Text** pane of the System Preferences application. Click the **Formats** tab. Choose the region whose time and date format you want to use, or click the **Customize** button for the format you want to change to customize it.

Save Energy

When you first think of saving energy, you might think of lowering your electric bill or reducing the need for electricity. However, your MacBook Pro uses so little energy that it is unlikely that you can make any difference in either of these areas by changing how your computer uses energy.

However, when you are running your MacBook Pro on battery power, saving energy is very important because the rate at which the computer consumes power determines how long you can work while using the battery.

Save Energy

1 Open the System Preferences application and choose the **Energy Saver** pane.

2 Click the **Battery** tab.

3 Drag the upper slider to set the idle time after which your MacBook Pro goes to sleep.

4 Drag the lower slider to set the amount of inactive time after which the display sleeps.

Note: The display is a major user of power. You should set it to sleep after a couple of minutes of inactivity to conserve battery power.

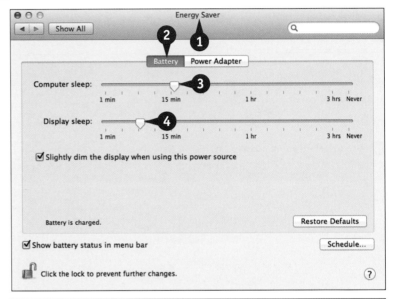

5 If you want the display to dim slightly while running on battery power, check the **Slightly dim the display when using this power source** check box.

6 If you want to see the battery icon ( ) in the menu bar, check the **Show battery status in menu bar** check box.

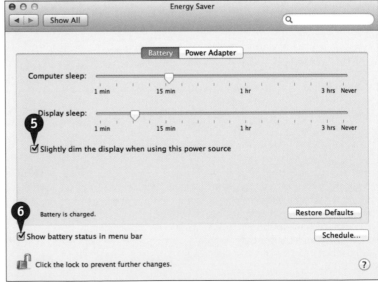

7 Click the **Power Adapter** tab.

8 Drag the upper slider to set the idle time after which MacBook Pro goes to sleep.

9 Drag the lower slider to set the amount of inactive time after which the display sleeps.

10 To enable devices connected to MacBook Pro through the Wi-Fi network to be able to wake it up, check the **Wake for Wi-Fi network access** check box.

11 Click **Schedule**.

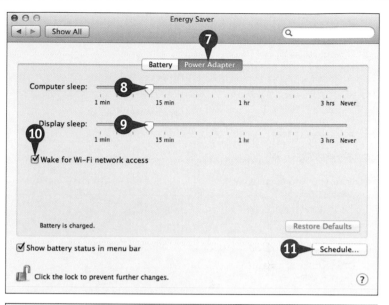

12 Use the **Start up or wake** controls to have MacBook Pro automatically start up or wake up at a specific time.

13 Use the lower controls to have MacBook Pro automatically sleep, restart, or shut down at a specific time.

14 Click **OK**.

15 To return to what Apple considers optimum power settings, click **Restore Defaults**.

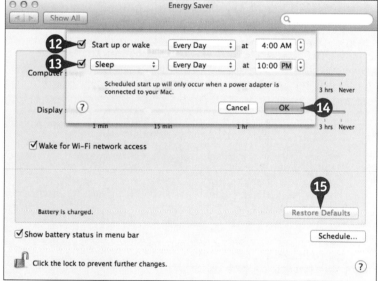

TIPS

Do I need to tell MacBook Pro which power settings to use?
OS X detects whether your computer is running on battery power or is connected to the power adapter and uses the energy saver settings for that power source automatically.

How else can I make my battery last longer?
Put MacBook Pro to sleep whenever you are not using it; close its lid or choose **Sleep** on the **Apple** menu (). Because the display is a major power drain, lower its brightness by pressing F1 until the screen is as dim as possible while you can still see it comfortably. Turn off transmitting or receiving functions that you are not using (such as Wi-Fi).

Configure the Display

The MacBook Pro's display is what you look at while you use it, and so it is important to know how to configure the screen so it matches your viewing preferences. You can configure the display's resolution, brightness, and color profile.

Although the physical size of MacBook Pro's display is fixed, the amount of information that it can show (its resolution) is not. That is because each pixel (short for *picture element*) that makes up the display's images can be larger or smaller. When pixels are larger, what is on the screen is shown on a larger, zoomed-in scale. When pixels are smaller, more content is shown on the screen, but on a smaller, zoomed-out scale.

Configure the Display

Configure the Display's Resolution

① Open the System Preferences application and click the **Displays** icon.

② Click the **Display** tab.

③ Click the **Best for built-in display** option to use what Apple thinks is the best setting for your MacBook Pro.

   If this setting works for you, skip to step **7**.

④ Click **Scaled**.

⑤ Click a resolution.

A The MacBook Pro's screen updates to the selected resolution. The current resolution is highlighted on the list.

Note: Notice how much less screen space the Displays pane takes on this figure. This is because the display is set to a higher resolution.

6 Experiment with resolution settings until you find the highest resolution still comfortable for you to see.

7 Drag the **Brightness** slider to the right to make the screen brighter, or to the left to make it dimmer.

8 To have OS X automatically adjust brightness based on the lighting conditions in which you are using the computer, click the **Automatically adjust brightness** check box.

TIPS

How else can I set screen brightness?
The MacBook Pro includes two keys that you can use to change the screen's brightness. Press F1 to lower the brightness or F2 to increase it. These do the same thing as the Brightness slider on the Displays pane. Each time you press one of the keys, an indicator appears on the screen to show you the relative brightness level you have set.

How do I use the Color tab?
The Color tab is used to configure a color profile for the display. You will not likely need to do this unless you are doing very precise color printing work, in which case, you can configure a screen profile to match your printer output.

Control Sound

From sound effects to music and movies, sound is an important part of the MacBook Pro experience. Additionally, you may want to use sound input for audio and video chats, record narration for movies, and so on.

The Sound pane of the System Preferences application is your primary stop for managing audio settings on your MacBook Pro.

Control Sound

Configure Sound Effects

1. Open the System Preferences application and click the **Sound** icon.

2. Click the **Sound Effects** tab.

3. Click a sound on the alert sound list.

4. Click the **Play sound effects through** menu to select where effects should play..

5. Drag the **Alert volume** slider to make the alert sound louder or quieter.

6. To hear sound effects for system actions, such as when you empty the Trash, click the **Play user interface sound effects** check box.

7. If you want audio feedback when you change the volume level, click the **Play feedback when volume is changed** check box.

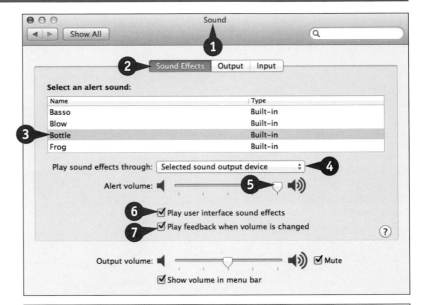

Configure Sound Out

1. Open the System Preferences application and click the **Sound** icon.

2. Click the **Output** tab.

3. Select the output device over which you want MacBook Pro to play sound.

4. Drag the **Balance** slider to set the balance between the left and right speakers.

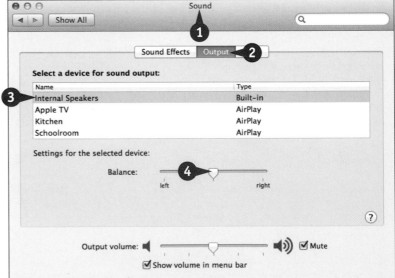

Control System Volume

1 Open the System Preferences application and click the **Sound** icon.

2 Click the **Output** tab.

3 Drag the **Output volume** slider to the right to increase the volume or to the left to decrease it.

4 To mute all sounds, check the **Mute** check box.

5 To configure the volume menu on the menu bar, check the **Show volume in menu bar** check box.

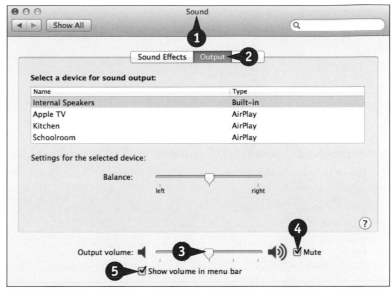

6 To set the volume using the volume menu (◀), open it and drag the slider up to increase volume or down to decrease it.

Configure Sound Input

1 Open the System Preferences application and click the **Sound** icon.

2 Click the **Input** tab.

3 Select the input device you want to use.

4 Play the sound you want to input.

5 Drag the **Input volume** slider to the left to reduce the level of input sound or to the right to increase it.

6 Keep trying levels until the gauge looks about right, about three-fourths of the length of the bar.

7 If the area you are in is noisy, check the **Use ambient noise reduction** check box.

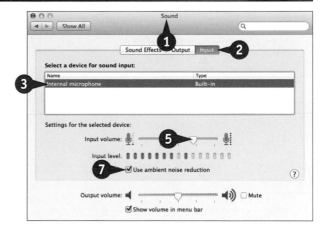

TIP

How can I use external speakers?
You can connect external speakers to your MacBook Pro's Headphone/Audio Out port. These can be powered computer speakers or you can use headphones. When you have speakers connected, click the Output tab and click the speakers you want to use. Sound will play from those speakers. You can use the controls to configure how it plays. See Chapter 9 for more details.

Create and Configure User Accounts

OS X is a multiuser system. What this means is that you can create user accounts for each person who uses your MacBook Pro. Each person who uses it then has a unique desktop, folders, files, and preferences so that MacBook Pro is tailored specifically to her.

A Standard user account can access all the MacBook Pro's resources, but it cannot perform administrator tasks, such as installing applications in the Applications folder; you should use the Standard type for most users. An administrator account allows access to the administration tasks, many of which are discussed in this chapter. (Other account types are explained in the tips at the end of this section.)

Create and Configure User Accounts

Create a User Account

① Open the System Preferences application and click the **Users & Groups** icon.

Ⓐ The Users & Groups pane appears. In the accounts list on the left side of the window, you see the accounts that currently exist.

② Click **Add** (⊞).

The New Account sheet appears.

③ Choose the type of account on the **New Account** pop-up menu.

Note: See the tip to learn about account types.

④ Enter a name for the account in the Full Name field. This can be just about anything you want, but it is usually the person's name.

OS X creates a shortened account name based on what you enter.

⑤ Edit the account name as needed.

⑥ If you manually create a password for the user, do so and then skip to step **11**. Otherwise, go to step **7**.

⑦ Alternatively, if you want help creating a password, click the **key** icon (🔑).

The Password Assistant appears.

8 Click the **Type** pop-up menu and select a password type.

B OS X generates a password for you. If there are tips related to the type you selected, you see them in the Tips box.

9 Drag the **Length** slider to the right to increase, or to the left to decrease, the length of the password.

C As you make changes, the Quality gauge shows you how secure the password is. Green indicates a secure password, yellow is less secure, and red is not secure.

10 When you are happy with the password, click back in the New Account sheet while leaving the Password Assistant window open.

11 Re-enter the password in the Verify field.

Note: If you did not keep the Password Assistant open, you need to remember the password you configured to be able to type it in.

12 If you want to provide a hint when users cannot remember their password, type the hint in the **Password hint** field.

13 Click **Create User**.

D The user account is created and appears on the list of accounts.

14 To associate an image with the user account, click the image well.

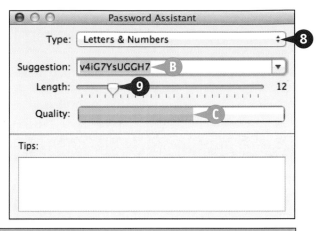

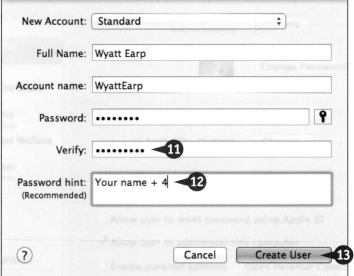

continued ▶

As you create new user accounts, be careful about the kind of account you provide to other people. In most cases, you will want to give other people a Standard or Managed with Parental Controls user account so that those people have limited access to OS X's administrative functions.

You should have at least two user accounts. One should be an Administrator account (which is the type created when you first started up MacBook Pro) that you use regularly. The other should be an Administrator account that you create but do not use so that it remains in the default state. You use this second account during troubleshooting.

Create and Configure User Accounts (continued)

15 To use one of the default images, click **Defaults**.

16 Click an image icon.

17 Click Done and skip to step **19**.

Ⓐ Alternatively, you can drag an image file from the desktop onto the image well.

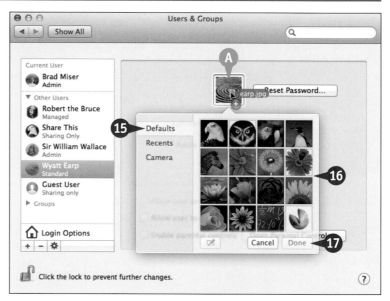

The edit tools appear.

18 Drag the **Size** slider to the right to zoom in on the image of the user's icon, or to the left to zoom out.

19 Drag the image within the selection box until the part of the image you want to use is enclosed in the box.

Ⓑ To take a photo with the MacBook Pro's camera to use as a user account's image, click the **Camera** tab. Place the subject in front of MacBook Pro's camera and adjust the image until it is what you want to use. Click the **Camera** button. After a few seconds, the image is captured. Use the edit tools to configure the image.

20 Click **Done**.

The image is associated with the user account.

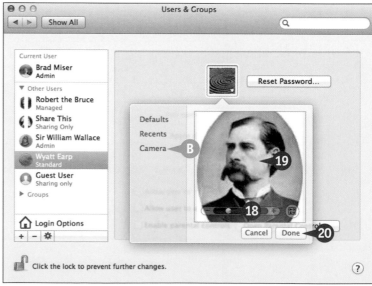

㉑ If the user has an Apple ID, click **Set**.

㉒ Type the user's Apple ID in the Apple ID field.

㉓ Click **OK**.

㉔ Click the **Allow user to reset password using Apple ID** check box if you set an Apple ID and want the user to be able to reset his OS X user account password based on his Apple ID.

㉕ Click the **Allow user to administer this computer** check box if you want the user to administer MacBook Pro.

㉖ Give the username and password you created to the person whom you want to use MacBook Pro.

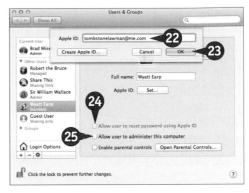

Configure Login Items for a User Account

① Log in under the user's account.

Note: You must be logged into an account to set Login Items for it.

② Open the System Preferences application and click the **Users & Groups** icon to open the Users & Groups pane.

③ Click the **Login Items** tab.

④ Click **Add** (⬚).

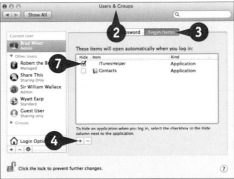

⑤ Navigate to locate and select the application or types of file, such as a document, that you want to open automatically.

⑥ Click **Add**.

⑦ Click the **Hide** check box for any items you want to be hidden by default.

The next time the user logs in, the items you configured open automatically.

TIP

Do I have to configure a password for a user account?
A user account does not have to have a password. If you leave the Password and Verify fields empty, you see a warning that not providing a password is not secure. If you are sure that is not a problem for you, clear the warning prompt and complete the user creation. The user is able to log in to the MacBook Pro without entering a password, which can mean that anyone who has access to the MacBook Pro can use it. This is usually not a good idea because it leaves your computer vulnerable.

Protect Users with Parental Controls

The phrase *parental controls* is a bit misleading. Although these can certainly be used to protect children from interactions on the Internet that might not be good for them, you can use the same tools to tailor any user's access to the MacBook Pro and the Internet.

You can also use Parental Controls to limit access to applications and system functions. Further, you can set up a user account such that the user can use the MacBook Pro only during times you specify.

Protect Users with Parental Controls

① Open the System Preferences application and click the **Parental Controls** icon.

② Select the user account for which you want to configure Parental Controls.

Note: Parental Controls can be applied only to Standard or Managed with Parental Controls user accounts.

③ Click **Enable Parental Controls**.

The Parental Controls tabs appear.

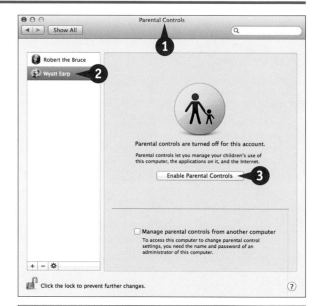

④ Click the **Apps** tab.

⑤ To limit the access of the user to specific applications, check the **Limit Applications** check box.

⑥ Choose **All** on the **Allow App Store Apps** menu to allow the user to access any applications downloaded from the App Store.

⑦ Uncheck the check box for the groups or individual applications you do not want the user to be able to use.

⑧ To allow the user to change the Dock, check the **Allow User to Modify the Dock** check box.

9 Click the **Web** tab.

10 To attempt to prevent access to adult websites automatically, click **Try to limit access to adult websites automatically**.

Note: Click the Customize button to open the Customize sheet, on which you can allow or prevent specific websites.

11 To limit access to only specific websites, click **Allow access to only these websites**. In the dialog that appears, click **Add** (⊞) and type the URLs of the websites you want to allow.

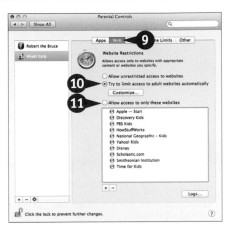

12 Click the **People** tab.

13 To limit the user's interaction with people through the Game Center, uncheck the two Game Center check boxes.

14 To limit e-mail, check the **Limit Mail** check box.

15 To limit messaging, check the **Limit Messages** check box.

Note: The e-mail and messages controls work only with OS X's Mail and Messages applications.

16 Click **Add** (⊞).

The Contacts sheet appears.

17 Configure the Parental Controls sheet for the person with whom you want to allow e-mail or chat interaction.

18 Click **Add**.

The person is added to the allowed list.

19 Repeat steps **16** to **18** for each person with whom you want to allow interaction.

20 If you want to receive an e-mail requiring you to grant permission when someone not on the list is involved in an e-mail exchange with the user, click the **Send permission requests to** check box and enter your e-mail address.

TIPS

What is the Time Limits tab for?
You can use the Time Limits tab to limit the amount of time the user can access the MacBook Pro. You can configure time on weekdays and weekends. You can also configure "bedtimes" during which the user is unable to access MacBook Pro.

What is the Other tab for?
On the Other tab, you determine whether profanity appears in the Dictionary application, limit printer administration, prevent CD or DVD burning, and disable password changes.

Set Login Options

You can configure the login process for MacBook Pro in a number of ways. In the Login window, you can present a list of users so that to log in, a user clicks his username and enters a password. Or, you can present an empty username and password field and the user has to complete both to log in. There are also a number of other ways to configure the Login window by showing or hiding specific buttons. You can also disable or enable Automatic Login. Fast user switching is another option, which allows multiple people to be logged in to MacBook Pro at the same time. Each user can quickly move back into his or her account because it is left open, instead of each user logging out before another logs in.

Set Login Options

Configure Automatic Login

1. Open the System Preferences application and click the **Users & Groups** icon.

2. Click **Login Options**.

   The Login Options pane appears.

3. Click the **Automatic login** pop-up menu and choose the name of the user that you want to be automatically logged in.

4. Type the user's password.

5. Click **OK**.

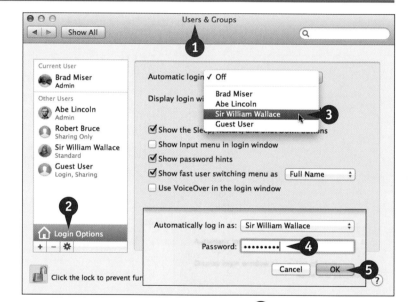

Configure the Login Window

1. Open the System Preferences application and click the **Users & Groups** icon.

2. Click **Login Options**.

3. To show a list of users in the Login window, click an option.

4. To put the MacBook Pro to sleep, restart it, or shut it down from the Login window, click the **Show the Sleep, Restart, and Shut Down buttons** check box.

5. To choose the language layout from the Login window, click the **Show Input menu in login window** check box.

6. To show a hint when a user forgets his or her password, check the **Show password hints** check box.

7. To have MacBook Pro read the text in the Login window, click the **Use VoiceOver in the login window** check box.

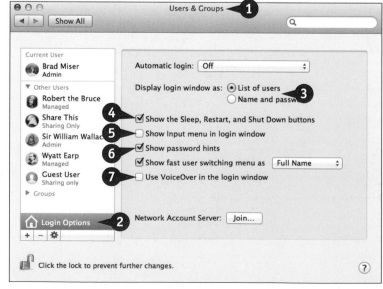

Configure and Use Fast User Switching

1. Open the System Preferences application and click the **Users & Groups** icon.

2. Click **Login Options**.

3. Check the **Show fast user switching menu as** check box.

4. Open the pop-up menu, then choose **Long Name** to see the current user's full name at the top of the Fast User Switching menu, **Short Name** to see the user's short name, or **Icon** to see a silhouette.

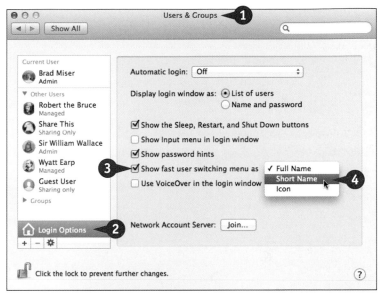

The Fast User Switching menu appears on the menu bar.

5. Open the **Fast User Switching** menu.

Ⓐ All the user accounts on MacBook Pro are shown. The users currently logged in are marked with a check mark.

6. Choose the user to switch to.

7. Enter the user's password.

8. Press **Return**.

The user is logged in and his or her desktop appears. The previous user remains logged in; select that user's account on the menu to move back to it.

TIPS

What happens to running applications when another user logs in using fast user switching?

Because a user does not log out when another one logs in using fast user switching, the applications and processes running under a user account continue to run in the background even while another user is using MacBook Pro. As soon as the previous user logs back in, the results of the activity that was ongoing are seen, such as new e-mails, web pages, and so on.

How I can leave myself logged in so my applications continue to work, but no one else can see or use what I am doing?

On the Fast User Switching menu, choose **Login Window**. The Login window appears, but you remain logged in (you see a check mark next to your username). All applications and processes continue to run in the background. To start using MacBook Pro again, choose your user account, enter your password, and press **Return**. You go back to where you left off.

Create Mail, Contacts, and Calendar Accounts

A number of applications require a user account to access the services those applications provide. The most obvious example is Mail, in which you configure your e-mail accounts. Each of the applications has the tools you need to create and manage your accounts.

However, you can also create and manage these accounts using the Mail, Contacts & Calendars pane of the System Preferences application. When you configure an account there, applications that need to access those accounts can obtain them from the same place. So, you only need to configure the accounts in one place for your applications (instead of managing the accounts in each application separately).

Create Mail, Contacts, and Calendar Accounts

1 Open the **Mail, Contacts & Calendars** pane.

A On the Accounts list, you see the accounts available to you; these may have been created using the pane's tools, or they may come from an application (such as Mail if you created an account there).

When you select an account, you see configuration information and tools in the right pane of the window.

2 Click **Add** (⊞).

3 Click the type of account you want to create.

The pane includes tools to make the accounts you see simple to create.

Note: If the account you are creating is not one of those listed, select Other. You are prompted to provide information to guide you through creating an account of that type. The steps you use will be slightly different from those shown here for one of the default account types.

4 Enter the account's full name.

5 Type the e-mail address for the account.

6 Enter the account's password.

7 Click **Continue**.

The application checks the information you entered.

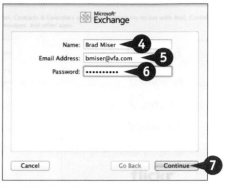

If it is valid, you see the summary sheet. If not, you are prompted to correct it.

8 Click **Continue**.

9 Check the check boxes for the services you want to access through that account, such as **Mail**, **Contacts**, **Calendars& Reminders**, or **Notes**.

10 Click **Add Account**.

The account is added to your Accounts list and applications will be able to use its information.

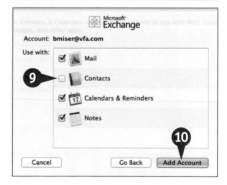

TIPS

I do not see the accounts I created in my e-mail application. Why not?

Applications have to be written to obtain account information from the System Preferences application. All of Apple's applications that need it have this capability, but applications from other sources may not. If not, use that application's tools to create and manage accounts in it.

How can I change an account?

Select it on the Accounts list. Its information appears in the right part of the pane. Check the check boxes to enable or uncheck them to disable services. Click **Details** and use the resulting sheet to change the account's information. To delete an account, select it and click **Delete** at the bottom of the Accounts list.

PART II

Getting Connected

A MacBook Pro really shines when it is connected to the Internet. As you move around, you need to know how to keep connected without risking the computer or its data. You will also want to connect devices to your MacBook Pro. In this part, you learn how to get and keep your MacBook Pro connected.

Chapter 7: Connecting to a Network and the Internet . . 120

Chapter 8: Connecting MacBook Pro to Other Devices . . 146

Chapter 9: Traveling with MacBook Pro 162

Understanding Networking Concepts

The topic of networking is the most technical in this book. Fortunately, OS X manages most of the details of networking your MacBook Pro for you, but a number of concepts are helpful to understand as you create your own network.

Network

Simply put, a *network* is two or more devices connected. Its purpose is to enable the devices on it to communicate with each other. This is done using various *protocols* to provide different services. For example, the Transmission Control Protocol/Internet Protocol (TCP/IP) is the basic "language" that devices speak over the Internet. There are other protocols for a variety of services, but the data for all of these services is communicated over a network. Networks can be large or small, simple or complicated, but they all have the same basic purpose.

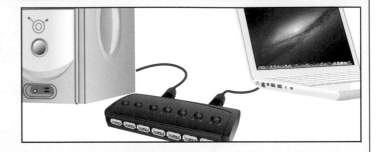

Internet

The Internet is the largest network possible because it literally spans the globe, and millions upon millions of devices and people are connected to it. The Internet makes communication and information available way beyond anything that was possible before it came to be. Many services are available over the Internet, such as email, searching the web, chats, and file transfers. Connecting your MacBook Pro to the Internet is just about as important as being able to charge its battery.

Local Network

A *local network*, also known as a local area network or *LAN*, is a network that covers a defined physical space. LANs can be quite large, such as in a business or school, or fairly small, such as in a home. A LAN connects its devices together so they can communicate with one another and also connect to outside networks — most importantly, to the Internet. This chapter focuses on helping you create a small LAN, such as what many people use in their homes. The principles of larger LANs are the same, but the details can get much more complicated.

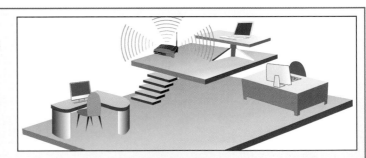

Ethernet

Ethernet is both a physical means of connecting devices together — for example, an Ethernet cable — and the protocol used to communicate over the physical connection. Ethernet can support various communication speeds, and all of them are quite fast. Some MacBook Pros have an Ethernet port that you can use to connect them to other devices; for those that do not, you can use an adapter. In addition to their speed, Ethernet connections offer other benefits, including simplicity and security. The primary downside to Ethernet is the need for cables for the physical connection between the devices.

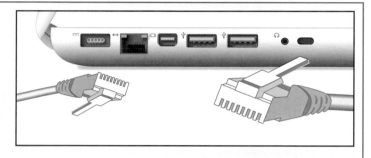

Wi-Fi Network

Wi-Fi is a general term for a set of wireless communication standards and technologies defined in the Institute of Electrical and Electronics Engineers (IEEE) 802.11 specifications. Like Ethernet networks, Wi-Fi enables devices to communicate, but uses radio transmissions instead of physical wires to connect devices. This offers ease of configuration and makes it possible to move around while remaining on a network. The downside of Wi-Fi is that it is not as secure as Ethernet networks and not as fast as either.

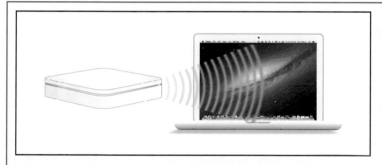

AirPort

Apple uses the term *AirPort* for its implementation of Wi-Fi in its wireless base stations, such as the AirPort Extreme Base Station. The software used to configure one of these devices is called the AirPort Utility. Under earlier versions of OS X, the wireless networking capability of MacBook Pros was called AirPort too, but with the Lion version this was changed to be the more generic standard, Wi-Fi. AirPort is fully compatible with standard Wi-Fi technologies, such as those used for Windows PCs and networking equipment.

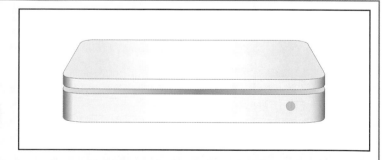

continued ▶

Hub/Router/Access Point

All networks need a device that controls the flow of information among the various computers, printers, and other resources on the network. These devices are called hubs, switches, routers, or access points. There are many kinds of these devices, and they all offer different features and benefits. They can support Ethernet, Wi-Fi, or both kinds of networks. Because AirPort Extreme Base Stations offer a lot of nice features and support

is built into OS X, they are the focus of this chapter. However, because it supports standard Wi-Fi technology, your MacBook Pro can be used with other kinds of routers/hubs as well. Some of the key features of hubs are the capability to share an Internet connection among many devices and to shield those devices from Internet attacks.

Internet Service Provider

The Internet must be accessed through specific entry points. To do this, you need the services of an Internet Service Provider (ISP). The ISP provides the means that you use to connect your network to the Internet using various connection technologies, such as cable, Digital Subscriber Line (DSL), dial-up (though no longer supported by MacBook Pros without additional hardware), or even satellite.

Internet Account

To access the Internet, you need an Internet account with an ISP. If you access the Internet through a business or school, that organization acts as your ISP. The cost and technical details (such as connection speed, server space, and so on) of accounts vary, depending on the specific ISP you use. Typically, ISPs require you to have only one Internet account for your network, but you are responsible for everything connected to the modem (the device that communicates from

your LAN to the ISP) on "your side," whereas the ISP is responsible for ensuring that the signal to the modem is working. Depending on the type of Internet access you use, you might need a username and password to connect to your account, or it might be based on your physical location (such as with a cable connection).

IP Address

An Internet Protocol (IP) address is the way devices on the Internet are identified. Put another way, to be able to connect to and use the Internet, a device must have an IP address. IP addresses include a set of four numbers with periods between each number, as in 169.155.12.3. In most networks, you do not need to worry about the details of IP addresses because the hub/router uses Dynamic Host Control Protocol (DHCP) to automatically assign addresses to devices as they are needed. You just need to be able to recognize whether or not a device has a valid IP address, which is usually pretty clear because when you do not have one, you cannot connect to the Internet.

Internet Services and Applications

The reason to connect devices to the Internet is to be able to access the services delivered over it. To access these services, you use Internet applications. Obvious examples are Mail for email and Safari for web browsing. Many kinds of services are available on the Internet, and many different applications use each of those services, but you will likely end up using just a few of them. Because OS X includes powerful and easy-to-use Internet applications, they are a good place to start.

Internet Dangers

Although the Internet offers amazing capabilities, they do not come without risk. Unfortunately, just like in the physical world, on the Internet there are many people who want to hurt other people. The dangers of Internet life include the annoying, such as pornography and spam, and the truly dangerous, such as viruses, hacking, or identity theft. Fortunately, with some basic precautions and common sense, you can protect yourself from most Internet dangers relatively easily.

Local Network Services

Similar to the Internet, you can take advantage of services that you can provide over your local network. These include file and printer sharing, screen sharing, and messaging. Configuring and using local network services is pretty straight forward because these services are built into OS X.

Obtain an Internet Account

To connect your network or MacBook Pro to the Internet, you must have an Internet account. Different kinds of Internet accounts allow you to connect in different ways. The most common high-speed technologies for homes are cable and DSL. Satellite connections are also available. Some communities provide free wireless networks that you can use. Before you decide on an Internet account, you should know the options available in your location.

If your location has cable TV service, contact the provider to see if Internet access is available and the cost. Then locate providers of Internet access through DSL. Check your community's website to see if it provides a wireless network.

Obtain an Internet Account

Determine What Types of Internet Accounts Are Available

1. If cable service is available to you, contact the cable provider to get information about Internet access, including monthly cost, speed options, and installation or startup costs.

2. If you have access to a computer connected to the web, go to dsl.theispguide.com.

3. Use the tools to search for DSL access in your location.

Note: When you contact a potential provider, ask if Macintosh is supported. Although you do not really need formal support because Macs work with standard technologies, Mac-literate technical support can be a factor when you are choosing a provider.

4. Contact DSL providers that serve your area to get details about their service, including monthly cost, installation costs or startup fees, and length of contract.

Note: Make sure you have potential providers check your actual phone number to ensure that DSL is available. DSL availability in your area does not guarantee service at your specific location.

Note: If cable or DSL is available to you, skip to step **1** in the next section. Satellite is the best option only when cable or DSL is not available.

5. If cable or DSL is not available, access the web and move to www.dbsinstall.com.

6. Follow the links on the DSL provider's website to search for satellite providers of Internet access.

Choose, Obtain, and Install an Internet Account

1 Compare your options.

If you have only one option for a broadband connection, the choice is made for you and you can skip to step **3.**

2 If you have a choice between cable and DSL, consider which is best for you based on cost, the provider's reputation for service, and other factors.

3 Contact the provider you want to use to obtain an account and schedule installation.

The provider activates your account, and if you choose to have the provider install the modem, they schedule an appointment with you. Some providers allow a self-install kit to be used.

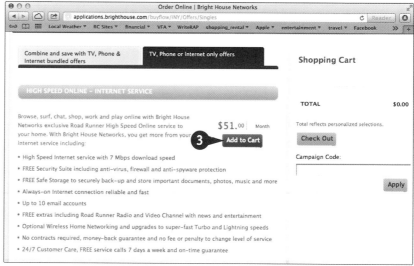

TIPS

What about dial-up Internet accounts?
Internet accounts that you access over a standard phone line and dial-up modem are available just about everywhere, though you need to add a USB modem to be able to use one with your MacBook Pro. Dial-up is very slow and unreliable, and you must connect each time you want Internet access. The speed is so slow that using the Internet requires extreme patience. Broadband connections are available in many areas, and so this chapter focuses on them.

If I need an Internet account to connect, why can I use Wi-Fi at public places without an account?
No matter how you connect to the Internet, you are using an Internet account of some sort. In public places, the organization that controls that place can make a wireless network available to you. Through that network, you can access the organization's Internet account. In some cases, you can do this for free. In others, you need to purchase access from the organization providing the network.

Set Up a Local Network

After you have a working Internet connection, you are ready to build a local network. You can include a lot of devices on the network, including both wired and wireless devices. The heart of any network is the hub/router you use. The best hub choice for most Mac users is an AirPort Extreme Base Station or a Time Capsule because support for administering the AirPort networks they provide is built into OS X. Also, these base stations shield your network from Internet attacks. The rest of this chapter assumes the use of one of these devices. The steps to install other kinds of hubs are similar. These steps also assume that you have a working Internet connection and modem.

Set Up a Local Network

Install an AirPort Extreme Base Station/Time Capsule

1 Connect the output cable of the modem to the modem (WAN) port on the base station.

2 Connect power to the base station.

Note: The only difference between a Time Capsule and an AirPort Extreme Base Station is the inclusion of a hard drive in the Time Capsule. For the purposes of this chapter, these devices are referred to as a base station.

3 Start up your MacBook Pro.

As long as you have not disabled Wi-Fi, the MacBook Pro can communicate with the base station wirelessly. You can also connect the MacBook Pro directly to one of the Ethernet ports on the base station using an Ethernet cable (and adapter if required).

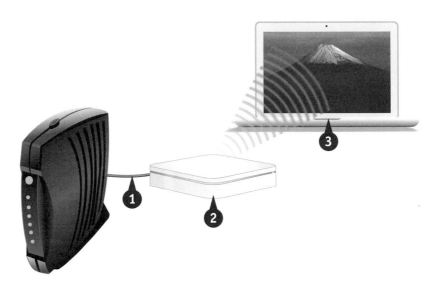

Configure an AirPort Extreme Base Station/Time Capsule

Note: The specific screens and options you see in AirPort Utility depend on the type of base station you are configuring and its current status. These steps show a Time Capsule that has been restored to factory settings.

1 On the Wi-Fi menu, choose the new base station.

The AirPort Utility application opens and identifies the base station you selected.

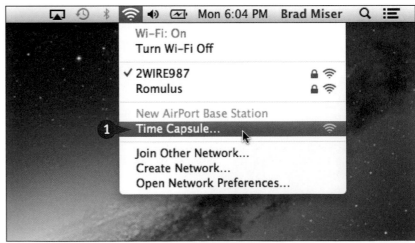

2 If you do not want to use the default network name, change it.

3 To change the default base station name, change the text in the Base Station Name box.

4 Enter the password for the wireless network you are creating in the Password and Verify boxes.

5 Click **Next**.

The AirPort Utility completes the configuration of the base station. When the process is done, you see that the new network is available.

6 Click **Done**.

The Wi-Fi network is ready to use.

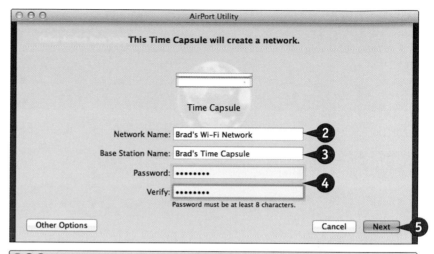

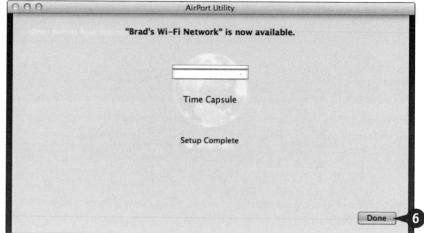

TIPS

What do the lights next to devices in the AirPort Utility mean?

The status light next to each device shows you how the device is functioning. If green, everything is working correctly. If flashing orange, there is a problem. If no light, the device is currently not communicating.

What does the Other Options button do?

By default, a new base station is set up to provide a wireless network. If you click the Other Options button, you can choose to add the device to another network or to replace an existing device. In most cases, the default choice is what you want to use.

continued ▶

In addition to setting up a new or restored base station, you can use the AirPort Utility to manually configure a base station. This is useful when you want to change something about how the base station works, such as the name or password of the wireless network.

You can configure many different options using the AirPort Utility. However, for a home or other small network, you usually need to set only a few of these. This section shows you how to change some of the more useful options.

Set Up a Local Network (continued)

Use AirPort Utility to Configure a Base Station

1. Open the Utilities folder, such as by clicking **Go** and then click **Utilities**.

2. Double-click the **AirPort Utility** application.

   The application opens and shows you the devices with which it can communicate.

3. Click the device you want to configure.

4. Click **Edit**.

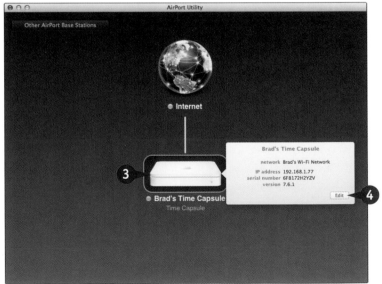

5 Click the **Base Station** tab.

6 Change the base station's name by typing a new name in the Base Station Name field.

7 To set an administrative password for the base station, enter it in the Base Station Password and Verify boxes.

Note: A base station's administrative password is required to make any changes to the base station's configuration. This password should be different from the password associated with the network the base station is providing.

8 Click the **Remember this password in my keychain** check box.

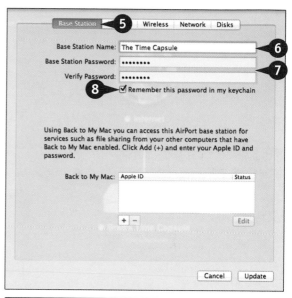

9 Click the **Wireless** tab.

10 Enter the name of the wireless network the base station is providing.

11 Choose the level of security you want the network to have.

Note: Any of the security options, except None, provides a reasonable level of security. You should always use some level of security to prevent unknown people from using your wireless network.

12 Enter the password for the wireless network.

13 Click the **Remember this password in my keychain** check box.

14 Click **Update**.

The changes you made are copied onto the base station and take effect after it restarts.

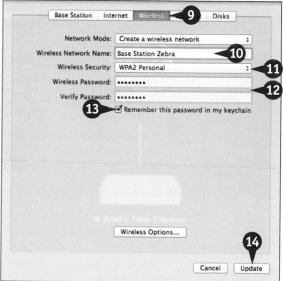

TIPS

What is the difference between an Extreme Base Station and an Express Base Station?
The most significant difference is that you cannot have a wired network connected to an Express Base Station because it has only one Ethernet port, which is connected to the modem. Typically, you should use an Extreme Base Station (or Time Capsule) for the primary hub on the network; you can add Express Base Stations to expand the range of the network as needed.

How do I expand the range of my network?
If an Extreme Base Station or Time Capsule does not provide sufficient coverage of the area in which you use MacBook Pro, you can chain base stations together. Use the AirPort Utility to connect to an Express Base Station and configure it to expand the existing network. You can do this by selecting the Express Base Station and choosing **Extend a wireless network** on the Network Mode pop-up menu on the Wireless tab.

Protect MacBook Pro from Internet Attacks

The Internet connects you to an unlimited number of people and organizations. This opens you up to Internet attacks. The worst of these are attempts to steal your identity and hack into your computers to steal the information they contain, or to use them to launch attacks on other computers. You also need to be mindful of the threat from viruses.

Fortunately, although the dangers of these attacks are very real, you can protect yourself with relatively simple techniques. An AirPort Extreme Base Station or Time Capsule protects you from most attacks automatically. If you ever connect MacBook Pro directly to the modem, such as for troubleshooting, make sure you configure its firewall before doing so.

Protect MacBook Pro from Internet Attacks

Check a Base Station

1 Open the AirPort Utility application.

Note: See the section "Set Up a Local Network" for details.

2 Click the device you want to configure.

3 Click **Edit**.

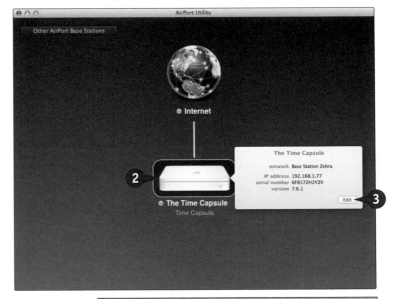

4 Click the **Network** tab.

5 Select **DHCP and NAT** on the Router Mode pop-up menu.

6 Click **Update**.

The new configuration is copied to the device and it restarts. After it does, the new settings take effect.

Note: When NAT is active, the only IP address exposed to the Internet is the base station's. This shields the devices connected to the Internet through the base station from Internet attacks because devices outside your base station cannot identify the devices on the network; they see only the base station, which cannot be hacked like a computer can.

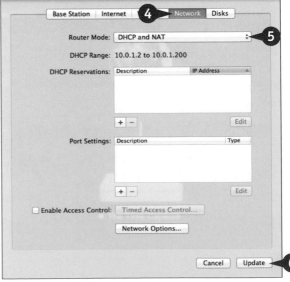

Protect with the OS X Firewall

1 Open the System Preferences application and click the **Security & Privacy** icon.

The Security & Privacy pane opens.

2 Click the **Firewall** tab.

3 Click **Turn On Firewall**.

Note: You must authenticate yourself to be able to configure the firewall.

The firewall starts up and protects your MacBook Pro.

Note: Chapter 9 explains performing more advanced configuration of the firewall.

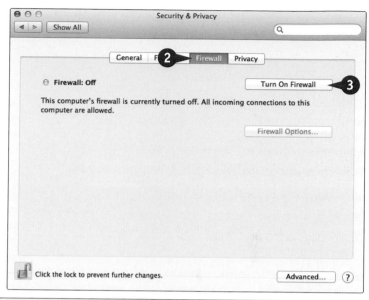

Protect MacBook Pro from Viruses

1 Purchase and install an antivirus application.

2 Configure the antivirus application so that it updates its virus definitions and scans MacBook Pro automatically (see the instructions for the particular application you use).

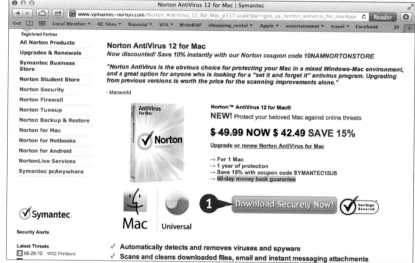

TIPS

Do I really need antivirus software?

OS X is less vulnerable to virus attacks than Windows PCs are. To be as safe from viruses as possible, it is a good idea to install and use antivirus software. However, being smart about how you deal with the Internet can be almost as effective. In general, be cautious about moving any files onto MacBook Pro unless you are very sure of the reliability of the source.

What other options are there for a wireless network?

If you click the Wireless Options button on the Wireless tab, you can change the protocol of connections allowed on the network. For example, if you choose 802.11n only, only those devices that support the most current standard can connect. You can use the Radio Channel pop-up menu to change the channel over which wireless signals are sent. This can be useful if the default channel has interference.

Connect to the Internet with Wi-Fi

The whole point of having a MacBook Pro is that you can move around with it. By connecting to a wireless network, you can connect to the Internet and a local network from any location covered by that network. Once connected, you can surf the web, chat, send and receive e-mail, and all the other great things that you can do over the Internet. With a Wi-Fi connection, you can do these from wherever you are, maybe even on the couch. Being free of wires is a good thing indeed. You use the same steps to connect to a Wi-Fi network outside your LAN as well.

Connect to the Internet with Wi-Fi

Connect to a Wi-Fi Network

1. Open the System Preferences application.

2. Click the **Network** icon.

Ⓐ The Network pane appears. In the pane on the left side of the window, you see all the ways you can connect to a network that are currently configured on MacBook Pro. When you select a connection to configure it, tools for that type of connection appear in the right part of the window.

3. Click **Wi-Fi**.

4. Click **Turn Wi-Fi On** if it is not on already.

Wi-Fi services start.

Note: You might see a window that shows the available networks as soon as you turn Wi-Fi on. Select the network you want to join and click Join, or click Cancel to follow the rest of these steps.

5. On the **Network Name** pop-up menu, choose the network you want to join.

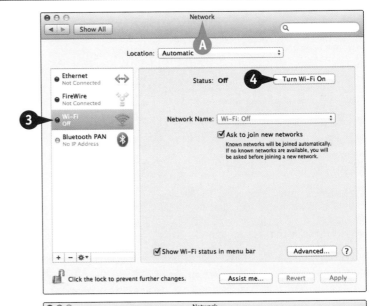

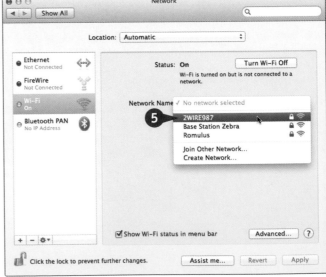

6 If prompted to do so, type the network's password.

7 Check the **Remember this network** check box.

8 Click **Join**.

The MacBook Pro connects to the Wi-Fi network, and you return to the System Preferences application window. The status of the network becomes Connected.

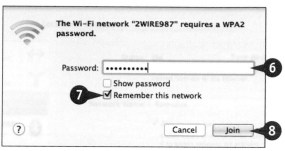

9 Check the **Show Wi-Fi status in menu bar** check box.

10 If enabled, click **Apply**.

11 Quit the System Preferences application.

12 Open Safari and go to a web page.

The web page opens, showing that MacBook Pro is connected to the network and the Internet through Wi-Fi.

If the web page does not open, troubleshoot the problem.

Note: See the section "Troubleshoot an Internet Connection," later in this chapter, for information on how to troubleshoot connection problems.

Use the Wi-Fi Menu

1 Open the **Wi-Fi** menu (📶).

B You can determine the signal strength of the network by the number of waves at the top of the menu.

More waves mean a stronger and faster connection; one or two waves may result in slow or intermittent performance.

2 Choose another network you want to join by selecting it on the menu.

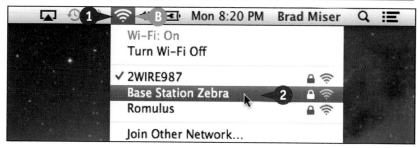

TIPS

How can I connect directly to another Mac using Wi-Fi?
Open the **Wi-Fi** menu on the Finder menu bar and choose **Create Network**. Name the network, give it a password, and click **OK**. Other Mac users can connect to your network using the same steps they use to connect to a network provided by an AirPort Base Station.

I see only one or two waves and MacBook Pro seems to lose its connection. What can I do?
The most likely cause is that the MacBook Pro is too far away from the base station. The most common solutions are to move MacBook Pro closer to the base station so that the signal is stronger or use Wireless Distribution System (WDS) to add another base station to the network to expand its coverage as described in the tip earlier in this chapter.

Connect to the Internet with Ethernet

Because some MacBook Pros have Ethernet support built in, you can connect MacBook Pro to the Internet by connecting it to a wired network over which an Internet connection is being shared. For those MacBook Pros that do not have an internal Ethernet port, you can purchase an Ethernet adapter so you can connect to an Ethernet network.

There are two steps. You can connect MacBook Pro to the network and then configure it to access the Internet over the network. This section assumes you are using an AirPort Extreme Base Station or Time Capsule. If you have a different network configuration, the details might be slightly different.

Connect to the Internet with Ethernet

Connect MacBook Pro to an Ethernet Network

① Connect an Ethernet cable to one of the available ports on the Extreme Base Station or Time Capsule.

② Connect the other end to the Ethernet port on MacBook Pro.

Configure MacBook Pro to Access the Internet over an Ethernet Network

① Open the System Preferences application.

② Click the **Network** icon.

Ⓐ The Network pane appears.

③ Select **Ethernet** in the left part of the pane.

Ⓑ The status should be Connected. If it is not, the cable is not connected correctly or the base station is not working.

④ On the **Configure IPv4** menu, choose **Using DHCP**.

⑤ If enabled, click **Apply**.

The MacBook Pro gets an IP address from the base station and should be able to access its Internet connection.

⑥ Quit the System Preferences application.

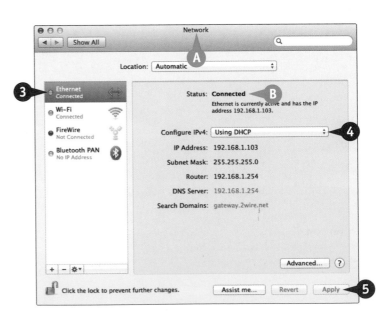

7 Open Safari by clicking its icon on the Dock.

8 If Safari does not load a web page automatically, type a URL in the address bar and press **Return**.

C Safari goes to the website if MacBook Pro is successfully connected to the network via Ethernet. If not, troubleshoot the problem.

Note: See the section "Troubleshoot an Internet Connection," later in this chapter, for information on troubleshooting connection problems.

Note: For detailed information about using Safari, see Chapter 11.

TIPS

Why use Ethernet when wireless is available?
Wireless connections are great because you are not tethered to one spot. However, the best wireless connection is not as fast as an Ethernet connection. So if you are "parked" in a location where an Ethernet connection is available, you get better performance if you use it instead of the wireless network. Additionally, an Ethernet connection is more secure because a device has to be physically connected to the network to use it.

Can I have more than one connection active at a time?
A MacBook Pro can have multiple connections to networks active at the same time. You can use the steps in this section to configure your MacBook Pro for Ethernet access and the steps in the previous section to configure it for wireless access. OS X chooses the connection to use at any point in time based on how you configure it and the connections available.

Use AirDrop to Share Files

When you work with other people, sharing your files with them, and using files they share with you, can be useful. There are many ways to do this, but perhaps the easiest is with OS X's AirDrop feature.

AirDrop automatically locates other Macs running OS X Lion or later that have Wi-Fi on, that are in range of your MacBook Pro, and whose users have their AirDrop folder selected. You see an icon for each person; to share files with someone, you simply drop the file on that person's icon. Likewise, people can share files with you by dropping them on your icon on their computers.

Use AirDrop to Share Files

Use AirDrop to Share Files with Others

1. Open a Finder window.

2. Click **AirDrop**.

3. Ask the people with whom you want to share a file to select AirDrop on their computers.

   Ⓐ Your AirDrop icon appears at the bottom of the window.

   Ⓑ Each Mac on the same network as MacBook Pro and with an AirDrop window active appears above your icon. Each user is identified with the image associated with the active user account.

4. Open a new Finder window and move to a file you want to share.

5. Drag the file you want to share onto another user's icon.

Note: You can share multiple files at the same time by pressing and holding ⌘ while you click each file you want share; then drag the group of files onto the other user's icon.

6. Click **Send**.

   If the person accepts the file you sent, you get no feedback. If the person declines to receive the file, you see a message so indicating.

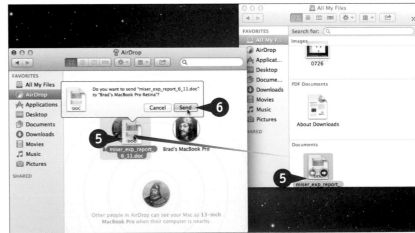

Use AirDrop to Receive Files Shared with You

When someone sends you a file via AirDrop, you see a notification. You see the name of the computer from which the file is coming, the name of the file being sent, and a preview of its content.

1 Respond to the notification.

C To save the file in your Downloads folder, click **Save**.

Note: Never accept a file unless you are absolutely sure about the computer sending the file to you. If you accept files from people you do not know, your Mac and its data could be in jeopardy.

D To save the file in your Downloads folder and open it, click **Save and Open**.

If you click **Save** or **Save and Open**, you see the file's icon "jumping" from the AirDrop folder to the Downloads icon on the Dock.

E To prevent the file from being moved onto your computer, click **Decline**.

2 If you accepted the file, you can work with it.

TIPS

Why can I not see other people in the AirDrop window when I know our Macs are on the same network?
In order to have AirDrop work, it must be selected in at least one Finder window on each computer. If a user closes the AirDrop window, you no longer see her icon in the window. As soon as she selects AirDrop, her icon reappears in your AirDrop window.

How can I keep AirDrop available without using up screen space on a Finder window just for that purpose?
Open a Finder window and select **AirDrop**. Minimize the window so it shrinks down to the Dock. Open other Finder windows on your desktop to use them to access files and folders. As long as the window showing AirDrop remains open, AirDrop is available, even if the window is minimized.

Share Files on a Local Network

Just like services you access over the Internet, you can provide services over a local network. These include sharing files, printers, an Internet connection, and iTunes sharing and streaming. Any computers that connect to the network, whether they use Ethernet or Wi-Fi, can access any of the services you make available.

File sharing is one of the most useful local network services because you can easily share resources among multiple computers. You can configure MacBook Pro to share files with others, and you can access files being shared with you.

Share Files on a Local Network

Share Files with Others

1 Open the System Preferences application.

2 Click the **Sharing** icon.

The Sharing pane appears.

Ⓐ In the list in the left part of the window, you see the services you can provide over a local network. When you select a service, the tools you use to configure it appear in the right part of the window.

Ⓑ You see Public folders for the other Mac users on your network on the Shared Folders list.

3 Type a name for your MacBook Pro in the Computer Name field.

This is the name others on the network choose to access your MacBook Pro. This is the name with which your AirDrop icon is labeled, too.

4 Check the **File Sharing** check box.

File sharing starts. By default, the Public folder within your Home folder is shared on the network.

5 To share specific folders, click **Add** (⊞).

6 Move to and select the folder you want to share.

7 Click **Add**.

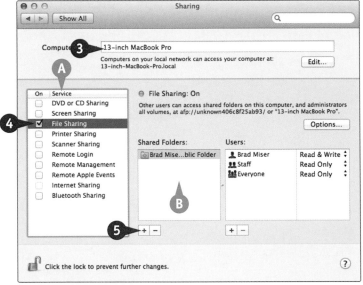

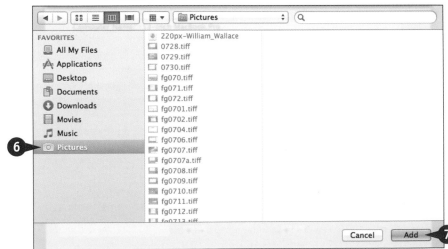

C The folder you selected appears on the Shared Folders list.

8 To allow everyone with whom you share files to access the folder, make sure the folder is selected and click **Everyone** ⬍ next to the Users list and choose the permission level from the pop-up menu that appears.

Note: See the tip for an explanation of permission levels.

9 To configure more users, click **Add** (⊞) at the bottom of the Users list.

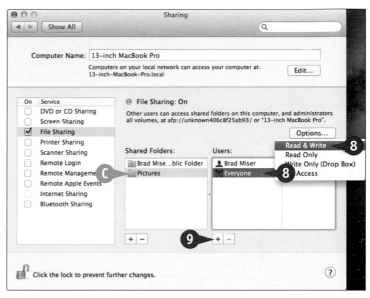

The Select Users sheet appears.

10 Choose the users for whom you want to configure access.

Note: If the user with whom you want to share files is not on the list, click New Person and create a username and password for that person.

11 Click **Select**.

The users appear on the Users list.

12 Repeat step **8** to configure the user's access to the shared folder.

13 Repeat steps **5** to **12** to share other folders and configure users to access your shared files.

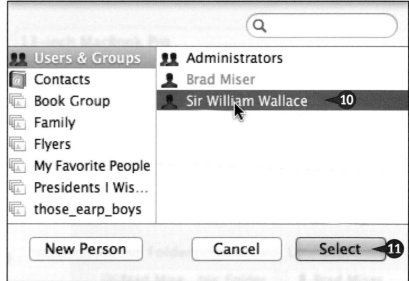

TIPS

What are the permissions I can assign to folders that I share?
With **No Access**, no one can use an item. **Write Only (Drop Box)** enables people to place items within the shared folder, but not to view or change its contents. **Read Only** allows people with whom you share a folder to view, but not change, its contents. **Read & Write** enables people who can access the shared folder to view and change its contents.

When should I use Write Only (Drop Box) access?
Use this when you need input, but you do not want people to be able to see each other's input. Suppose you are teaching and want your students to place assignments on your computer. You can create a Submission folder and share it with Write Only (Drop Box) access. Your students can then place files in the folder, but they cannot see files in that folder.

continued ▶

Share Files on a Local Network (continued)

When you connect to a local network, your MacBook Pro automatically identifies resources on the network that are sharing files. It collects all these resources in the Shared section of the Sidebar so that you can access them easily.

When you connect to a sharing resource, what you can do with the content of that resource is determined by the permissions that you have been granted for it. For example, if you have Read & Write access, you can use a shared folder just like one you created. If you have Read Only access, you can see its contents, but you cannot change those contents.

Share Files on a Local Network (continued)

Access Files Being Shared with You

1 Move to the desktop and open a Finder window.

A In the Shared section of the Sidebar, you see all the computers sharing files on the network.

2 Select the computer whose files you want to access.

B MacBook Pro connects to that computer as a Guest, and you see the resources to which guest accounts have access.

Note: By default, the Public folder in each user's Home folder is available to everyone on the network.

3 Click **Connect As**.

4 To connect as a guest, click **Guest** and skip to step **9.**

5 To connect as a registered user, click **Registered User**.

6 Type the username of the account under which you want to connect.

7 Type the password for the username you typed in step **6.**

8 Check the **Remember this password in my keychain** check box.

9 Click **Connect**.

Your MacBook Pro connects to the resource under the user account you entered.

C The Finder window that appears shows the resources available to you based on the kind of access the user account you used has.

D The user account under which you are logged in is shown here.

E At the top of the window, you see the Sharing icon indicating that the resource you are using is stored on a different computer on the network.

10 Open a shared resource.

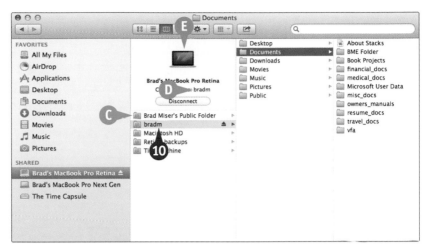

11 Open folders on the shared resource.

12 Double-click files to open them.

13 To copy a file or folder from the shared resource to your MacBook Pro, drag it from the shared resource folder onto a folder stored on your MacBook Pro.

TIPS

When are the files that I share available to others?

In order for people to access files you are sharing, your MacBook Pro must be awake and connected to the network. If a MacBook Pro is configured to go to sleep automatically, people lose access to shared files when it sleeps. Likewise, if your MacBook Pro is no longer connected to the network, its files are not available.

How can I share files with Windows computers?

Turn on File Sharing by clicking its check box. Click **Options**. Select the **Share files and folders using SMB (Windows)** check box. Select the check box next to each user and type the password for that user's account. The user can access the files by typing **smb://*ipaddress***, where *ipaddress* is the current IP address of your MacBook Pro; this address is shown on the Sharing pane.

Share Screens on a Local Network

With screen sharing, you can control another Mac on your local network just as if you were sitting in front of it. For example, you can log in to a different Mac on your network and run an application like you would if that application was installed on your MacBook Pro. This is also useful for helping other users on your network because you can "take over" the other computer to solve problems. Like file sharing, you must configure screen sharing permissions on each computer to determine who can access this feature.

Share Screens on a Local Network

Configure Screen Sharing on MacBook Pro

1 Open the Sharing pane of the System Preferences application.

2 Select the **Screen Sharing** service.

Ⓐ The controls for screen sharing appear.

3 Click **Computer Settings**.

4 Check the **Anyone may request permission to control screen** check box if you want to allow anyone who can access your MacBook Pro to request to share your screen.

5 Check the **VNC viewers may control screen with password** check box and enter a password if you want people using Virtual Network Computing connections to be able to control your MacBook Pro.

6 Click **OK**.

7 Click **All users** to allow anyone who can access your MacBook Pro over the network to share its screen, or **Only these users** to create a list of user accounts that can share your screen.

Note: To create a user list, click Add (➕). The User Account sheet appears. Select the user accounts you want to share and click Select.

8 Check the **On** check box for Screen Sharing.

Screen sharing services start, and your MacBook Pro becomes available to users on your local network.

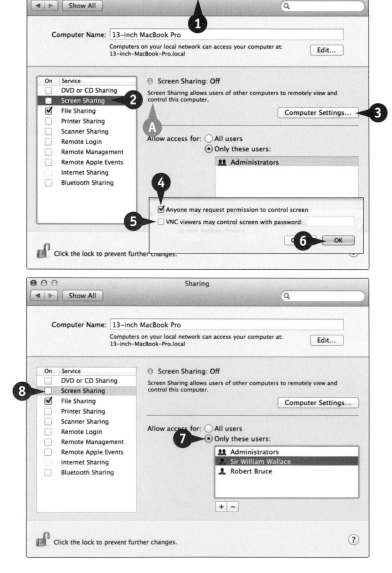

Share Another Computer's Screen

1 Open a Finder window.

2 In the Shared section of the Sidebar, select the Mac whose screen you want to share.

3 Click **Share Screen**.

4 Click **Share Display**.

After the other Mac grants permission for you to share, the Screen Sharing application opens.

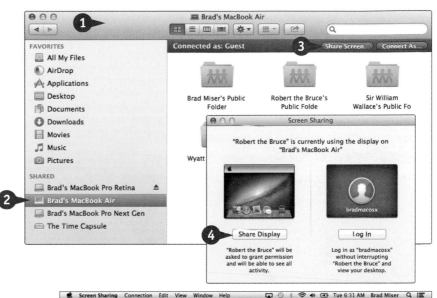

B Within the Screen Sharing application's window, which has the other computer's name as its title, you see the other computer's desktop. When you move your pointer within the window, the pointer is resized according to the resolution of the other computer.

5 Within the Screen Sharing window, you can control the shared Mac.

You can use any application or command on the sharing computer as you would if you were sitting in front of it.

TIPS

What happens when someone wants to share my screen?

If you allow anyone to request to share your screen, when someone wants to share your MacBook Pro, you see a permission dialog on your screen. To allow your screen to be shared, click **Share Screen**. The person sharing your screen can then control your MacBook Pro.

How can I share another computer's screen if that computer is not on my local network?

If you have an iCloud account, you can also share screens across the Internet. On the iCloud pane of the System Preferences application, register your iCloud username and password on each computer among which you want to share screens, and then use the Back To My Mac check box to enable it. You can access any shared services over the Internet like you can on a local network.

Troubleshoot an Internet Connection

You can troubleshoot your Internet connection if you have problems with it. Fortunately, you probably will not need to do this very often. Networks are typically pretty reliable, and once configured correctly, you can usually just keep using them. However, as in the real world, things in the virtual world do not always go according to plan.

If an error message appears, determine if the problem is a network issue or if it is related just to one computer by trying the same action on a different computer on the same network.

Troubleshoot an Internet Connection

Troubleshoot a Network Problem

1. Check the status lights on the modem to make sure the modem is working.

   If the modem appears to be working, go to step **2.** If not, go to step **7.**

2. Check the status of the AirPort Extreme Base Station or Time Capsule.

   If the status lights indicate the base station is working, go to step **3.** If not, go to step **8.**

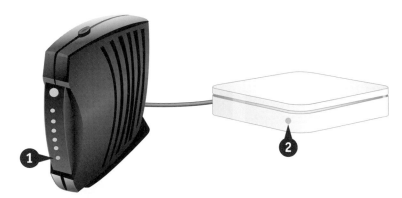

3. Disconnect power from the base station and from the modem and wait about 20 seconds.

4. Connect power to the base station and then to the modem.

5. Try the task that you had a problem with.

   If it is successful, you are done; if not, continue with the next steps.

6. If the modem's power light is on but the connection light is not, contact the ISP to make sure service is available. It probably is not, in which case you need to wait until service is restored.

7. When you are sure that your Internet service has been restored, remove power from the base station, wait 20 seconds, and connect it again.

8. Try the task that you had a problem with.

   The problem should be solved.

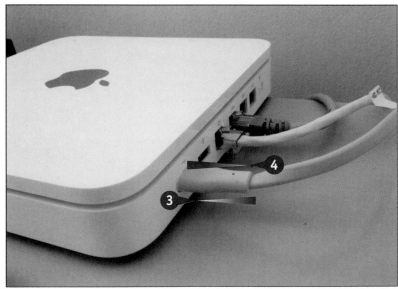

Troubleshoot a MacBook Pro Problem

1 Open the Network pane of the System Preferences application.

2 Check the status of the various connections.

If the status is Not Connected for a connection, you need to reconfigure that connection using steps shown in the section "Connect to the Internet with Wi-Fi" or "Connect to the Internet with Ethernet" earlier in this chapter.

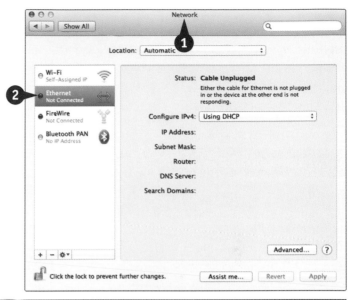

3 If the status is Connected, click the **Apple** menu (🍎), and then click **Restart**.

4 Click **Restart** at the prompt.

5 After the MacBook Pro restarts, try the activity again.

Restarting is always good when you have a problem; it is easy to do and solves a lot of different issues.

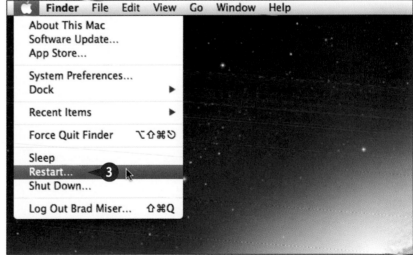

TIPS

How can I get help diagnosing a problem?
Move to the Network pane of the System Preferences application. Click **Assist Me**. At the prompt, click **Diagnostics**. Follow the on-screen steps to diagnose the issue. When the application finds a problem, it identifies it and provides some hints about how to solve it. However, using the steps outlined in this section is usually faster because they include most of what the application tells you to do.

What can I do if none of these steps helped?
Visit www.apple.com/support. Search for the problem you are having. Disconnect everything from your network and connect a computer to the modem (turn the firewall on first). If it works, the problem is related to the network; add devices one by one until you find the source of the problem. If the connection does not work, you need help from your ISP.

Expand Storage Space with an External Hard Drive

Your MacBook Pro includes a drive on which you store the operating system, applications, and your own files and folders. Over time, you might run low on available space, especially if you do large video or DVD projects. More importantly, you should back up your files using Time Machine, which requires a drive outside your Mac, such as an external hard drive. You can connect an external hard drive to your MacBook Pro to expand the working storage space available to you or to use Time Machine.

Two basic steps are involved in preparing an external hard drive to work with MacBook Pro. First, you make the connection between the computer and the hard drive. Second, you use the Disk Utility application to format and partition the hard drive.

Expand Storage Space with an External Hard Drive

Connect and Power an External Hard Drive

① Connect the hard drive to a power source and turn it on.

② Use the appropriate cable to connect the hard drive to the compatible port on the MacBook Pro.

Note: Most hard drives include the cable you need to connect to MacBook Pro. However, some do not. Check the package information to make sure the cable is included. If it is not, you have to buy a cable separately.

The hard drive is ready to format and partition.

Format and Partition an External Hard Drive

① Open the Applications folder, open the Utilities folder, and then double-click the **Disk Utility** application.

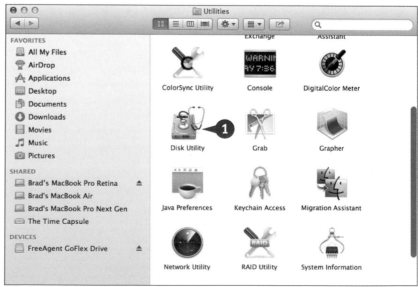

Ⓐ When Disk Utility opens, you see all available disks in the left pane.

② Select the external hard drive.

③ Click the **Partition** tab.

Ⓑ You see the number of partitions in which the disk is currently organized; a new disk has one partition.

④ On the **Partition Layout** pop-up menu, choose the number of partitions you want to create on the disk.

Ⓒ The space on the disk is grouped into the number of partitions you selected. Each partition is named "Untitled *X*," where *X* is a sequential number.

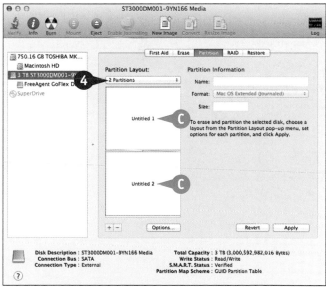

TIPS

What kind of drive works with a MacBook Pro?
All current models can work with USB 2.0, USB 3.0, or Thunderbolt drives; non-Retina models also support FireWire 800. The drive should be at least twice as large as the drive in your MacBook Pro. You can also use Mac- or Windows-compatible hard drives. If a hard drive is formatted for Windows, you should reformat and partition it before using it.

Which interface is best?
USB 2.0 is least expensive, but also the slowest. USB 3.0 is faster and a bit more expensive. FireWire 800 is similar to USB 3. Thunderbolt is the fastest; you pay a premium for that speed. If you are going to use it only for backing up, the interface speed does not really matter. If you are using it for active projects, you want the fastest interface you can get, so go with Thunderbolt.

continued ▶

Although being able to access more storage space is useful for current projects and documents, it is even more important for backing up the information you have stored on MacBook Pro.

With an external hard drive, you can use the OS X Time Machine feature to back up your important data. Should something happen to this data on MacBook Pro or to the MacBook Pro itself, you can easily recover the data from the external drive so that you do not lose files that you can never recover, such as your photos. For more information about Time Machine, see Chapter 17.

Expand Storage Space with an External Hard Drive (continued)

5 Select the top partition.

A Its information is shown in the Partition Information section.

6 Type a name for the partition in the Name field.

7 On the **Format** pop-up menu, choose **Mac OS Extended (Journaled)**.

8 Enter the size of the first partition in the Size field and press `Return`.

Note: You can also change the size of partitions by dragging the resize handle located in the horizontal bar between the Partition Layout box.

The partition is named and sized.

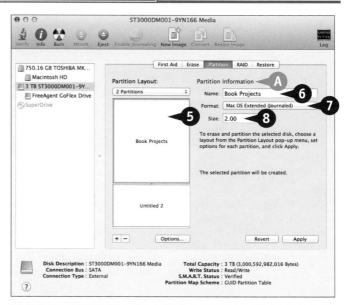

9 Select the next partition.

10 Repeat steps **6** to **8** to name, format, and size the partition.

11 Repeat steps **9** and **10** until you have configured each partition.

Note: The total size of the partitions equals the usable size of the hard drive.

12 Click **Apply**.

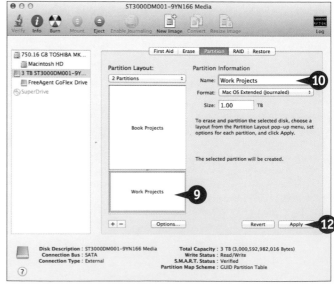

The partition warning appears.

Note: When you partition a disk, all the data it contains is erased, so make sure you do not need its data before continuing.

⑬ Click **Partition**.

Disk Utility partitions the drive according to your settings.

⑭ If the Time Machine dialog appears, click **Decide Later**.

Note: See Chapter 17 for information about configuring Time Machine.

⑮ Quit the Disk Utility.

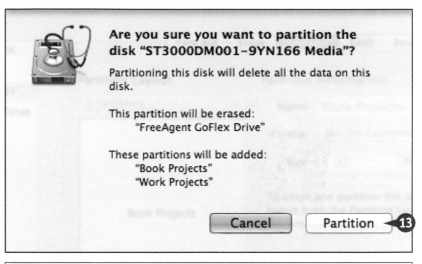

⑯ Open a Finder window.

Ⓑ You see the partitions on the external drive, and they are ready to be used just like the MacBook Pro's internal drive.

Note: Before disconnecting a hard drive from MacBook Pro, click Eject (⏏) next to its icon in the Sidebar or press ⏏ and wait for the disk icon to disappear from the Sidebar. Disconnecting a drive without ejecting it first can damage its data.

TIPS

Why can I not partition a new hard drive?
Some drives come in a format incompatible with OS X, and the partition process fails while displaying an error message. Before you click **Apply** on the **Partition** tab of the Disk Utility application in step **12**, click **Options**. On the resulting sheet, click **GUID Partition Table** and then click **OK**. The sheet closes. Continue with the rest of the steps as described.

What is a partition and how many should I create on my drive?
Partitions are logical volumes, which means that they behave as if each partition is its own drive, even though they are on the same physical device. You can create partitions for various purposes, such as to organize data. You should use only one or two partitions on a drive to avoid ending up with a lot of partitions too small to be usable.

Connect and Use an External Display

You can never have too much screen space to work with. In addition to making your document windows larger so that you can see more of their contents, more screen space helps you work efficiently because you can have more windows open so you can use them at the same time.

To add screen space to MacBook Pro, you can connect an external display to it. This enables you to use the MacBook Pro's internal display and the external display at the same time. You can use both as a single large desktop, or you can mirror the displays, which means they both show the same thing.

Connect and Use an External Display

Connect the Required Adapter to the External Display

Note: Some Apple displays include a cable with a Mini DisplayPort/Thunderbolt connector, and you do not need an adapter. If that is the case for you, skip to step **4.**

1. If required, purchase the Mini DisplayPort adapter appropriate for the display you are using.

2. Plug the small end of the adapter into the Mini DisplayPort/Thunderbolt port on your MacBook Pro.

3. Connect the other end of the adapter to the cable connected to the VGA or DVI input port on the display.

4. Connect the display to a power source, and power it up.

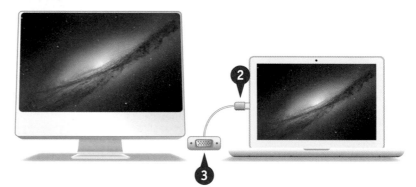

Configure the External Display

1. Open the System Preferences application and click the **Displays** icon.

    A Displays pane opens on the MacBook Pro display and on the external display.

2. Click the **Arrangement** tab on the Displays pane on the MacBook Pro screen.

    Ⓐ You see an icon representation of each display.

3. Drag the external display's icon to match the physical location of the display compared to MacBook Pro (on its left or right side).

4. If you want the external display to be the primary display, drag the menu bar from the MacBook Pro display's icon onto the external display's icon.

5. If you want the displays to show the same information, check the **Mirror Displays** check box and skip the rest of these steps.

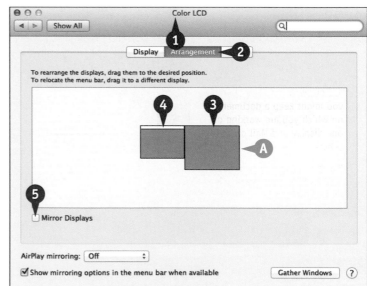

150

6 Select the **Displays** pane visible on the external display.

7 Click the **Display** tab.

8 Choose the resolution for the external display by selecting it from the list of available resolutions.

9 If the **Refresh Rate** pop-up menu appears, choose the highest rate available.

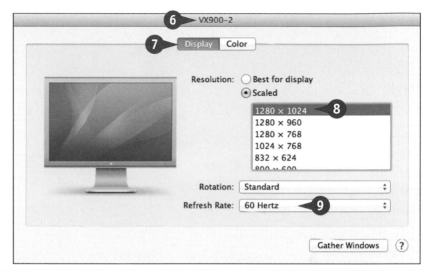

10 Click the **Color** tab.

11 Select the color profile for the display you are using.

12 Quit the System Preferences application.

You now can use the external display. When video mirroring is off, the two displays act as a single, large desktop area. You can move windows onto either display. For example, you might keep a document on which you are working on one display and Mail on the other.

When video mirroring is on, you see the same information on both screens.

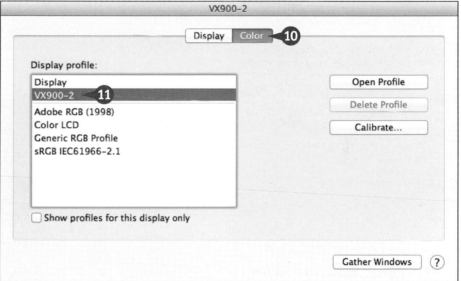

TIP

What kind of external display should I get for my MacBook Pro?
MacBook Pros support many different displays and resolutions. The three most important considerations are interface, size, and cost. If you have a Retina model, an HDMI display is an excellent choice; if not, DVI or VGA is fine. Larger displays are better because they give you more working space. They also tend to be more expensive, although that depends on the specific brand you choose. Be wary of very inexpensive displays because they tend to have poor image quality. In most cases, if you choose a display from a reputable manufacturer or reseller, it will work well for you.

Use an Apple TV to Display on an HDTV

With an Apple TV, you can wirelessly broadcast your MacBook Pro's display on the device to which the Apple TV is connected. This ability has many uses, such as to watch content you have stored on your MacBook Pro on a big-screen TV, or you might want to see the web on the big screen. It is also useful for presentations where you want to show the activity on your MacBook Pro to a group of people.

To broadcast to an Apple TV, your MacBook Pro uses AirPlay. This technology enables MacBook Pros (and most other Apple devices) to send a signal to an Apple TV for it to display on a television. One of the best things about AirPlay is its ease of use, as you will see.

Use an Apple TV to Display on an HDTV

Set Up the Apple TV for AIrPlay

1 Set up the Apple TV by connecting it to a television.

2 Connect the Apple TV to a wireless network.

3 Open the Apple TV's Settings screen.

4 Select **AirPlay**.

5 Turn AirPlay on if not on already.

Broadcast from a MacBook Pro to an Apple TV

1 Open the Wi-Fi menu.

2 Join the network to which you connected the Apple TV in step **2** in the previous section.

Note: If the MacBook Pro and the Apple TV are not on the same network, you cannot use AirPlay.

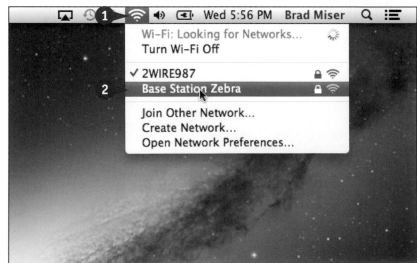

3 Open the Displays pane of the System Preferences application.

4 On the AirPlay Mirroring menu, choose **Apple TV**.

Your MacBook Pro's desktop appears on the television to which the Apple TV is connected. By default, mirroring is used, so the same image appears on your MacBook Pro and on the television.

5 Check the **Show mirroring options in the menu bar when available** check box.

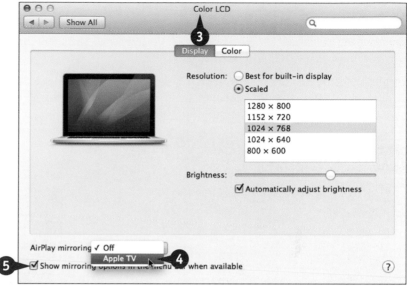

6 Open the mirroring menu.

7 To match the MacBook Pro's desktop to the Apple TV, choose **Apple TV**.

Your MacBook Pro's display adjusts to match the resolution of the Apple TV.

Note: Some applications use the display on your MacBook Pro to present controls instead of the content. For example, when you play a movie in iTunes via AirPlay, the iTunes window contains controls while the content plays on the television.

8 To stop broadcasting to the Apple TV, choose **Turn Off AirPlay Mirroring**.

TIP

Why do I not see any AirPlay devices available on my MacBook Pro?
There are a couple of most likely causes. The first is that the devices are not on the same network. Check the network configuration of each device to make sure they are on the same network. Second, if the devices are on the same network but you do not see any AirPlay devices, the network you are using may not support the protocols AirPlay uses; in some public areas, networks are designed to prevent streaming of content. If you cannot use a different network, you must see if the available one can be reconfigured to support AirPlay.

Connect and Use a Bluetooth Mouse

You might find that the MacBook Pro trackpad works really well for you and that you never want to use anything else; or, you might prefer a mouse when you are working with MacBook Pro in one place. It is mostly a matter of personal preference. If you do want to use a mouse, a Bluetooth mouse is a good option since there are no wires to fuss with.

If you have already configured a Bluetooth device, you see those devices when you open the Bluetooth pane. If not, you see the screens shown in this task. The steps work similarly in either case.

Connect and Use a Bluetooth Mouse

① Insert batteries into the mouse and turn it on.

② Place the mouse in discovery mode.

Note: See the documentation for the specific mouse you use to see how to do this.

③ Open the System Preferences application and click the **Bluetooth** icon.

④ Check the **On** check box to turn Bluetooth on.

⑤ Check the **Discoverable** check box if you want other Bluetooth devices to be able to locate your MacBook Pro.

⑥ Check the **Show Bluetooth in menu bar** check box to enable the Bluetooth menu so that you can control Bluetooth from the desktop.

⑦ Click **Add** (⊞), or the **Set Up New Device** button (which appears when you have not set up a device before).

The Bluetooth Setup Assistant appears. It looks for any devices it can discover and presents them on the list.

⑧ Click the device you want to set up.

⑨ Click **Continue**.

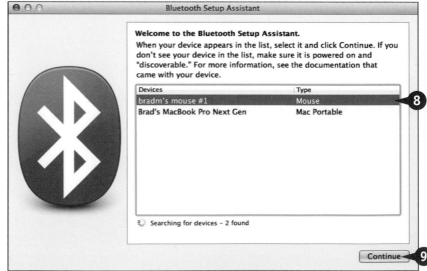

The MacBook Pro attempts to connect to the device. If successful, you see the Conclusion screen.

⑩ Click **Quit** in the Conclusion screen.

You go back to the Bluetooth pane where you see the mouse you configured.

Ⓐ You see connection status information about the mouse you configured.

⑪ Click **Advanced**.

The Advanced sheet appears.

⑫ Check or uncheck check boxes to complete the configuration; for example, check **Allow Bluetooth devices to wake this computer** if you want to be able to wake MacBook Pro by moving the mouse.

⑬ Click **OK**.

Note: Once you have set up the mouse, use the Mouse pane of the System Preferences application to configure it, such as by setting which actions are assigned to its buttons and other controls.

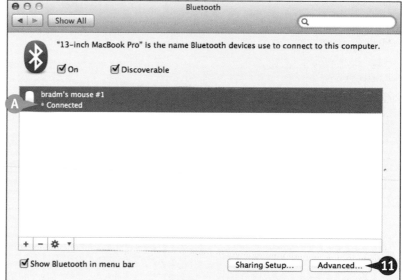

TIP

What is the best kind of Bluetooth mouse?
Choosing a mouse is a personal decision in that one person's favorite mouse might be unusable to someone else. The most important consideration when choosing a mouse is the comfort of the mouse in your hand. If possible, you should try using a mouse before buying it. Next, consider the number of controls, buttons, and other features a mouse offers. At the least, a mouse should have two buttons and a scroll wheel. Some devices have more controls; for example, the Apple Magic Mouse replicates the gesture features of the MacBook Pro trackpad by allowing you to make gestures on the top of the mouse.

Connect and Use a Bluetooth Keyboard

The MacBook Pro's keyboard is great, but it might be more convenient when you are working at one location to use an external keyboard. For example, when you are working at an office desk, an external keyboard is often easier to use, especially if the desk has a keyboard tray.

A Bluetooth keyboard is great because you do not need any cables to connect it to your Mac. You simply pair the keyboard with your MacBook Pro and then you can use it. There are many types of keyboards from which you can use; ideally, you will be able to try them "hands on" before buying one to make sure you get one that is comfortable for you to use.

Connect and Use a Bluetooth Keyboard

① Insert batteries into the keyboard and turn it on.

② Place the keyboard in discovery mode.

Note: See the documentation for the specific keyboard you use to see how to do this.

③ Open the System Preferences application and click the **Bluetooth** icon.

The Bluetooth pane appears.

④ Click **Add** (⊞), or the **Set Up New Device** button (which appears when you have not set up a device before).

The Bluetooth Setup Assistant appears. It looks for any devices it can discover and presents them on the list.

⑤ Click the device you want to set up.

⑥ Click **Continue**.

The MacBook Pro attempts to connect to the keyboard. You see the pairing screen.

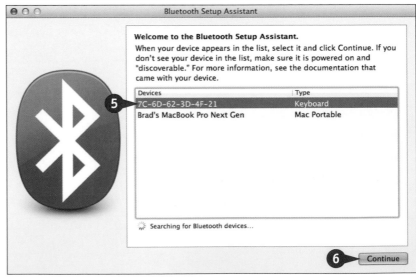

7 On the Bluetooth keyboard, type the passkey.

If successful, you see the Conclusion screen.

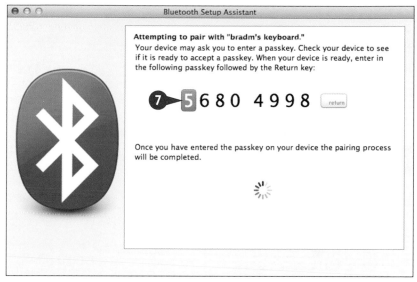

8 Click **Quit** in the Conclusion screen.

You go back to the Bluetooth pane where you see the keyboard you configured.

How can I configure a Bluetooth keyboard?
Open the Keyboard pane of the System Preferences application. Click **Set Up Bluetooth Keyboard**. Use the resulting controls to configure the keyboard. The options you see depend on the specific keyboard you use as they have different features and options.

How can I use a wired keyboard?
To use a wired keyboard, simply connect it to your MacBook Pro. Your MacBook Pro connects to it and you can use it right away. You can configure its options using the Keyboard pane of the System Preferences application.

Connect and Use External Speakers

Your MacBook Pro has speakers, but their sound quality is somewhat less than spectacular. With iTunes, streaming video, and all the other great applications for which sound is an important element, you should consider using external speakers when you use MacBook Pro in one location.

You can use a variety of speakers with MacBook Pro as long as they are *powered* (also called *computer*) speakers. Some speaker sets have two speakers (left and right), whereas others have three (left, right, and subwoofer). For the ultimate in sound, consider a digital 5.1 sound system.

Connect and Use External Speakers

① Connect the speaker input to the Audio port; on the 15-inch model, use the Audio Out port.

② Make the connections between the speakers, such as between the left and right speaker and the subwoofer.

③ Power up the speakers.

④ Open the System Preferences application and click the **Sound** icon.

The Sound pane appears.

⑤ Click the **Output** tab.

⑥ Select the speakers you want to use for sound output.

This option appears as Headphones even when you attach a set of speakers.

Note: You can also connect any pair of analog headphones to the MacBook Pro audio port, which is a great way to enjoy good sound quality on the move.

⑦ If controls for the speakers appear, use them to improve the sound.

For example, you might be able to set a balance level and system volume level.

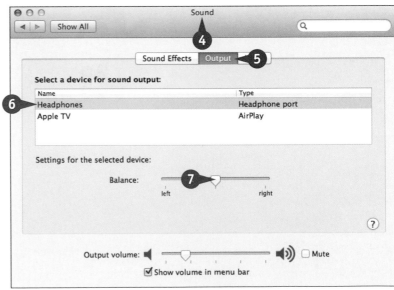

8 Play sound with an application such as iTunes.

Note: For more information about iTunes, see Chapter 18.

9 Use the application's controls to set the specific volume level.

10 Adjust the volume level and other settings using the speaker system's controls.

TIPS

Does a MacBook Pro support digital audio?
Yes. To use a digital speaker system with MacBook Pro, you need a TOSLINK adapter that connects to the digital audio cable and plugs into the Audio port on MacBook Pro (which supports both analog and digital audio). When you connect the other end to the speaker system, you can enjoy the benefits of digital, such as surround sound coming from multiple speakers.

How can I play audio on an Apple TV or other devices?
You can use AirPlay to broadcast your MacBook Pro's audio to an Apple TV, to AirPort Express base stations to which you have connected speakers, or directly to AirPlay-enabled speakers. Set up the AirPlay device and then choose the AirPlay device on the Output tab.

Connect To and Use a USB Hub

Many devices use USB to connect to a computer. Examples of these include external hard drives, mice, iPhones, iPads, digital cameras, and printers. MacBook Pros have two USB ports, and so you are able to connect only two devices to it at a time, which can be inconvenient.

For situations in which you want to connect more than two USB devices to your MacBook Pro at the same time, you can use an external USB hub. You connect the hub to MacBook Pro and then connect USB devices to the ports on the hub. MacBook Pro can access these devices just as if they are connected to its USB port.

Connect To and Use a USB Hub

Obtain an External USB Hub

1 Visit your favorite retailer.

2 Look for a USB 2 or USB 3 hub with the number of ports matching or exceeding the number of devices you want to have connected at the same time.

Note: You should also consider whether the hub gets its power from the MacBook Pro or requires an external power source. An external power source is a nuisance because you have to carry it with you, but a self-powered hub uses power from the MacBook Pro, which shortens life when operating on battery power.

3 Purchase a hub.

Install a USB Hub

1 Connect the input port on the hub to a USB port on the MacBook Pro.

2 Connect the hub to a power source, if required.

3 Connect USB devices to the hub.

The devices are ready to use.

Connect To and Use Ethernet Devices

Macbook Pro is designed to be wireless when it comes to connecting to many devices — most importantly, local networks and the Internet. However, Ethernet, which is a wired technology, does offer some benefits over wireless connections. Ethernet is faster, and so achieves the best network performance. Ethernet is also more secure than wireless because you have to be physically connected to a network to access it.

To connect to a network or devices (such as a printer) with Ethernet, you can use MacBook Pro's Ethernet port on those models that have one; for models that do not, you need an Ethernet adapter. Use an Ethernet cable to connect the port (or adapter) to an AirPort Base Station, network hub, or other Ethernet device (such as a printer).

Connect To and Use Ethernet Devices

1 Connect an Ethernet cable to the MacBook Pro's Ethernet port or adapter.

2 Connect the other end of the cable to an Ethernet device, such as an AirPort Extreme Base Station.

3 Configure the Ethernet connection using the appropriate pane of the System Preferences or other application.

For example, you can use the Network pane to configure an Ethernet network connection.

Connect to the Internet with Wi-Fi

When you are on the move, you can still easily connect to the Internet. In most public places, businesses, hotels, restaurants, and other locations, Internet access is readily available through a wireless (Wi-Fi) network connection.

Connecting to the Internet using Wi-Fi is a two-step process. First, you establish the connection between your MacBook Pro and the network. Second, you register your MacBook Pro to access the Internet over the network. The second step is required most of the time, especially when you are charged a fee to access the Internet for a specific period of time. When access to the Internet is free, all you typically have to do is agree to terms and conditions.

Connect to the Internet with Wi-Fi

Connect to a Wi-Fi Network

Note: When your MacBook Pro turns on or wakes up, it scans the area for available wireless networks. If it does not find one of your preferred networks (one that you have used before, such as the one in your home), it presents a list of available networks to you.

1 Click the **Wi-Fi** menu (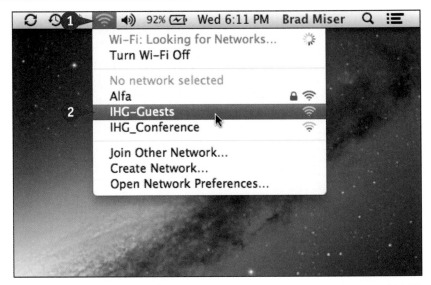).

Note: If the lock icon appears along the right side of the window for a network, it is secured and you need a password to join it.

2 Select the wireless network you want to join.

The MacBook Pro connects to the network. Depends on the kind of network you are connecting to, you are prompted to join the network by providing required information or by accepting fees or terms and conditions.

3 Type in the required information.

4 Click **Accept** or **Logon**.

Typically, you see the home page for the network's provider.

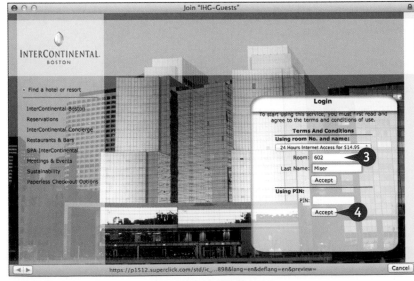

5 Go to any web page.

If the page appears, the MacBook Pro is connected to the Internet, you can skip the remaining steps.

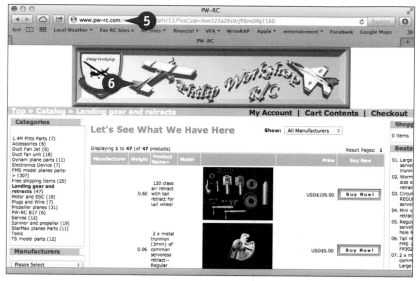

6 If a page does not appear, click the **Apple** menu (🍎) and choose **System Preferences**.

7 Click the **Network** icon to open the Network pane.

8 Click the **Network Name** menu to select a different network.

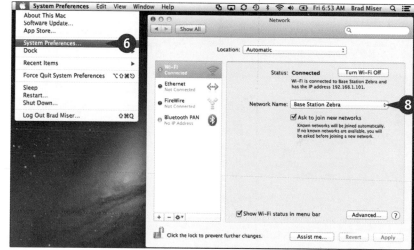

TIPS

What does Wi-Fi stand for?
Wi-Fi stands for wireless fidelity. It applies to a set of standard protocols used to ensure that wireless devices and the software they use are compatible. The technical specifications fall under the Institute of Electrical and Electronics Engineers (IEEE) 802.11 series. The MacBook Pro's wireless capabilities are Wi-Fi or 802.11 compatible so that you can connect to any network or device that uses these standards.

What if there is only an Ethernet connection available?
Some places, such as hotel rooms or meeting rooms, have only an Ethernet connection available. In that situation, you have three options: connect wirelessly through an AirPort Express Base Station connected to the Ethernet network, connect using an Ethernet cable (and adapter if required), or connect wirelessly with a broadband wireless modem. You can find more information on the first and third methods later in this chapter.

Connect to the Internet with an AirPort Express Base Station

An AirPort Express Base Station is a small, portable wireless base station that you can use to easily create your own wireless networks. For example, if you happen to stay in a hotel that only has wired Internet access in its rooms, you can use an AirPort Express Base Station to quickly create a wireless network there. This also is very useful if you have multiple devices, because all the devices can share the same connection, avoiding multiple access fees. There are two steps to setting up a temporary wireless network with an AirPort Express Base Station. First, you connect the base station to the wired network. Second, you configure the base station to provide a wireless network.

Connect to the Internet with an AirPort Express Base Station

Connect the Base Station to the Network

1 Using an Ethernet cable, connect the wired network to the Ethernet Wide Area Network (WAN) port on the base station.

2 Connect the base station to power.

Note: This exercise assumes that the wired network provides an Internet connection using Dynamic Host Configuration Protocol (DHCP).

Configure and Access a Wireless Network

3 On the **Wi-Fi** menu (), choose the AirPort Express Base Station.

The AirPort Utility application opens and connects to the base station.

4 If you are prompted to join the provider's network, configure the login sheet to gain access to that network for the base station.

Note: If it is fee-based access, you usually have to select the period and fee you want to use and click Accept.

Note: You may not be prompted to provide information required to join the network until after the base station is set up, so some of these steps might occur in a different order.

⑤ Enter the name you want to give to the wireless network that the base station will provide.

Note: The AirPort Utility application creates default names for the network and base station.

⑥ Enter the name by which you will identify the base station itself.

⑦ Enter the network's password in the Password and Verify fields.

⑧ Click **Next**.

The AirPort Utility completes the network configuration and starts providing a wireless network and Internet connection. The MacBook Pro connects to the new network automatically.

⑨ Click **Done**.

The base station provides the wireless network. You can quit the AirPort Utility.

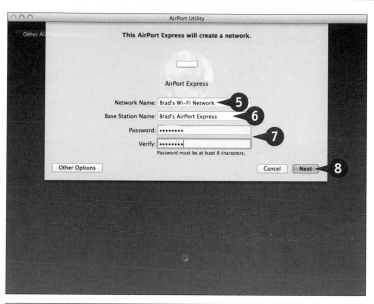

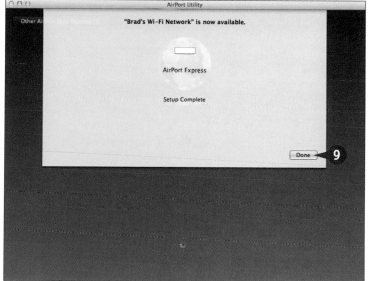

TIPS

Do I have to reconfigure the base station when I take it to a new location?

No, an AirPort Express Base Station remembers the configuration of the last location in which you used it. As long as each network you connect it to provides access through DHCP, you can simply connect the base station to the new network.

How do I correct base station errors?

Open the AirPort Utility (within the Utilities folder located in the Applications folder), select the base station, and click **Edit**. Use the resulting sheet to make changes to the base station's configuration. For example, on the Network tab, you might need to change the Router Mode to DHCP and NAT. After you make changes, click **Update**.

Connect to the Internet with a Broadband Wireless Modem

If you travel a lot, you should consider a broadband wireless modem, with which you can connect to the Internet anywhere within the network's coverage area. National networks provide broad coverage areas, and so you can usually get a connection wherever you are. This can also save money because you use one account and all your access is included in one monthly fee.

With a broadband wireless modem, you use the same network every time you connect so you do not have to find and sign onto networks in various locations. One of the best types is a portable Wi-Fi hotspot that provides a network to which you can connect multiple devices at the same time.

Connect to the Internet with a Broadband Wireless Modem

Obtain a Broadband Wireless Modem

1. Explore the major cell phone company websites to determine which ones offer a modem you can use; obtaining a broadband wireless modem is a lot like buying a cell phone.

2. Make sure the modem you consider connects using USB either directly or via a cable.

3. Check the specifications or features to ensure the modem and accompanying software are OS X compatible and to determine the connection speed under ideal conditions.

4. Determine the cost of the modem (many are free when you sign up for an account) and monthly service.

Note: Many wireless broadband accounts have a maximum amount of data that can be transferred under the account's monthly fee. If you exceed this amount, the overage charges can be quite expensive.

5. Check the contract terms; many providers require two-year agreements.

6. Check the coverage area for the provider to make sure it includes the areas you are mostly likely to be in.

   You want to be sure you frequent the highest-speed areas of the network.

7. After you have compared your options, choose and purchase the modem and account that makes the most sense to you.

8. If required, install the software for the broadband wireless modem using the modem's installer application.

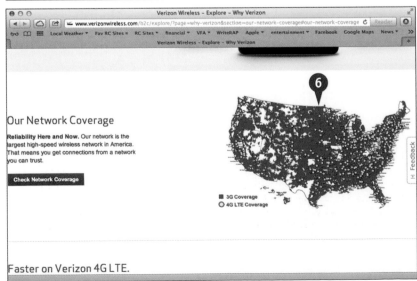

Use a Broadband Wireless Modem to Connect to the Internet

1. Turn the device on.

2. If necessary, launch the broadband wireless modem's connection application.

   If you are using a MiFi device, you do not need to run any software on your MacBook Pro. After you power up the device, it starts providing the network after its startup process is complete.

3. Click the **Wi-Fi** menu ( ) and select the device.

4. If prompted, enter the network's password.

5. Select the **Remember this network** check box.

6. Click **Join**.

   The MacBook Pro connects to the wireless network and provides you with an Internet connection.

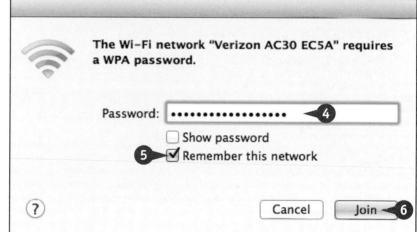

TIP

Why not use a wireless modem all the time?
If a broadband wireless modem provides sufficient connection speeds in the locations you use MacBook Pro the most, you can use it as your primary Internet connection (and so you do not need another account with a cable or DSL provider). However, most accounts have limits on the amount of data that can be transferred per month at the account's monthly cost. If that amount is sufficient for your Internet use, you can use the wireless modem for all your Internet activity. If not, you will need another option because overage charges are usually quite expensive (often enough to cover the cost of another type of account). And, even though performance is usually pretty fast, a broadband wireless modem is still significantly slower than a cable or DSL connection.

Manage Your MacBook Pro's Power

Your MacBook Pro needs power to operate, just like any other electronic device. Because it has an internal battery, you do not need to be connected to an outlet for MacBook Pro to run (which is what makes it a mobile computer). One of the most important tasks as you travel with your MacBook Pro is to manage its power so that you do not run out of power at an inconvenient time.

You can do a number of things to manage power on your MacBook Pro. First, you can configure the MacBook Pro to use as little power as possible. Second, you can monitor the MacBook Pro's power status. Third, you can build a power toolkit.

Manage Your MacBook Pro's Power

Configure the MacBook Pro to Minimize Power Use

1 Use the Energy Saver pane of the System Preferences application to configure the MacBook Pro so that it uses a minimum amount of power while running on the battery.

Note: See Chapter 6 for details.

Monitor the Battery Power

1 Look at the battery icon (■) in the menu bar.

As battery power is used, the filled part of the icon shrinks to give you a relative idea of how much battery power remains.

2 To access more detailed information, open the battery menu by clicking the battery icon (■).

A The amount of operating time you have left is shown at the top of the menu.

3 To display the percentage of charge remaining next to the battery icon, choose **Show Percentage**.

Build a MacBook Pro Power Toolkit

1 When you travel with MacBook Pro, bring its power adapter with you so that you are able to recharge when you can; when possible, work with the power adapter connected to keep your battery fully charged so that you have maximum working time when running on battery power.

2 If you frequently travel on long plane flights, purchase an Apple MagSafe Airline Adapter. This enables you to connect MacBook Pro to the power outlets provided in some airplanes.

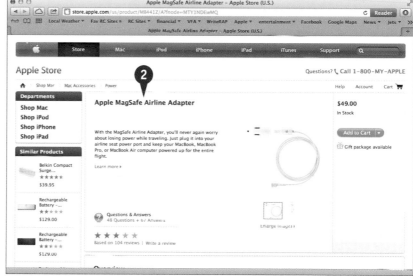

TIP

What are some other tips to extend my working time on the road?
Put the MacBook Pro to sleep when you are not using it (such as by closing its lid). When it sleeps, the computer uses very little power. If you have an iPod or iPad, use it to listen to music or watch video instead of iTunes on your MacBook Pro. iTunes uses significant amounts of power because it requires a lot of disk activity. In general, the more disk activity required to run an application, the faster the MacBook Pro runs out of power, so be aware of the applications you use; keep only those applications that you are actively using open, to prevent unnecessary activity. Also, turn off Wi-Fi and Bluetooth to save the power they consume. Making your screen dimmer helps too.

Protect Your Data with FileVault

When you use your MacBook Pro while traveling, you incur a higher risk of someone either accessing your MacBook Pro or stealing it. In either situation, data stored on your MacBook Pro can be compromised. This can lead to the loss of sensitive information, identity theft, or other harmful outcomes.

The OS X FileVault feature encrypts your data so that it cannot be used without a password. Even if someone does get into your MacBook Pro, he or she cannot access its data without the password, rendering the information stored on your computer unusable. (Ensure that Automatic Login is turned off or anyone who turns your computer one can access its data.)

Protect Your Data with FileVault

① Open the System Preferences application.

② Click the **Security & Privacy** icon.

③ Click the **FileVault** tab.

Note: You need to be authenticated to configure FileVault.

④ Click **Turn On FileVault**.

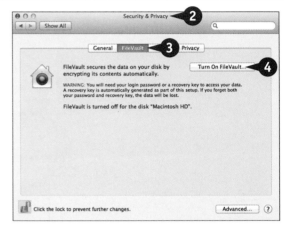

Ⓐ You see a list of all user accounts on your MacBook Pro. Each user must provide a password to be able to unlock the disk.

Ⓑ Users with passwords set are marked with a check mark.

⑤ Click the **Enable User** button.

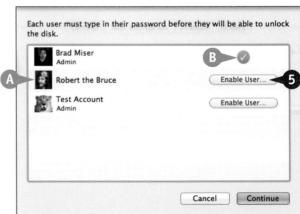

⑥ Enter the user's password.

⑦ Click **OK**.

⑧ Repeat steps **5** to **7** until all users have been enabled.

⑨ Click **Continue**.

You are prompted to document a recovery key. If you forget passwords, the data on MacBook Pro is unusable. The recovery key enables you to gain access to the data as a safety precaution.

10 Click the **Show Recovery Key** arrow.

The recovery key appears.

11 Copy the recovery key exactly as it appears and store it in a very safe location.

12 Click **Continue**.

You are prompted to store the recovery key with Apple. This enables you to have a backup of the recovery key that you can access by contacting Apple. In general, you should do this, just in case.

13 Select the **Store the recovery key with Apple** radio button.

14 Create your security questions and answers, which are required for you to get the key from Apple.

15 Click **Continue**.

16 Click **Restart**.

Your MacBook Pro restarts and the encryption process begins. This process can take a long time. You can monitor the process on the FileVault tab.

Note: When you are logged in to your user account, your data is available. Make sure you log out whenever you are not using MacBook Pro if any risk exists of someone you do not know or trust accessing it. Only when you are logged out is your data encrypted.

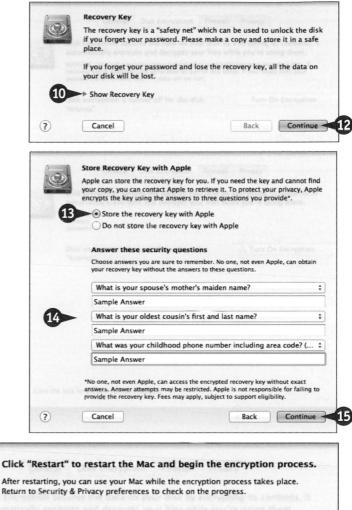

TIPS

When I log in and FileVault is on, I do not notice any difference. Is it working?

FileVault protects access to your data from outside your user account. For example, if someone tries to access your hard disk as if it were an external hard drive, the data is encrypted and cannot be used. When you are logged in under your user account and FileVault is on, you will probably not notice any difference.

What happens if I forget my password?

You have to use the recovery key to be able to access your data. If you cannot locate the key, contact Apple to get it, assuming you enabled that option. If you or Apple cannot get to your recovery key, *all* the data on your MacBook Pro is lost. So make sure you keep your key in a safe location, and you should store it with Apple too.

Protect MacBook Pro with General Security

I f other people use your MacBook Pro, or some chance exists that they will, consider adding some extra security to prevent unwanted access to the data stored on the computer.

For example, you can require that a password be entered to wake the MacBook Pro up or to stop the screen saver. This is good if you sometimes leave the MacBook Pro running when someone else can possibly access it. Without your password, other users cannot access your information even if they can physically access your MacBook Pro.

Protect MacBook Pro with General Security

1 Click the **Apple** menu (🍎) and choose **System Preferences**.

2 Click the **Security & Privacy** icon.

3 Click the **General** tab.

4 Click the **Require password** check box and choose the amount of time from the pop-up menu if you want a password to be required to start using MacBook Pro after it goes to sleep or the screen saver activates.

5 To display a message when the screen is locked, check the **Show a message when the screen is locked** check box, and in the text box enter the message that appears.

6 If you want to prevent automatic login, click the **Disable automatic login** check box.

7 Choose the gatekeeper level of security that you want for applications to be installed.

A You can use the controls on the Privacy tab to prevent diagnostic information from being sent to Apple and to disable location services.

Protect Your MacBook Pro with Its Firewall

When you are using a known network to access the Internet, it should be equipped with its own firewall or Network Address Translation (NAT) protection to prevent computers you do not control from being able to see or access your MacBook Pro. However, if you are not sure about how much protection a network provides, such as when you are connecting to a network in a public place, you should use the OS X firewall to block attempts to access your computer from the Internet. You might have to tweak the firewall a bit to be as secure as possible while still allowing you to do what you want.

Protect Your MacBook Pro with Its Firewall

1 Open the System Preferences application.

2 Click the **Security & Privacy** icon.

3 Click the **Firewall** tab.

4 Click **Turn On Firewall**.

The firewall starts working.

5 Try your normal tasks.

If they work as expected, you can skip the rest of these steps. If not, configure the firewall to allow specific tasks.

6 Click **Firewall Options**.

7 To add applications through which you want to allow incoming connections, click **Add** (⊞).

Note: To prevent any network access to MacBook Pro, check the Block all incoming connections check box.

8 Use the resulting sheet to select the applications or services you want to allow and click **Add** (⊞).

Services and applications allowed to have incoming connections are shown on the list.

9 To prevent services you did not request from detecting the MacBook Pro on a network, such as through Bonjour, check the **Enable stealth mode** check box.

10 Click **OK**.

PART III

Using the Internet

A MacBook Pro is ideal for using the Internet. With iCloud, you can store your information online where all your devices can access the same data. Safari is OS X's excellent web browser. Using Mail, you can send, receive, and organize e-mail. To communicate with people near and far, use FaceTime and Messages for text, audio, and even video chats.

Chapter 10: Using iCloud Online Services 176

Chapter 11: Surfing the Web 188

Chapter 12: E-Mailing with Mail. 216

Chapter 13: Communicating in Real Time 238

Explore iCloud

An iCloud account gives you access to a number of useful services and online applications that you can use as much as you want. Because your iCloud account is integrated with your MacBook Pro, you can consider iCloud to be an extension of your MacBook Pro desktop onto the Internet.

You can use iCloud to keep information and documents in sync among several devices, such as your MacBook Pro, other Macs, an iPhone, an iPad, and even a Windows PC. An iCloud account provides you with online e-mail, calendars, contacts, documents, photos, and more. You can access this through applications on your MacBook Pro and through your iCloud website.

The iCloud

With iCloud, you have an online storage space. This is so useful because you can access that space from many devices at the same time, keeping your information and documents in sync. For example, you can start a document on your MacBook Pro and save it to the Cloud. You can make changes to the document on an iPad; those changes are also saved to the cloud, from where they are copied back to your MacBook Pro. So, no matter which device you are using at any point in time, you have the same information available to you.

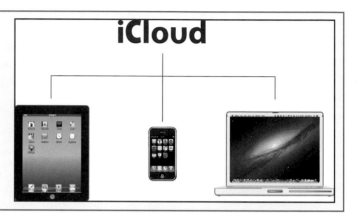

iCloud Account

To use iCloud, you must have an iCloud account. If you already have an Apple ID, you also have an iCloud account. If you do not, creating an iCloud account is simple. You can use many of iCloud's services for free, so you have no reason not to try it to see if it will be useful to you. After you have an iCloud account, you configure it on each of your devices to be able to take advantage of all that iCloud offers.

iCloud Website

In addition to being able to access iCloud data and services from your MacBook Pro and other devices, you can also use your iCloud website to access your information through the online applications it provides. This is very useful for those times you might not have one of your devices with you. You can log in to your account from any compatible web browser and check your e-mail, create an event on your calendar, and so on.

E-Mail

Another great feature of iCloud is that you get an e-mail account, with an e-mail address that is *AppleID*@me. com, where *AppleID* is the username of your Apple account (if you have an existing e-mail account, you can associate that with your iCloud account). You can send and receive e-mail from your iCloud account just like you do with other e-mail accounts that you may have, using an e-mail application such as Mail; using an iPhone, iPad, or iPod touch; or directly from the Mail application on your iCloud website. You can also create e-mail aliases that enable you to use multiple addresses at the same time.

Calendars and Contacts

Similar to e-mail, iCloud enables you to store contact and calendar information on the cloud so that you can access it through applications on your MacBook Pro and iPads, iPhones, and iPod touches. You can also use the online applications to work with this information from any computer using a compatible web browser.

Find My Mac

iCloud can identify the current location of your MacBook Pro through its network connection. This can be helpful if your MacBook is lost or stolen because you can identify where it is and you can take steps to protect the information stored on it, such as by wiping its drive.

iCloud and Windows PCs

iCloud works with Windows PCs, too. If you also use a Windows PC, you can configure its applications, such as Outlook, to access your iCloud account so that you can share information on a PC. The software necessary to configure iCloud on a Windows PC is downloaded and installed the same time as iTunes; you can open the iCloud control panel to configure your iCloud account. This is similar to configuring it on your MacBook Pro, which is described in the next section.

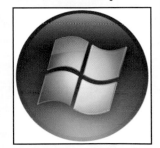

Obtain and Configure an iCloud Account

A s mentioned previously, to use iCloud services you need an iCloud account. An iCloud account is free (some services or upgrades require a fee). If you have an Apple ID already, you also have an iCloud account, so you just need to make sure your account is configured on your MacBook Pro.

To obtain or configure an iCloud account, you use the iCloud pane of the System Preferences application. This pane has two modes. If you have not logged in to an account, the pane enables you to do so. If you have logged in, you can use the controls on the pane to configure your account.

Obtain and Configure an iCloud Account

Obtain an iCloud Account

1 Click **Apple** (🍎) and select **System Preferences**.

2 Click **iCloud**.

Note: If you already have an Apple ID, skip to the "Configure an iCloud Account" section.

3 Click **Create an Apple ID**.

The Create an Apple ID sheet appears. This guides you through each step of the process. When you are done, your Apple ID and password are entered in the iCloud pane automatically and you jump to step **5** in the next section. Click **Back** to be able to start at step **1** in the following task, or just pick up with step **5**.

Configure an iCloud Account

① Follow steps **1** and **2** to open the iCloud pane.

② Type your Apple ID.

③ Type your password.

④ Click **Sign In**.

⑤ Deselect the top check box if you do not want your information synced on the cloud.

⑥ Deselect the lower check box if you do not want to use Find My Mac to be able to locate your MacBook Pro.

⑦ Click **Next**.

The basic configuration of your iCloud account is complete. The iCloud pane is reconfigured to show that you are signed into your account. You can use the controls you see to do further configuration of your account; some examples are provided later in this chapter.

TIPS

How do I change iCloud accounts?

To switch to a different iCloud account, move to the iCloud pane and click **Sign Out**. You are prompted to keep on or delete from your MacBook Pro the information that has been synced, such as contacts, calendars, and so on. After you have deleted or kept each type of information, you return to the iCloud pane and can sign into a different account.

How can I stream music to all my devices?

The iTunes Match service uploads all the music in your iTunes library to the cloud. From there, each of your devices can access, download, and play that music. This is useful because you do not have to bother with selecting only parts of your music collection to sync on a device. All your music is available all the time. iTunes Match requires a fee to use; see http://www.apple.com/itunes/itunes-match/ for more information.

Work with Your iCloud Website

Your iCloud account provides access to a website that includes online applications and tools you can use to manage your iCloud account. Because the online applications get data from the cloud, you share the data in these applications and any devices with which you have synced your account.

Your iCloud website enables you to access your information from any computer running a compatible web browser (which includes Safari, Firefox, Internet Explorer on a Windows PC, and Chrome). This is convenient for those situations in which you do not happen to have any of your devices with you.

Work with Your iCloud Website

1 Move to www.icloud.com.

The iCloud Login page appears.

2 Type your Apple ID, if needed.

3 Type your password.

4 Click the **Keep me signed in** check box if you want to remain logged in to your account.

5 Press **Return**.

You move to the iCloud website. You see icons for the applications available to you.

6 Click the icon for the application you want to use; for example, to use the Contacts application, click **Contacts**.

The application you selected opens and you can work with it.

⑦ Work with the online application.

Note: The iCloud applications work very similarly to the OS X desktop applications.

⑧ To access commands in the application, click the Action button (⚙).

⑨ To move into a different application, click the **iCloud** button (☁).

You move back to the iCloud home page and see the application icons again.

⑩ To move into a different application, click its icon.

⑪ To exit your iCloud website, click **Sign Out**.

TIPS

How can I change my account?
When you are logged in to your iCloud website, click your name located in the upper right corner of the window. The Account sheet appears. Here you can add a photo and set the language and time zone. If you click your Apple ID, you move to the My Apple ID website where you can reset your password and perform much more advanced administration of your account.

How can I add more disk space to my account?
Your iCloud account includes 5GB of storage space by default. For most people who are just using it for e-mail, calendars, and contacts, that is enough. If you store a lot of documents on the cloud and need more room, open the iCloud pane and click **Manage**. Click **Buy More Storage** and follow the on-screen instructions to increase the amount of online storage available to you. Note that content from the iTunes Store, App Store, iTunes Match, and Photo Stream does not count against your storage space.

Synchronize Information Among Multiple Devices

If you have more than one Mac, you can use iCloud to keep a variety of information synchronized on each Mac. For example, you can make sure you have the same set of contacts in the Contacts application on each computer, or ensure that all your favorite bookmarks are available when you need them.

To get started, you need to configure each computer to be part of the synchronization process. After you do that, the synchronization process happens automatically and you do not even have to think about it.

Synchronize Information Among Multiple Devices

1 Click **Apple** (🍎) and select **System Preferences**.

2 Click **iCloud**.

3 If necessary, sign into your iCloud account as described in the section "Obtain and Configure an iCloud Account" earlier in this chapter.

4 Select the check boxes for information that you want to sync.

5 Deselect the check boxes for any information you do not want to be synced.

6 Click **Delete from Mac** if you are sure that you do not want to keep the information on your MacBook Pro; if you change your mind, click **Cancel** instead.

7 Repeat steps **4** to **6** until you have configured all the data available for syncing.

8 Press ⌘+Q to close the System Preferences application.

Repeat steps **1** to **7** on each Mac that you want to keep in sync.

Note: You can only sync information from one iCloud account under each user account on your MacBook Pro (each user account can use a different iCloud account).

TIP

How do I keep information synced on my iOS devices?
To use the same information on an iPhone, iPad, or iPod touch, configure your iCloud account on each of those devices. Open the Settings app, tap **iCloud**, and enter your account information. Once your information is verified, set the status switch for each type of information you want to keep in sync, such as Mail, Contacts, and so on to the ON position. This causes the data on the device to sync with the cloud, which in turn syncs with your MacBook Pro.

Use iCloud Photo Stream

Photo Stream provides online storage for your photos and other images, making it easy to have your photos available on all your devices. For example, a photo you take with an iPhone is automatically uploaded to your Photo Stream. Any other devices configured to use Photo Stream can automatically download the photos.

Photo Stream also provides a temporary backup for your photos. Suppose you take photos with your iPhone and then lose the phone. Any photos that were uploaded to your Photo Stream are still available to download.

Use iCloud Photo Stream

Set Up Photo Stream in OS X

1 Click **Apple** (🍎), click **System Preferences**, and then click **iCloud** in the System Preference window.

2 Ensure the **Photo Stream** check box is selected.

3 Press ⌘+Q to close the System Preferences application.

Set Up Photo Stream in iPhoto

1 Click the **iPhoto** icon on the Dock.

iPhoto opens.

2 Click **iPhoto** menu and select **Preferences**.

3 Click the **Photo Stream** tab.

4 Select the **Enable Photo Stream** check box.

5 Select the **Automatic Import** check box.

6 Select the **Automatic Upload** check box if you also want photos or other images you add to iPhoto to be uploaded to your Photo Stream.

7 Close the Preferences dialog.

Any photos uploaded to your Photo Stream automatically download into iPhoto. If you selected the check box in step **6**, any photos or other images that you add to iPhoto automatically upload to your Photo Stream. From there, they automatically download to other devices accessing your Photo Stream.

TIPS

How can I configure Aperture to use Photo Stream?
Open Aperture. Open the **Aperture** menu and choose **Preferences**. Click the **Photo Stream** tab. Select the three check boxes, which are the same as those in steps **3**, **4**, and **5**. Close the Preferences dialog.

How can I remove photos from my Photo Stream?
Log in to your iCloud website. Click your name located in the upper right corner of the window. On the Account sheet, click **Advanced**. Then click **Reset Photo Stream**. After you confirm at the prompt, all the photos in your Photo Stream are deleted. Photos stored on your devices are not removed.

Use iCloud to Store Documents Online

$\mathbf{I}$n addition to information, you can also store documents on the cloud. This makes working on documents on multiple devices convenient because the same versions of those documents are available to you on each device, which includes MacBook Pros, other Macs, iPads, iPhones, and iPod touches.

Not all applications support iCloud document storage; an application must be iCloud-enabled for this to be available. Currently, Pages, Numbers, and Keynote are among the Apple applications that support iCloud documents. Over time, more applications will likely have this capability added.

Use iCloud to Store Documents Online

Set Up Online Documents in OS X

1 Click **Apple** (), click **System Preferences**, and then click **iCloud** in the System Preference window.

2 Click the **Documents & Data** check box option.

3 Press + to close the System Preferences application.

Work with Online Documents in Pages

Note: These steps show how to use the Pages application with online documents. Other applications support online documents similarly.

1 Click **Pages** on the Dock.

2 Click **File** and then click **Open**.

The Open dialog appears.

③ Click **iCloud**.

Ⓐ You see the Pages documents stored on the cloud.

④ Click the document you want to work with.

⑤ Click **Open**.

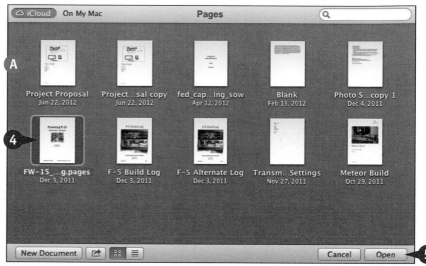

Ⓑ The document downloads to your MacBook Pro and opens.

⑥ Change the document.

⑦ Close the document when you are done.

The updated version is saved on the cloud. You can open it from any device that can access your Pages documents, including other Macs, iPads, and iPhones.

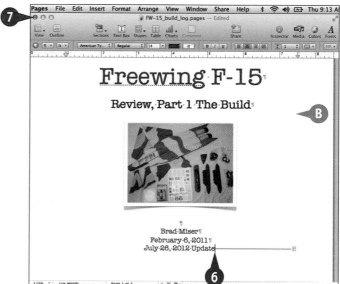

TIP

How do I access my documents on an iPad or iPhone?
Open the Settings app and tap **iCloud**. Tap **Documents & Data**. Set the status switch for **Documents & Data** to the **ON** position. If you want documents to be synced even when you are using a cellular connection, set the **Use Cellular Data** status switch to the **ON** position. Open an iCloud-enabled app on the device. Tap **Use iCloud**. You see the documents associated with that application stored on the cloud. Tap a document to work with it. Any documents you change or create are stored on the cloud from where they are synced onto other devices.

Explore Safari

Safari is an elegant application, meaning that it offers a lot of functionality and is a pleasure to use at the same time. As soon as you open it, Safari is configured for easy use, and you can set various preferences to tailor the way it works for you.

Safari in Browse Mode

A Back and Forward

Click ◄ to move back to the previous page. Click ► to move forward to the next page.

B Show iCloud Tabs

As you browse through iCloud, you can click ⌂ to jump to Safari tabs open on other devices.

C Address and Search Bar

Shows the current web address (Uniform Resource Locator, or URL). You can also type information here to perform a search.

D Title

Shows the title of the web page being shown.

E Refresh or Stop Loading

Refresh (⟳) gets the current version of the page, or stops loading (✕) a page.

F Bookmarks Bar

The Bookmarks bar provides quick access to your favorite bookmarks.

G Top Sites

Clicking ▦ provides thumbnails of your favorite web pages that you can click to visit.

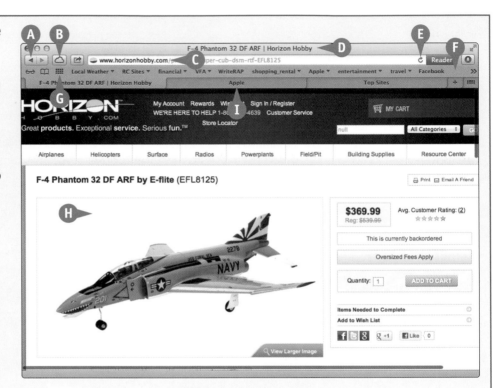

H Web Page

Provides access to the information and tools on the web page.

I Tab Bar

Each tab can show a different webpage; click a tab to jump to its page.

Safari in Bookmarks Mode

Ⓐ Bookmarks Mode Button

Click 🖿 to toggle between Browse and Bookmarks mode.

Ⓑ Collections

Special groups of bookmarks, such as those on the Bookmarks bar.

Ⓒ Selected Source

Select a source of bookmarks to see them on the list.

Ⓓ Bookmarks

Shows individual bookmarks and folders containing bookmarks.

Ⓔ List of Websites or Bookmarks in Selected Source

Shows the websites or bookmarks and folders of bookmarks in the selected source.

Ⓕ Bookmark Name

A descriptive name that you can assign to bookmarks.

Ⓖ Address

The URL to which the bookmark points.

Ⓗ Search Tools

Enables you to search for bookmarks.

Ⓘ Cover Flow Browser

Enables you to flip through the web pages or bookmarks in the selected source to preview and navigate to them.

Navigate to Websites

The most basic task when you use the web is to move to the website you are interested in and then navigate within that site's pages. You can do this in a number of ways, and you will probably use all of them as you explore the web.

Moving to a website by entering its URL address is the most flexible method, and is the one you can always use. For most sites that you use regularly, you need to type the URL only once. After that, you can move back to it with a bookmark or by using the Safari History menu.

Navigate to Websites

Navigate to a Website by Entering a URL

① Launch Safari by clicking its icon on the Dock.

② Type the address of a website.

Although a full web address begins with either http:// or https://, you do not need to type either of these prefixes because Safari automatically adds them to any address that you type. If the address begins with www, you do not need to type the www part, either. For example, go to http://www.apple.com, you just need to type **apple.com**.

Note: In many cases, you do not need to type .com because Safari assumes addresses include it if you do not type it. If you navigate to a different domain type, such as .org, you do need to type it in the address.

Ⓐ As you type in the address bar, Safari tries to match what you type with a top site, popular searches, sites you have visited previously, and your bookmarks, and shows you the matches on a list under the address bar.

③ When the address becomes the one you want or when you finish typing it, press **Return**.

Safari moves to the address and you see its content.

Navigate to Websites with a Bookmark

1 To use a bookmark on the Bookmarks bar, click the bookmark.

B Bookmarks can be organized in folders on the Bookmarks bar. Click a folder to see the bookmarks it contains and then click the bookmark you want to use.

Note: Folders on the Bookmarks bar have a downward-pointing triangle.

2 To access a bookmark stored on the Bookmarks menu, click **Bookmarks**.

Note: When you select a folder of bookmarks on the menu, its contents appear.

3 Select the bookmark you want to use.

That web page opens.

C To move to any bookmark you have saved using Safari's Bookmarks mode, click **Show All Bookmarks**.

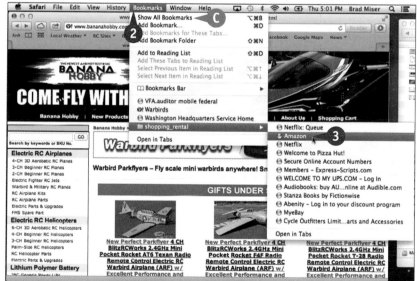

TIPS

How can I on the same bookmarks on all my devices?
If you use more than one Mac, you are likely to create different bookmarks as you surf the web on each computer. Fortunately, if you use iCloud, you can synchronize the bookmarks on each Mac you use so that whether you use your MacBook Pro, a different Mac, or an iOS device, you always have the same set of bookmarks available to you.

How do I know specifically where a bookmark points?
Because you can name a bookmark anything you want, and you usually use an abbreviated name when you add a bookmark to the Bookmarks bar, you might not remember where a bookmark points. To see a bookmark's address, point to the bookmark on the Bookmarks bar without clicking it. After a second or two, the full address for the bookmark appears.

continued ▶

As you move to web addresses, a new page opens, which is also what happens when you click a link that points to a different address (on the same website or elsewhere). As you navigate through pages, you create a chain of pages that you can move back and forward through. You can do this because Safari remembers each page as you move through it, and each page is temporarily stored (the technical term is *cached*) on your MacBook Pro.

You can also move to web pages from outside Safari by clicking hyperlinks in documents, such as email and text documents. When you click a web link, OS X recognizes it as an address and opens it in your default web browser.

Navigate to Websites (continued)

Ⓐ The Bookmarks window replaces the website, which means that Safari is in Bookmarks mode.

④ Choose a location in which the bookmark you want to visit is saved.

If the selected source includes folders, click their disclosure triangles to view the bookmarks they contain (▶ changes to ▼).

⑤ Drag the scroll bar to flip through the bookmarks using the browser.

⑥ Single-click a bookmark in the browser or double-click the bookmark that you want to visit in the lower pane.

Whichever method you used to access a bookmark, once you click it, its web page fills the Safari window.

Navigate to Websites Using History

① Open the **History** menu.

In the fourth section of the menu, you see a list of web pages you have visited most recently.

② If the page you want to return to is on the list, select it.

③ If the site is not on the list, select the folder for the time period in which you visited it.

④ Select the site you want to visit on the resulting menu.

The site you selected opens.

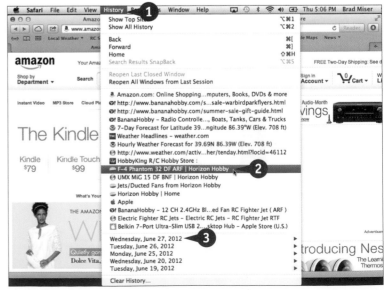

Navigate to Websites Using a Link

1 Click a link in an email or other document.

Safari opens and moves to the website.

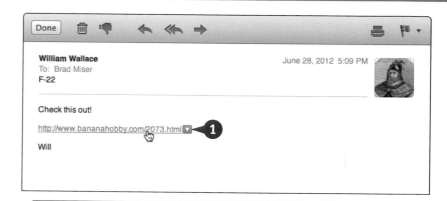

Move Through Web Pages

1 Click a link to move to web pages.

2 Click **Back** (◄) to move to a previous page.

3 Click **Forward** (►) to move to a later page in the current "chain" of pages you have been browsing.

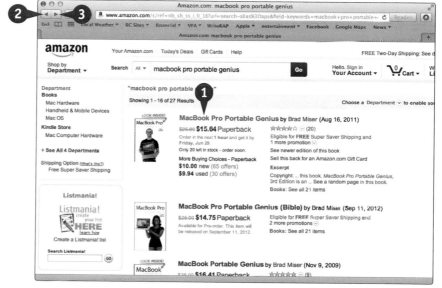

TIPS

What does the http that Safari adds to the front of URLs stand for?

The http prefix stands for Hyper Text Transfer Protocol, and is the basic *protocol*, or language, that web browsers employ. You can access other protocols with Safari, such as FTP (File Transfer Protocol), in which case the URL starts with ftp: instead of http:. The vast majority of sites that you will visit with Safari use http, and so Safari assumes that this is the kind of site you want. To move to a different kind of site, you have to add that prefix at the beginning of the URL, such as ftp://.

What is https?

A lot of websites deal with information that needs to be protected, such as bank accounts and credit cards. These sites use Secure Socket Layer (SSL) technology to encrypt and therefore protect the data being sent between the web page and Safari. These sites use the https protocol (Hyper Text Transfer Protocol Secure). You typically do not have to add https at the beginning of addresses to move to them; when you reach the secure part of the site, https is employed automatically.

Search the Web

One of the most useful things to do on the web is to search for information, and one of the best search engines is Google. Google searching is by default built into Safari to make web searches fast and easy.

You can perform a Google search by using the Safari built-in Search tool. (You can use a different search engine by changing a preference.) Of course, you can also move directly to the Google Search page by entering the URL google.com in the address bar and pressing Return, but using the Safari Search tool is easier and faster.

Search the Web

1 Type the information you want to search for in the address bar.

A When you type something other than a web address, Safari goes into search mode and you see the type of search you are doing in the address bar.

B As you type, Safari presents a list showing you suggested searches and your previous searches; click one of these to perform that search.

2 To search on the term you entered, press **Return** or click the search term you want to use on the list.

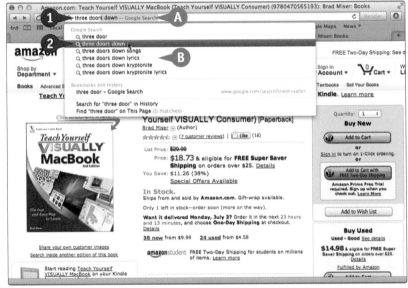

The search is performed and you see the Google results page.

3 Click a link to visit one of the search results.

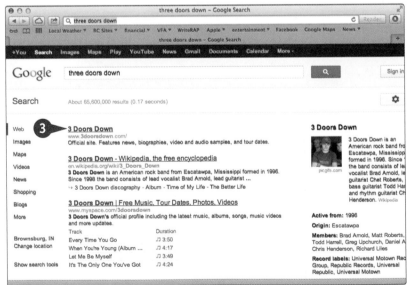

That web page appears.

④ View and use the web page.

⑤ Click **History** and **Search Results Snap Back.**

Note: You can also press Option+⌘+S to return to your search results.

You return to the search results page.

⑥ Scroll the page to explore other results.

Note: When you get to the bottom of a search results page, you see how many pages are in the results. Click Next to move to the next page of results, or click a page's number to jump to it.

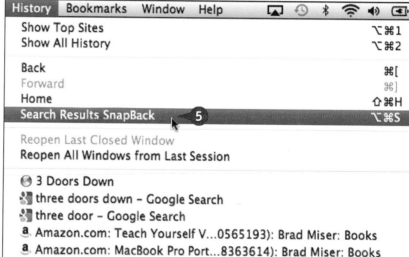

TIPS

How can I repeat a previous search?
Safari remembers the most recent searches you have performed. Start to repeat the search by typing the same text you did the first time. When the sheet appears, look in the Bookmarks and History section; click the search you want to repeat.

Can I use any search page with Safari, or do I have to use Google?
You can use any search page by moving to its URL. For example, to search with Yahoo!, type **yahoo.com**. The search page appears and you can use its tool to search the web. By default, when you search using the Safari address bar, you search using Google. You can change this to use Bing or Yahoo! instead with a preference covered later in this chapter.

Download Files

There are all kinds of great files that you can download from the web. These include images, PDF documents, applications, and so on.

After you download a file, how you use it depends on the kind of file it is. Most applications are provided in a disk image file (with the filename extension .dmg), which mounts automatically. Some files, such as PDF documents, are downloaded as they are. Other files are compressed so that you need to uncompress them before you use them.

Download Files

Download Files from the Web

1 Locate a file that you want to download.

2 Click the file's download link or button.

The file begins to download.

3 Click **Downloads** ( ) to open the Downloads window so you can monitor the progress of the download.

Note: You do not really have to monitor a file download because it downloads in the background. You can continue to do other things as files download.

When the download is complete, the file is ready for you to use.

Use Disk Images You Have Downloaded

1 Open a Finder window.

Note: Many disk images are self-mounting, in which case you select the mounted disk image instead of double-clicking it in step **2**.

2 Select or double-click the disk image that you downloaded.

The contents of the disk image are shown just like a hard drive or other volume you select.

3 Run the application installer, or install it with drag-and-drop (see Chapter 5 for details).

Use Document Files You Have Downloaded

1 Click the **Downloads** stack on the Dock.

The folder fans out onto the desktop, or it appears in a grid if you set that as your preference for the Downloads stack or if the folder contains a lot of items in.

2 Click the downloaded document you want to use.

Note: To open the Downloads folder in a Finder window, choose Open in Finder or *X* More in Finder (where *X* is a number of items).

The file opens using the application associated with it.

Note: When you download a group of files that have been compressed using the Zip format, they uncompress for you automatically. Instead of a single file, you see a folder with the Zip file's name. Open that folder to see the files it contains.

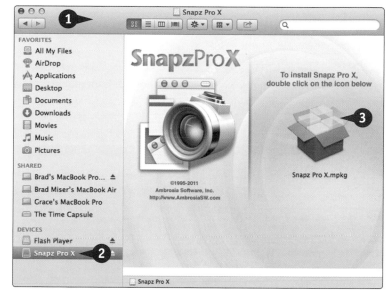

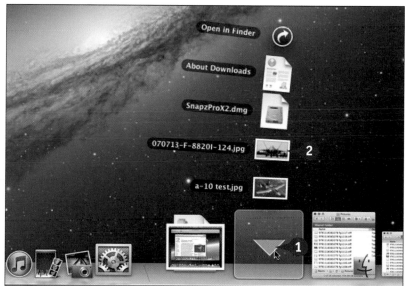

TIPS

What is a SIT file?
A SIT file is compressed with an older scheme. When OS X was introduced, support for the Windows standard compression (file extension .zip) was built into the OS, and so most files you encounter these days are compressed as ZIP files. However, there are a few older files that might have .sit as their filename extension; use the free StuffIt Expander application to be able to open SIT files.

What about FTP?
Some sites use FTP to provide files for you to download. The primary benefit of an FTP site is that files are usually downloaded faster than they are through HTTP. You can access FTP sites in Safari (their URLs start with ftp:// instead of http://), or you can use an FTP application, such as Fetch. Most FTP sites require you to have a username and password to be able to download files.

Browse the Web with Tabs

As you browse the web, you often want to see different information. For example, you might be comparing prices from several different online retailers or you may be looking at specifications for two similar products. Often, you will want to have several websites open at the same time. Opening each of these in its own window works, but it can result in screen clutter.

Tabs in Safari enable you to open as many web pages at a time as you want, while keeping all those pages in one window so that you do not clutter up your desktop. Moving to a page is as simple as clicking its tab.

Browse the Web with Tabs

Configure Safari's Tabs

1 Press ⌘+, .

The Safari Preferences window opens.

2 Click the **Tabs** tab.

3 Click the **Open pages in tabs instead of windows** menu and select how new pages open.

4 Click the top check box if you want to be able to press ⌘ when you click a link to open a web page in a new tab.

5 Click the second check box if you want to immediately move to new tabs and windows when they are created.

6 Review the keyboard shortcuts.

7 Close the Preferences window.

Open and Use Tabs

1 Open a Safari window and move to a web page.

2 Press ⌘+T .

A A new tab appears. By default, the Top Sites page appears.

3 Open a web page in the new tab using any of the techniques described earlier in this chapter.

The web page fills the tab.

4 To open a link in a new tab, press and hold ⌘ while you click the link.

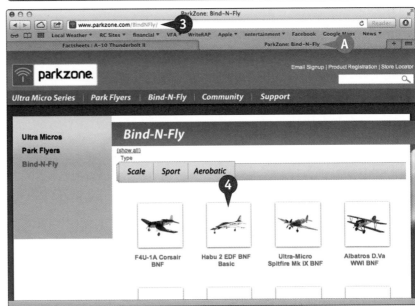

B A new tab opens and displays the destination page of the link. (If you did not enable the option to make new tabs active, you have to click the new tab to make it active.)

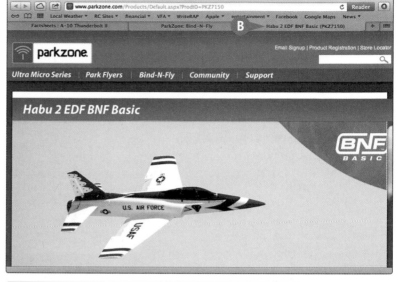

5 Click a tab to open it.

C The tab's web page appears.

6 To close a tab, click **Close** (), which appears when you point to the left side of a tab.

The tab disappears.

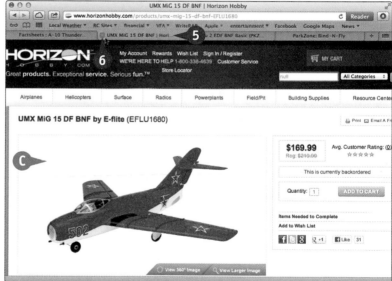

TIPS

How can I move through open tabs with the keyboard?
Press ⌘+} to move to the next tab, or press ⌘+{ to move to the previous tab.

When should I open more windows instead of tabs?
Tabs are great because you can have many pages open in the same window. However, you can see only one tab at a time. If you open multiple windows instead (press ⌘+N), you can arrange the windows so that you can see multiple windows at the same time. To convert a tab into a window, move to it, click the **Window** menu, and then click **Move Tab to New Window**.

Set and Organize Bookmarks

Bookmarks make returning to sites you have previously visited much faster and easier than typing URL addresses. By default, Safari includes a number of bookmarks that you can use, but as you explore the web, there will be a lot of sites that you visit regularly. You can create bookmarks for each of these sites so that it is simple to get back to them.

Because you are likely to end up with many bookmarks, you need tools to keep them organized. Safari also helps with that. It is a good idea to organize bookmarks are you create them so that they do not get out of hand.

Set and Organize Bookmarks

Create Bookmarks

1 Go to a web page that you want to bookmark.

2 Press ⌘+D.

You can also open the **Bookmarks** menu and then select **Add Bookmark**, or you can click **Add Bookmarks** (+).

The Bookmark sheet appears.

3 Select the location in which you want to store the bookmark from the menu.

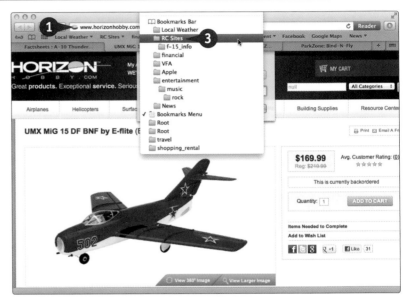

A The location you selected appears in the pop-up menu.

4 Type a name for the bookmark.

Note: You can leave the default name as is, edit it, or replace it with something completely different.

5 Click **Add**.

The bookmark is created in the location you selected. You can move back to the site at any time by choosing the new bookmark.

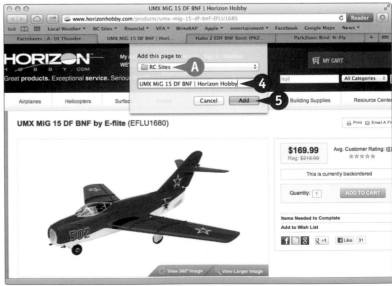

Organize Bookmarks

1 Click **Show all bookmarks** (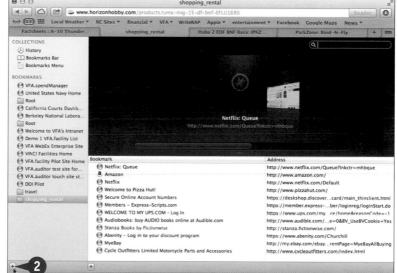).

Alternatively, you can press
Option + **⌘** + **B**, or choose **Show
All Bookmarks** from the **Bookmarks**
menu.

Safari opens the Bookmarks window.

2 To create a new folder for
bookmarks, click **Add** (+).

A new untitled folder appears. The
Bookmarks list is empty because
no bookmarks are in the folder.

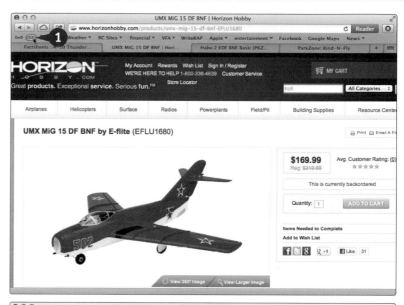

TIPS

How do I store bookmarks on the Bookmarks bar?
The Bookmarks bar is a convenient way to store and
access bookmarks from the top of the Safari window. You
can move to a bookmark just by clicking its button on
the bar. To add a bookmark to the bar, choose **Bookmarks
Bar** on the pop-up menu on the New Bookmark sheet.
Adding the bookmark places it on the left edge of the
bar, becoming the first bookmark on the bar.

How do I change the location of a bookmark on the Bookmarks bar?
The contents and organization of the Bookmarks bar are determined
by the contents of the Bookmarks Bar collection. To move a bookmark
toward the left side of the Bookmarks bar, drag its icon up the list of
bookmarks that appears when you select the Bookmarks Bar collection.
Drag a bookmark down the list to move it to the right on the
Bookmarks bar.

continued ▶

Set and Organize Bookmarks (continued)

In addition to making it much easier to move to websites, using bookmarks also reduces the chance for errors when you type a URL. Sometimes these errors are merely annoying, and at other times, they can lead you to places on the web where you would rather not be.

Over time, you are likely to create many bookmarks. You can use the techniques in this section to keep them organized. Place the bookmarks you use most often on the Bookmarks bar or on the Bookmarks menu so that you can get to them easily. Use folders to create sets of bookmarks related to specific topics or purposes, such as finance or news.

Set and Organize Bookmarks (continued)

3 Type a name for the folder.

4 Press **Return**.

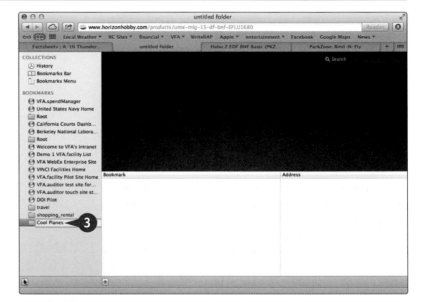

5 Select the location containing bookmarks you want to move into the folder.

6 Drag a bookmark from its current location onto the folder that you want to contain it; when that folder is highlighted in blue, release the trackpad.

7 Repeat steps **5** and **6** to place more bookmarks in the folder.

8 Select the folder you created.

The bookmarks you placed in it appear on the list.

9 To create a folder within the selected folder, click **Add** ($\boxed{+}$).

10 Type a name for the new folder and press **Return**.

11 Drag bookmarks onto the nested folder to place them in it.

12 Drag bookmarks and folders up and down in the folder to change the order in which they appear.

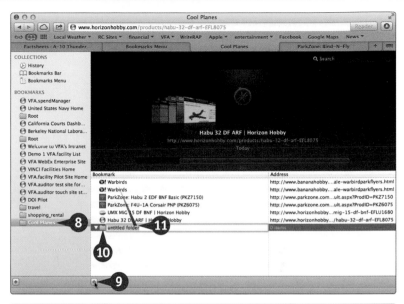

13 To add the bookmarks you use most frequently to the Bookmarks bar or Bookmarks menu, drag them onto the location in which you want them to be available.

14 Organize the contents of the Bookmarks bar or Bookmarks menu just like other locations.

Note: To delete a bookmark or a folder of bookmarks, select what you want to delete and press **Delete**.

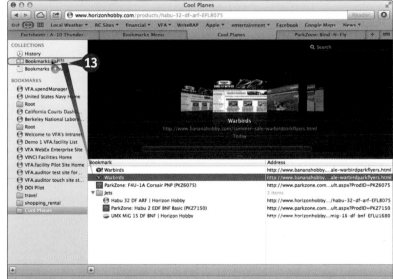

TIPS

When should I bookmark a site?

It is best not to think of bookmarks as permanent things. Although you will definitely want to bookmark some pages that you use over long periods of time, others are useful only in the short term. Bookmark these sites as you go so that you can get back to the ones you need. When you are done, delete the temporary bookmarks to prevent Safari from becoming cluttered with useless bookmarks.

Can I change the order in which folders are shown in the Bookmarks window?

Yes. To reorder folders in the Bookmarks section of the Source pane, drag them up or down into the order you want.

Use and Set Top Sites

Safari's Top Sites feature is a window where thumbnails of your favorite websites are stored. You can click a thumbnail to move to the website; in this respect, the thumbnails on your Top Sites page work just like bookmarks.

As you move through websites, Safari tracks the sites you visit and automatically adds those you visit most to your Top Sites page. Because of this, the contents of your Top Sites page can change over time. You can also manually add pages to your Top Sites page and "pin" them to the page so they are always there. You can also determine how many sites appear on the page.

Use and Set Top Sites

Use Top Sites

① Click **Top Sites** (▦) on the Bookmarks bar.

Ⓐ Your Top Sites page appears. A thumbnail represents each web page.

② Point to a thumbnail you are interested in.

A blue box encloses the thumbnail, and the page's name and URL appear at the bottom of the window.

③ To move to a page, click its thumbnail.

The web page replaces the Top Sites page.

Add a Web Page to Your Top Sites

① Click **Top Sites** (▦).

② Click **Edit**.

③ Press ⌘+N to open a new window.

④ Go to the web page you want to add to your Top Sites.

⑤ Click the icon at the left edge of the address bar to select the URL and drag it to the location on the Top Sites page where you want it to appear. (As you drag over thumbnails, they shift around to make room for the new one.)

When you release the trackpad button, the page's thumbnail is added to your Top Sites.

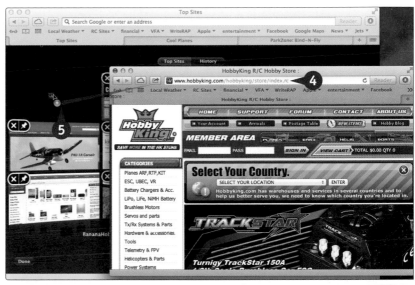

Organize Your Top Sites

① Open your Top Sites page and click **Edit**.

② To remove a page, click **Close** (✖).

③ To lock a page on the thumbnail so it will not be removed as Safari adds new pages, click **Mark as Permanent** (📌).

④ To unlock a page, click **Unmark as Permanent** (📌).

⑤ To change the location of thumbnails, drag them around the window.

⑥ To change the number of thumbnails shown, click **Small**, **Medium**, or **Large**.

⑦ Click **Done** when you are finished making changes.

TIPS

What are other ways to add pages to my Top Sites page?
You can drag a link from any document, such as an email message, and drop it onto the Top Sites page (it must be in Edit mode) to add it to your Top Sites. You can also open a new document, such as a text document, type a URL, and drag it from the document to your Top Sites page.

Why are some of the thumbnails on my Top Sites page marked with a star?
When new content is added to a website you have on your Top Sites page, the thumbnail is marked with a star and a "corner" of the thumbnail is folded down. This helps you know that something has changed on the site.

Open Several Web Pages at the Same Time

Using tabs, you know you can have many web pages open at the same time, which is useful. However, opening one tab after another takes longer than necessary. And who needs that? It would be nice if there were a way to open a lot of pages at the same time.

Fortunately, Safari allows you to do this. By using bookmarks, folders, and tabs, you can configure any collection of web pages to open with a single click. First, prepare the folder containing bookmarks for the pages you want to open. Second, open those pages.

Open Several Web Pages at the Same Time

Prepare a One-Click Bookmark Folder

1 Set bookmarks for the pages you want to open.

2 Click **Bookmarks** and select **Show All Bookmarks** from the menu.

Safari moves into Bookmark mode.

3 Create a folder for the group of pages you want to open at the same time.

4 Add the bookmarks you want to open to the folder you created in step **3.**

5 Drag the bookmarks up or down the list into the order in which you want them to open.

The bookmark at the top of the list becomes the first tab in the Safari window, the next one down is the second tab, and so on.

6 Select the **Bookmarks Bar** collection.

7 Drag the folder you created in step **3** onto the Bookmarks list in the order in which you want it to appear on the Bookmarks bar (the top of the window represents the left end of the bar).

8 Check the **Auto-Click** check box.

Ⓐ The folder you created appears on the Bookmarks bar. At the right side of its name on the Bookmarks bar, you see a box, which indicates it is an Auto-Click folder.

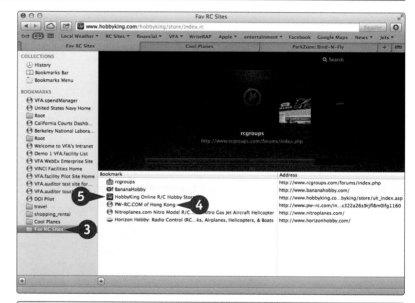

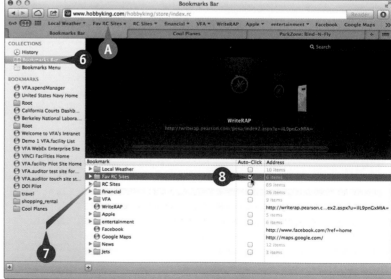

Open a Lot of Pages with a Click

1 When you want to open all the bookmarks in the Auto-Click folder, click it on the Bookmarks bar.

B Each bookmark in the folder opens in its own tab.

Watch Movies on the Web

Movies are common on the web. From trailers for the latest Hollywood productions to instructional videos, commercials, and other video content, there is a lot to watch. You can use Safari to view many of these movies through its embedded QuickTime player.

Different sites have different ways of presenting content to play. Apple's trailer site uses the Watch Now button on which you can click to choose the size you want to watch. Other sites use different interfaces. Movies come in different sizes; if you are using a broadband connection, you can usually choose the largest size.

Watch Movies on the Web

1 Go to a site containing a movie you want to watch.

2 Click the size of the movie you want to watch.

A The movie opens, starts to download, and begins to play.

3 Use the **Volume** menu (🔊) to change the volume.

4 Click **Pause** (⏸) to pause the movie.

5 Drag the playhead to the right to scan forward or to the left to scan backward.

Note: The shaded part of the timeline bar indicates how much of the movie has downloaded; you can watch only that part. If the connection slows down for some reason, the movie may stop; just restart it when more of the movie has downloaded.

Use AutoFill to Quickly Complete Web Forms

As you use the web, you will probably need to complete forms, such as when you are registering for an account on a website or when you are doing some online shopping. Many of these forms require the same basic set of information, such as your name, address, and telephone number. Using the Safari AutoFill feature, you can complete this basic information with a single click.

AutoFill can also remember usernames and passwords that you use to log in to websites so that you do not have to retype this information each time you want to access your account on a site. If you use AutoFill, keep your MacBook Pro secure because anyone who uses your OS X user account can access the AutoFill information.

Use AutoFill to Quickly Complete Web Forms

Configure AutoFill Information

1 Press ⌘+,.

2 Click the **AutoFill** tab.

3 To complete forms using the information on your card in Address Book, check the **Using info from my Contacts card** check box.

4 To have Safari remember usernames and passwords for websites you access, check the **User names and passwords** check box.

5 To have Safari remember information for other forms, check the **Other forms** check box.

6 Close the Preferences window.

Use AutoFill Information

1 Go to a website that requires your information.

2 Start to enter information.

3 Click the AutoFill prompt.

4 Click **AutoFill**.

Safari completes as much information as it can, based on the form and the contents of your Address Book card. The fields it completes are highlighted in yellow.

5 Manually complete or edit any of the fields that AutoFill did not correctly fill in.

Save or Share Web Pages

As you explore the web, you will probably find web pages that you want to view again. Because the web is always changing, there is no guarantee that a page you are viewing now will exist a day from now, or even five minutes from now. If you want to make sure you can view a page again in the future, you can save it on your MacBook Pro.

Some pages that you encounter are worth sharing. You can easily shares pages, such as sending links to web pages to others or sharing a web page via the Messages application.

Save or Share Web Pages

Save Web Pages

1. Go to a web page you want to save.

2. Open the **File** menu, and then select **Save As**.

Ⓐ The Save sheet appears.

3. Enter a name for the web page.

4. Choose the location in which you want to save it.

5. Choose **Web Archive** on the **Format** pop-up menu.

6. Click **Save**.

The page is saved in the location you specified.

Note: A page that you save is a copy of what it was at the time you viewed it. To see the current version, you need to return to it on the web.

Email a Link to a Web Page

1. Go to a web page you want to share.

2. Click the **Share** button (🔗).

3. Click **Email this Page**.

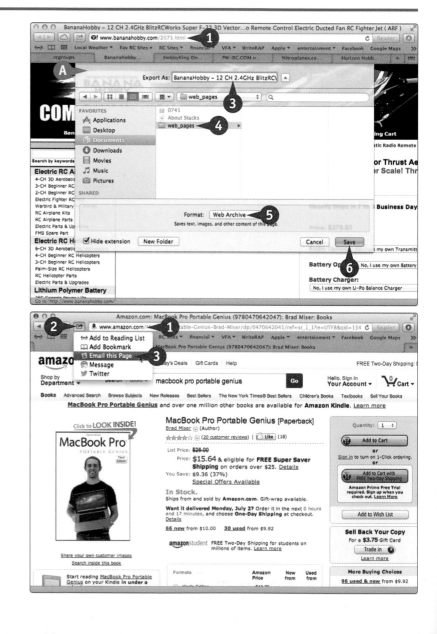

A new e-mail message is created in Mail with the title of the page as its subject.

4 Add recipients.

5 Click the **Send Web Content As** arrow and select **Link Only** from the pop-up menu.

6 Edit the subject line.

7 Type your comments in the body of the message.

Note: Do not change the link that was pasted into the e-mail message or it might not work.

8 Click **Send** (📨).

When the recipient receives the message, he or she can click the link to view the page.

Email the Contents of a Web Page

1 Perform steps **1** to **4** under "Email a Link to a Web Page."

2 Click the **Send Web Content As** arrow and select Web Page from the pop-up menu.

3 Edit the subject line.

4 Type your comments to the body of the message.

Note: Do not change the link that was pasted into the email message or it might not work.

5 Click **Send** (📨).

When the recipient receives the message, he or she can view the page in it.

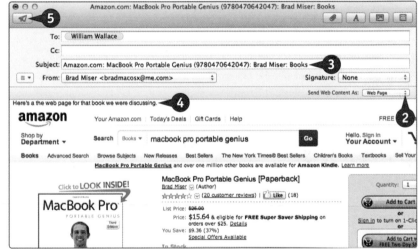

TIPS

How do I tell if I am viewing a page saved on MacBook Pro or one on the web?
Look at the URL. If it starts with file:///, you are viewing a saved web page. If it starts with http://, you are viewing a live page on the web.

Should I send a link or content?
When you are viewing a website that does not change frequently or that uses direct URLs to the resource you are viewing, sending a link is better because it reduces the size of the email. However, if you want to make sure your recipients see what you intend them to, send the content instead.

Use the Reading List

The Reading List is a way to save pages you want to read at a later time. You can collect the pages you want to read on your Reading List as you browse. When you want to read the pages you have collected, you open the Reading List and see the pages you have added there.

The Reading List is useful to store pages that you do not necessarily want to bookmark because your use of them is temporary. To be able to read any content linked to a page on your Reading List, you have to be connected to the Internet to read the linked content; you can read the pages on your Reading List without being connected.

Use the Reading List

Add Pages to Reading List

1 Go to a web page you want to add to your Reading List.

2 Click **Bookmarks**.

3 Click **Add to Reading List**.

Alternatively, you can press **Shift** + **⌘** + **D**.

The page you are viewing moves onto your Reading List.

Note: If you want to add all of the tabs you are viewing to your Reading List, click Bookmarks and then Add These **X** Tabs to Reading List, where **X** is the number of open tabs.

4 Repeat steps **1** and **3** to add more pages to your Reading List.

Read Pages on the Reading List

1 Click **Reading List** (⟨⟩).

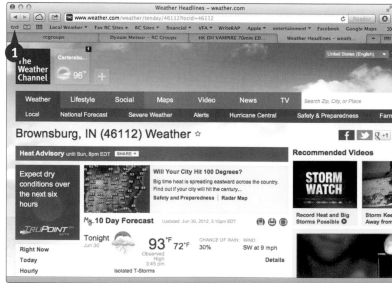

Ⓐ The Reading List pane opens.

② Select the page you want to read.

It appears in the right part of the window.

③ Read the page.

④ Continue selecting and reading pages.

⑤ If you navigate to another page you want to add to your Reading List, click **Add Page**.

Note: To view only pages you have not read yet, click Unread.

⑥ When you are done with your Reading List, click **Reading List** (⬚).

TIPS

How do I delete a page from the Reading List?
When you finish with a page on your Reading List, point to it and click the **Delete** button (⬚) that appears.

How do I delete all pages from the Reading List?
To clear your entire Reading List, click **Clear All** and then click **Clear** in the resulting prompt.

Set Safari Preferences

Safari includes a number of preferences that you can set to change the way it looks and works. You set other Safari preferences similarly to the Tab and AutoFill preferences. For more information, see the sections "Use AutoFill to Quickly Complete Web Forms" and "Browse the Web with Tabs."

You can also move to web pages from outside Safari by clicking hyperlinks in various documents you work with, such as email and text documents. When you click a web link, the application you are using recognizes it as an address and opens that address in your default web browser.

Set Safari Preferences

1 Press ⌘+. to open the Safari Preferences window.

2 Click the **General** tab.

3 On the **Default search engine** menu, choose the search engine you want to use in the Safari address bar; the options are **Google**, **Bing**, or **Yahoo!**.

4 On the **New windows open with** pop-up menu, choose the page you want to open automatically when you open a new Safari window.

5 On the **New tabs open with** pop-up menu, choose the page you want to open automatically when you open a new Safari tab.

6 Type the URL for your home page, or click **Set to Current Page** to make the page you are currently viewing your home page.

7 Use these settings to specify how Safari handles history items, downloads, and links.

8 Click the **Bookmarks** tab.

9 If you want to see your Top Sites pages, links in cards in your Address Book, or sites available via Bonjour as options on the Bookmarks bar, check the corresponding **Bookmarks bar** check boxes.

10 Check the related **Bookmarks menu** check boxes to include those items on your Bookmarks menu.

11 To include the Address Book and Bonjour collections in the Bookmarks window, check their respective check boxes.

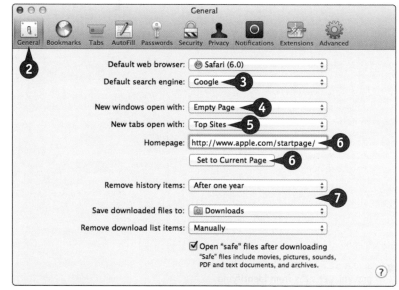

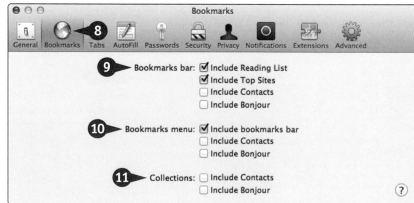

12 Click the **Security** tab.

13 Check the **Warn when visiting a fraudulent website** check box if you want to be warned when something seems amiss with a site you are heading to.

14 Use the **Web content** check boxes to enable plug-ins, Java, and JavaScript, or to block pop-ups. If you disable plug-ins or the Java features, many websites will not work properly. Some sites will not work with pop-ups blocked, but you should disable the pop-up blocker only when you need to use those specific sites.

15 Click the **Privacy** tab.

16 To remove web information stored on your computer, click **Remove All Website Data**.

17 Use the **Block cookies** radio buttons to determine how Safari deals with cookies.

Note: In most cases, you want to choose the From third parties and advertisers option so the cookies stored on your MacBook Pro are related to sites you actually use.

18 Select **Deny without prompting** to prevent websites from identifying the location of your MacBook Pro.

19 Close the Preferences window.

TIPS

What are Notification preferences?
Some websites can provide information to you through OS X's notifications feature. The Notifications tab shows you the websites that have requested permission to notify you. Select a website and click **Remove** to stop it from sending notifications to you.

What are the other preferences?
The Extensions preferences help you manage software that works with Safari. You can enable or disable this software, update it, and so on. The Advanced preferences enable you to set universal access features such as minimum font size and enabling web page navigation with Tab. You can also choose a default style sheet and configure a proxy server if you use one.

Explore Mail

E-mail is a very important means of communication for most people today. To e-mail, you need a device connected to the Internet and an e-mail application on your computer. Fortunately, OS X includes the Mail application, which is one of best applications available. Mail includes many useful features, and it wraps those features in an interface that makes sense and is easy to use. Mail provides all the capabilities that you want in an e-mail application so that you can work with e-mail efficiently and effectively.

A Mail Icon

The Mail Dock icon enables you to launch the Mail application and also shows you how many new messages you have.

A Toolbar

Contains tools you can use to work with e-mail.

B Inbox

Contains mailboxes for each e-mail account.

C Account Mailboxes

Contain e-mail for various accounts that you have configured in Mail.

D Account Mailbox Folders

Organize e-mail in different states, such as Sent or Draft, for each account.

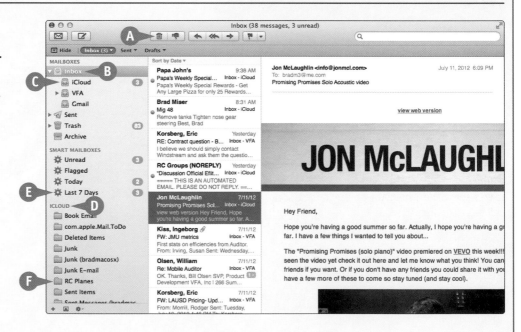

E Smart Mailboxes

Automatically organize e-mail based on criteria that you define.

F Mailboxes

Folders in which you can store and organize e-mail.

Ⓐ Selected Source

The source of e-mails you want to work with, such as those you have received in a specific account.

Ⓑ Message Pane

Shows the messages in the selected source.

Ⓒ Sort Criteria

Shows how the list of messages is sorted, such as by Date.

Ⓓ Read/Unread

A blue dot indicates a message that you have not read.

Ⓔ From

The name of the person who sent the message to you.

Ⓕ Date Received

The date and time you received the message.

Ⓖ Subject

The subject of the message.

Ⓗ Selected Message

To read a message, you select it; the selected message is highlighted in blue.

Ⓐ Reading Pane

Displays the selected message.

Ⓑ Message Details

Who the message is from, the subject of the message, when it was sent, and who the other recipients are.

Ⓒ Sender's Image

Shows the image associated with the sender in Contacts.

Ⓓ Body

The message's text.

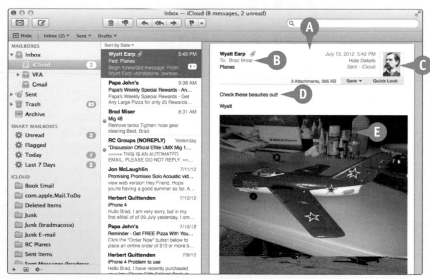

Ⓔ Attachments

Shows files attached to the message and enables you to save or view them; image files may be displayed within the body.

Set Up E-Mail Accounts

Before you can work with e-mail, you must obtain one or more e-mail accounts and configure Mail to access them. The details of configuring an e-mail account depend on the type of account it is; for example, configuring an iCloud account is slightly different from configuring an account you have received from your Internet service provider (ISP). However, in all cases, you enter the configuration details for each type of e-mail account in the appropriate fields in Mail.

You can also use the Mail, Contacts & Calendars pane of the System Preferences application to create accounts to use in Mail. See Chapter 6.

Set Up E-Mail Accounts

1. Launch Mail.
2. Press ⌘+,.

   The Mail Preferences window opens.
3. Click the **Accounts** tab.
4. Click **Add** (⊞).

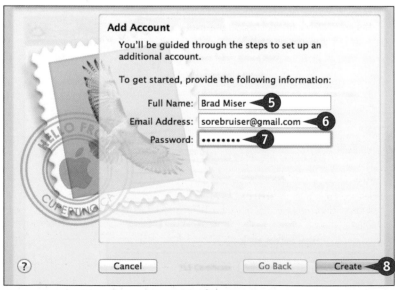

   The Add Account sheet appears.
5. Type the full name for the account.
6. Type the e-mail address for the account.
7. Type the password for the account.
8. If Mail recognizes and can automatically configure the account (such as for iCloud, Gmail, and other popular e-mail services), click **Create**.

   Depending on the type of account you are creating, you may see additional configuration sheets.

   Mail automatically sets up the account.

Note: If the Continue button appears instead of the Create button, Mail does not recognize and cannot automatically configure the account.

The Account Summary dialog appears.

9 Select the Notes, Calendars & Reminders, and Messages options to set up as desired.

10 Click **Create**.

The account is created and appears in the list of accounts along the left side of the Preferences window.

11 Click the **Mailbox Behaviors** tab.

12 If you want messages you have written but not yet sent to be stored online so you can access them from other computers, check the **Drafts** check box.

13 If you want messages you have sent to be stored online, check the **Sent** check box and use the pop-up menu to determine how long your sent messages are kept.

Note: If you choose to store messages on the server, those messages count against your total storage space for e-mail. Use the Delete pop-up menus to configure Mail so that messages stored on the server are deleted periodically.

14 If you want messages Mail has identified as spam to be stored online, check the **Junk** check box and use the pop-up menu to determine how long those messages are stored.

15 Use the **Trash** check boxes and pop-up menu to determine how Mail deals with messages you delete.

16 Click the **Advanced** tab for options such as temporarily disabling the account, including the account when Mail checks for e-mail, and storing messages and attachments.

17 Close the Preferences window and save your changes at the prompt.

The account's mailbox is added to your Inbox and is ready to use.

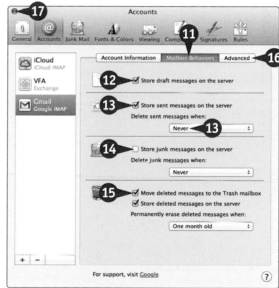

TIPS

An iCloud e-mail account was already set up when I launched Mail. How did that happen?

When you configure an iCloud account, either during the initial MacBook Pro setup or on the iCloud pane of the System Preferences application, the iCloud e-mail account is set up in Mail automatically. See Chapter 10 for more information about iCloud online services.

Where can I get free e-mail accounts?

You can obtain a Gmail account at www.google.com. You can also get a free e-mail account at www.yahoo.com. Having at least two e-mail accounts is a good idea so that you can use one to guard against spam. For more information, see the section "Avoid Spam."

Read and Reply to E-Mail

One of the reasons to use e-mail is, of course, to read it. Mail makes it easy to do that. You can read e-mail in the reading pane, as described in the following steps, or you can double-click a message to open it in its own window.

You can also easily reply to e-mail that you receive to start or continue an e-mail conversation, also called a *thread*. There are options in how Mail can display threads that you may want to explore as you use the application. Some may be more useful to you than others.

Read and Reply to E-Mail

Read E-Mail

1 Select the Inbox.

Note: You can also select a specific e-mail account to read e-mail that you have received only for that account.

2 Select the message you want to read.

The message you select appears in the reading pane.

3 Read the message.

If the message has images attached, they may appear in the message's body.

Note: After you have viewed a message in the reading pane, its blue dot disappears so that you know you have read it.

4 If the message is too long to fit into the current window, press `Spacebar` to scroll down in the message.

5 To open a message in its own window, double-click it.

The message appears in a new, separate window.

6 Read the message and look at the images contained in it within its window.

7 Close the message when you are done.

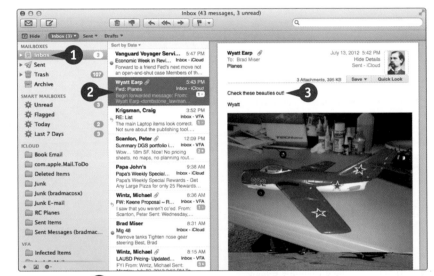

Reply to E-Mail

1 Select or open a message.

2 Click **Reply** (↩).

Note: If more than one person is listed in the From or Cc fields and you want to reply to everyone listed, click Reply All (↩↩) instead.

Ⓐ A new message appears, addressed to the sender of the message (and all recipients, except those that are Bcc'd if you clicked **Reply All**).

Ⓑ "Re:" is added to the beginning of the subject to show that the message is a reply.

Ⓒ The contents of the original message are pasted into the body in blue and marked with a vertical line to indicate quoted text.

3 If you have more than one e-mail account, choose the account through which you want to send the message on the **From** pop-up menu (by default, the account to which the original message was sent is selected).

4 Type your reply.

5 Click **Send** (✈).

The window closes, the e-mail is sent, and you hear the sent mail sound effect.

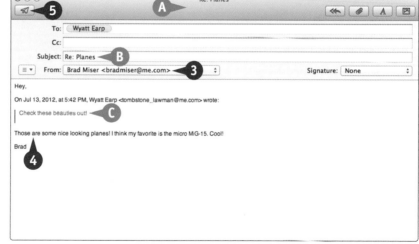

How do I delete a message I do not want to keep?

Select the message and click **Delete** (🗑) on the toolbar. The message is removed from the Message list and placed in the appropriate Trash folder. How long it remains there depends on the trash settings for that e-mail account. You can recover a message by opening the Trash folder and dragging a deleted message back into an Inbox.

Can I add more recipients to a reply?

Yes, you can add more addresses to a reply e-mail to include other recipients. In fact, all the tools available to you when you create a new e-mail message are also available when you reply to messages. For more information, see the section "Send E-Mail."

Send E-Mail

In addition to reading and replying to e-mail messages that you receive, you will want to create and send your own messages. When you want to communicate with someone, you can use the New Mail Message tool to create and send e-mail. You can send a message to as many people as you want.

People who are the primary recipients should be in the To field. People receiving a message for their information only should be in the Cc field. People who should be invisible to other people who receive the message should be included in the Bcc field.

Send E-Mail

1 Click **Compose New Message** (⬛) on the toolbar.

The New Message window appears.

2 Type the name or e-mail address of the first recipient in the To field.

Note: As you type, Mail attempts to match a previously used e-mail address or an address in Contacts to what you type. Select an e-mail address to insert it.

3 Press **Tab**.

Note: When it can, Mail replaces an e-mail address with the person's name.

4 Type another e-mail address.

5 Click in the Cc field or press **Tab** to move there, and type e-mail addresses of people who should receive a copy of the message.

6 Type the subject of the message in the Subject field.

7 On the **From** pop-up menu, choose the e-mail address from which you want to send the message; if you have only one e-mail account, skip this step.

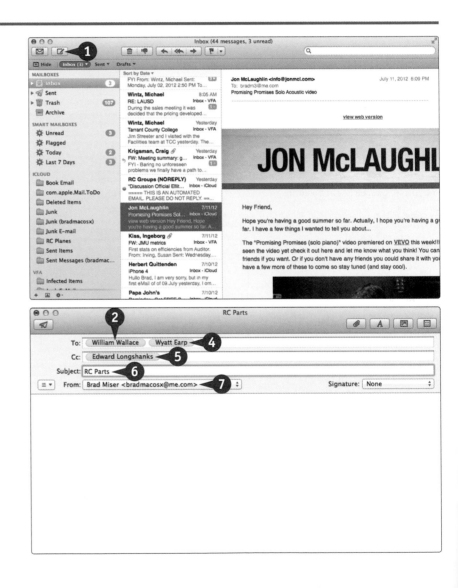

8 Type the message in the body.

Note: You can use Format (Ⓐ) to open the Format toolbar. You can use the tools on this toolbar to format new messages.

As you type, Mail checks your spelling. Misspelled and unrecognized words are underlined in red.

Note: Mail automatically corrects some mistakes for you. When it does so, the word changed is underlined with a dashed blue line. Perform a secondary click on that word to return to the previous spelling.

9 To correct a misspelled word, perform a secondary click on it.

10 Choose the correct spelling on the list.

Note: If the word is spelled correctly and you want to add it to the dictionary so that Mail does not flag it as a mistake in the future, choose Learn Spelling.

11 Review your message and make sure it is ready to be sent.

12 Click **Send** (◁).

The window closes, the message is sent, and you hear the sent message sound effect.

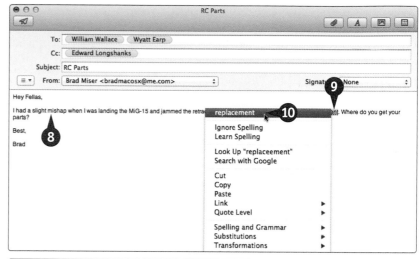

TIPS

How do I avoid having to type e-mail addresses?
You can store e-mail addresses in Contacts so that you can type an e-mail address by typing a person's name, which is usually much easier to remember. As you type an e-mail address, Mail searches e-mail that you have sent, e-mail that you have received, and cards in Contacts to identify e-mail addresses for you. You can select one of these to easily address a message.

From where else can I start a new e-mail message?
When you are using an OS X application, such as Contacts, and you see an e-mail address, you can almost always send an e-mail to that address by performing a secondary click on it and choosing **Send Email** on the contextual menu. A new message to that address is created in Mail, and you can then complete and send it.

Work with Files Attached to E-Mail

In addition to communicating information, e-mail is a great way to send files to other people, and for people to send files to you. Files can be documents, photos, and even applications. E-mail is a particularly useful way to share files because it is so easy to use for this purpose. However, you do need to be aware of the size of the files you send. In many cases, the recipient will not be able to receive files that are larger than 10MB.

In Mail, some file attachments, particularly photos, can be displayed within an e-mail message. In all cases, you can save attachments on your MacBook Pro for your use.

Work with Files Attached to E-Mail

1 Select a message containing attachments.

A The Attachments tools appear just above the body of the message.

2 To save the attachments on your MacBook Pro, open the **Save** menu to see the attachments to the message.

3 Scroll the message to see the attachments in or at the end of the body of the message.

B To preview the attachments, click **Quick Look**. The Quick Look viewer appears and you see the contents of the attachments.

C If the attachments can be displayed in the message (most images can be), you can view them in the body.

4 Choose **Save All** to save all the attachments, or choose a specific attachment to save it.

If you selected **Save All**, the Save sheet appears. If you selected an attachment, it is saved to your Downloads folder and you can skip steps **5** and **6**.

5 Choose the location in which you want to save the attachments.

6 Click **Save**.

The attachments are saved in the location you selected, and you can use them just like files you have created.

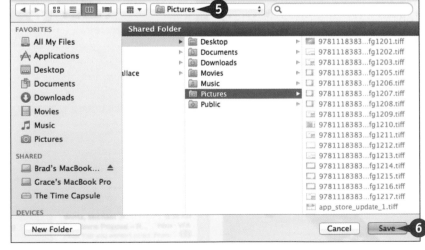

Attach Files to E-Mail

You can attach files to e-mail messages that you send in order to make those files available to other people. You can attach any file to a message and, assuming the recipient has a compatible application, anyone who receives the message can use the files that you attach.

When you attach files to a message, the size of the e-mail increases by the size of those files and more because of the encoding done to the file to create the attachment. If you attach only one or two small files, you can attach them as is. However, to attach many or large files, you should compress them and send the compressed file as an attachment instead. See Chapter 4 for more information about file compression.

Attach Files to E-Mail

① Create a new e-mail message by clicking **New Message** (📝) in the Mail toolbar.

Ⓐ A window appears for you to compose your message in.

② Compose the message by addressing it and typing the body.

③ Click **Attach** (📎).

Note: You can also attach files to a message by dragging them from the desktop onto the New Message window.

The Attach File sheet appears.

④ Move to and select the files you want to attach.

Note: You can select multiple files to attach by pressing and holding ⌘ while you click each file.

⑤ Click **Choose File**.

The files you selected are attached to the message.

⑥ Send the message.

When the recipients receive the message, they can work with the attachments you included.

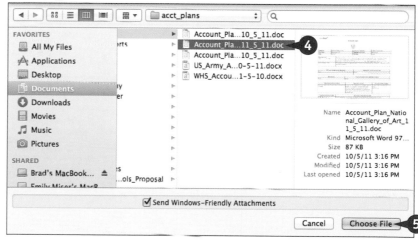

Organize E-Mail

As you use Mail, you are likely to end up with a lot of e-mail messages. Mail provides two great ways to keep your e-mail organized: Mailboxes and Smart Mailboxes. Mailboxes are like folders in the Finder. Smart Mailboxes automatically organize e-mail based on rules that you create.

However, one of the best ways to keep your e-mail organized is to delete messages that you do not need, which is probably most of those that you receive. The fewer messages you keep, the fewer you have to organize, and the less storage space your e-mail requires.

Organize E-Mail

Organize E-Mail in Mailboxes

1 To create a new mailbox, click **Add** (⊞).

2 Select **New Mailbox**.

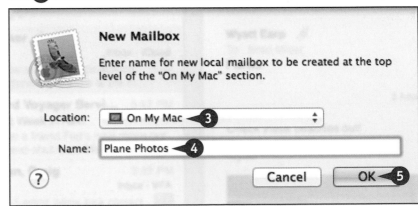

The New Mailbox sheet appears.

3 On the **Location** pop-up menu, choose **On My Mac**.

This setting stores e-mail on MacBook Pro instead of on the mail server.

Note: If you want the messages you store in the mailbox to be available from other devices, choose a location accessible over the Internet, such as a folder associated with your iCloud account.

4 Type a name for the mailbox.

5 Click **OK**.

(A) The mailbox appears in the On My Mac section of the Mailboxes pane.

6 Drag messages from the Messages pane onto the mailbox you created.

The message is moved into the mailbox.

Organize E-Mail with Smart Mailboxes

1 To create a new Smart Mailbox, click **Add** (⊞).

2 Select **New Smart Mailbox**.

The New Smart Mailbox sheet appears.

3 Name the new Smart Mailbox.

4 On the **Contains messages that match** pop-up menu, choose **any**.

5 Use the pop-up menus and fields to create a condition for the messages that you want to be included.

6 To add another condition, click **Add** (⊞).

7 Use the pop-up menus and fields to configure the condition.

8 Repeat steps **6** and **7** until you have added all the conditions you want.

Note: To remove a condition, click Remove (⊟).

9 Click **OK**.

The mailbox is created and any messages that meet its conditions appear in it automatically.

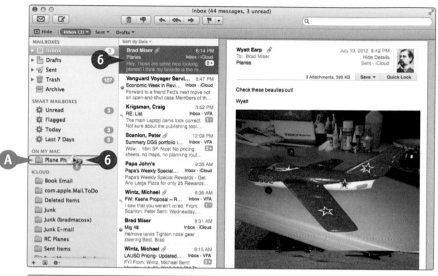

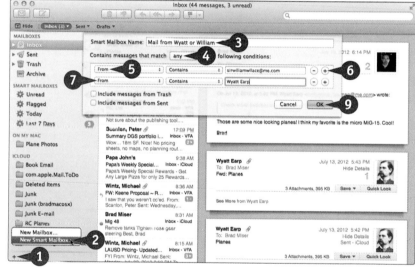

TIPS

How do I change how messages are listed on the Messages list?

Open the **Sort by** menu and choose how you want the list sorted. For example, choose **From** to sort messages by the sender. To change the order of how the list is sorted, open the menu and choose **Ascending Order**. You can also drag the right edge of columns to change their width.

I have received a message saying that I am over my mail storage quota. What can I do?

Most e-mail accounts have a limit on how much e-mail you can store on the server. To prevent e-mail server storage overload, store e-mail in mailboxes on your MacBook Pro. You should also check account settings to make sure mail is not being stored on the server unintentionally. See the section "Set Up E-Mail Accounts."

Search E-Mail

As you accumulate messages, you may want to be able to find messages that contain information or attachments you need. You can use the Mail Search bar to quickly find important messages. This is really useful because you can search for specific words and phrases in messages, which is much faster than browsing for specific messages in most cases.

One of the best ways to be able to find e-mail is to keep it organized. A little time spent organizing e-mail earlier prevents much of the effort to find it later. For more information, see the section "Organize E-Mail."

Search E-Mail

1 Type the information for which you want to search in the Search bar.

A As you type, Mail presents search options that relate to your search. For example, when you search for a name, it may suggest messages containing the name, people with that name, and so on.

2 Select the search option you want to use.

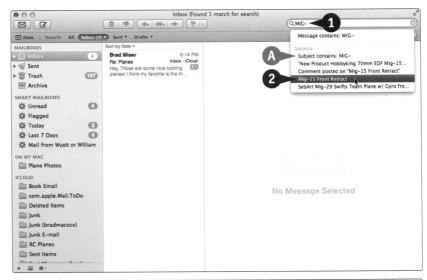

B The messages that meet the criteria you selected are shown.

3 To read a message, select it.

C The message opens in the reading pane that appears in the right pane of the window.

Note: By default, Mail searches the currently selected mailbox, which is highlighted in blue. You can change the search location or just select the mailbox you want to search before you search.

4 To search in all mailboxes, click **All**, or to search in the Sent folder, click **Sent**.

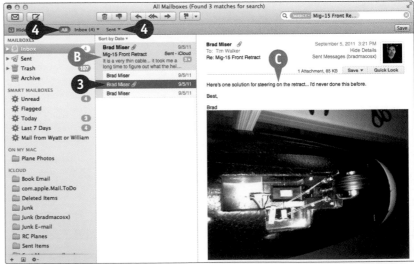

5 Click the menu that appears next to your search term to indicate what part of the messages you want to search.

For example, to search for messages by recipient, click **To**.

The results are refined, based on the choices you made.

Note: When you click Entire Message, Mail searches all parts of the messages.

6 To save a search as a Smart Mailbox so that you can run it again, click **Save**.

The Smart Mailbox sheet appears.

7 Configure and save the Smart Mailbox.

Note: For more information on configuring a Smart Mailbox, see the section "Organize E-Mail."

8 Click OK. You can repeat the search at any time by selecting its folder in the Smart Mailboxes section of the Mailboxes pane.

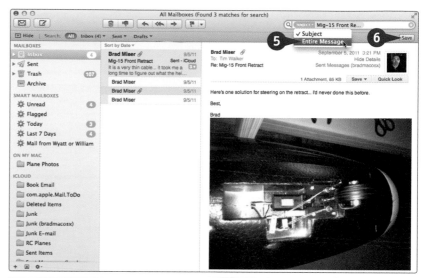

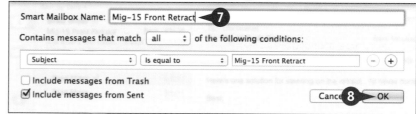

TIPS

Do I have to be using Mail to search e-mail?
The OS X Spotlight feature enables you to search for information on your MacBook Pro no matter where that information is found, including files, folders, and e-mail. If you are sure the information you need is in an e-mail, search in Mail. If not, use Spotlight instead. To learn how to use Spotlight, see Chapter 4.

Can I have the same e-mail in more than one mailbox?
An e-mail can exist in only one mailbox in the same location, such as the mailboxes stored on MacBook Pro. (Of course, you can make copies of messages and place the copies in different locations.) Because Smart Mailboxes do not actually contain the messages (a Smart Mailbox makes pointers to the actual e-mail messages), e-mail messages can be included in many Smart Mailboxes at the same time.

Avoid Spam

One of the perils of receiving e-mail is spam. Spam is annoying at best, with messages that stream into your Inbox with advertising in which you have no interest. At worst, spam contains offensive or dangerous messages that promise all kinds of rewards for just a few simple actions (usually an attempt at identity theft).

Notice that the title of this section is "Avoid Spam," as opposed to "Eliminate Spam" or "Prevent Spam." Unfortunately, spam is part of receiving e-mail, and the best you can do is to minimize your exposure to it as much as possible.

Avoid Spam

① Press ⌘+,.

The Mail Preferences window appears.

② Click the **Junk Mail** tab.

③ Check the **Enable junk mail filtering** check box.

④ Click **Mark as junk mail, but leave it in my Inbox** if you want Mail to highlight junk e-mail, but not do anything else with it.

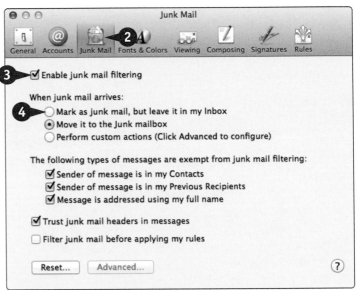

⑤ Click **Move it to the Junk mailbox** if you want Mail to move spam to the Junk mailbox.

⑥ Click **Perform custom actions (Click Advanced to configure)** if you want to define what Mail does using a mail rule.

⑦ Click the check boxes to specify e-mails that are exempt from junk mail filtering.

⑧ Close the Preferences window.

As you receive e-mail, Mail takes the action that you selected when you receive e-mail that it identifies as junk.

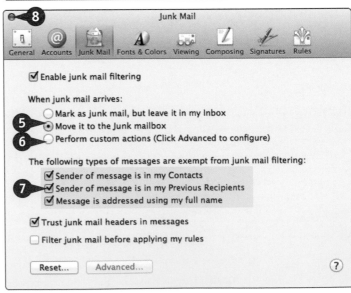

⑨ Click the **Junk** folder.

Ⓐ The contents of the Junk folder, which are all the messages that Mail has classified as junk, appear.

⑩ Select and review each message.

⑪ If a message is junk, do nothing; the message stays in your Junk folder.

Note: By default, Mail does not load any images in junk mail. If you want to see the images, click Load Images.

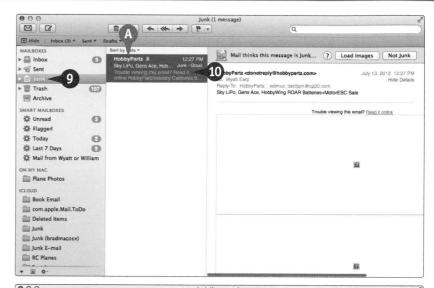

⑫ If a message is not junk, click **Not junk**.

Any images in the message are shown; you can move the message to a different folder if you want to keep it.

Over time, Mail learns from your actions and gets better at identifying junk mail.

⑬ Click **Delete** (🗑) to delete junk messages.

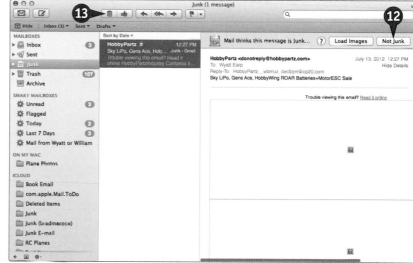

TIPS

I have received a message saying I need to update my account. What should I do?
One effective technique that criminals use is to model their spam e-mails so that they look just like e-mail from legitimate companies. They usually mention that your account is out of date or compromised, and that you need to provide information to correct the situation. These messages are always spam and you should never respond to them.

How can I tell if a message is legitimate or spam?
Many spam e-mails include a link, usually to your account so that you can verify some information, which means that they are trying to steal information from you. Point to these links (**do not click!**), and the URL pops up. You will see that the first part of the URL has nothing to do with the real company, which is a dead giveaway that it is an attempt to steal your identity.

Create and Use E-Mail Signatures

Including a signature at the end of your e-mails is good practice to make your communication more personal or to provide important information, such as your phone number or website address. You can even advertise in your signature.

You can configure Mail to make adding signatures easier and faster. You can create many different signatures and easily use the most appropriate one for a specific e-mail message that you send. You can also have a signature inserted into new messages automatically.

Create and Use E-Mail Signatures

Create Signatures

1 Press ⌘+.

2 Click the **Signatures** tab.

3 Click **All Signatures**.

4 Click **Add** (⊞).

A new signature is created, ready to be edited.

5 Type a name for the signature and press **Return**.

When a signature is selected in the center column, its contents appear in the far right column.

6 With the signature selected, type the content of the signature in the right column.

7 If you use a default font for your messages, check the **Always match my default message font** check box so that the signature uses that font.

8 If you use default quoting, check the **Place signature above quoted text** check box.

9 Repeat steps **4** to **6** to create as many signatures as you want.

10 Drag signatures from the center column onto the e-mail accounts with which you want to use them in the left column.

The number of signatures available for each account is shown under the account name.

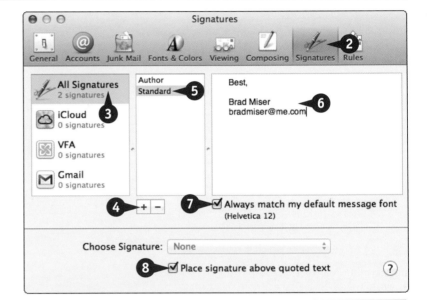

⑪ Click an e-mail account.

⑫ Choose the default signature for the account on the **Choose Signature** pop-up menu.

Whenever you send an e-mail from the account, the default signature is pasted in automatically.

⑬ Close the Preferences window.

Use Signatures

① Create a new message.

Ⓐ The default signature for the e-mail account, if you configured one, is pasted in the new message.

② To change the signature, choose the signature on the **Signature** pop-up menu.

Note: If you do not select a default signature for an account, you can choose a signature on the menu to add it to a message. The signatures available on this menu are those that you added to the account on the Signatures tab.

What are the other choices on the Choose Signature pop-up menu on the Signatures tab?
If you choose **At Random** on the **Choose Signature** pop-up menu, Mail selects a signature randomly each time you create a message. If you choose **In Sequential Order**, Mail selects the first signature on the list for the first message, the next one for the second message, and so on.

Can I put images or links in my signature?
Yes. To add an image to a signature, drag the image file from the desktop onto the right pane of the Signatures tab. You can also add links to a signature by typing the URL in the signature block or by copying and pasting it in.

Create E-Mail Rules

If you find yourself doing the same tasks with certain kinds of e-mail, you can probably configure Mail to do those tasks for you automatically by configuring rules, which are automatic actions that Mail performs for you.

To determine whether you can create a rule, you need to be able to define the conditions under which one or more actions should be taken, and the actions you want to happen every time those conditions are met. The following steps describe how to create a rule to automatically file e-mails from specific people in a folder and to alert you that they have arrived. You can configure other rules similarly.

Create E-Mail Rules

① Press ⌘+,.

② Click the **Rules** tab.

The center pane shows the configured rules.

③ Click **Add Rule**.

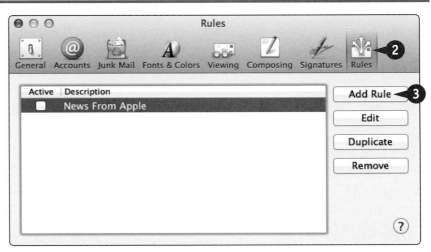

The New Rule sheet appears.

④ Name the rule.

⑤ Choose **any** on the pop-up menu if only one condition has to be true for the rule to apply, or **all** if all of the conditions have to be true for the rule to apply.

⑥ Select the attribute for the first condition on the left pop-up menu.

⑦ Choose the operand for the condition on the center pop-up menu, such as **Contains**.

⑧ Type the condition value in the box.

⑨ Click **Add** (⊕).

⑩ Repeat steps **6** to **8** to configure the new condition.

Note: To remove a condition, click Remove (⊖).

⑪ Repeat steps **9** and **10** to add and configure more conditions.

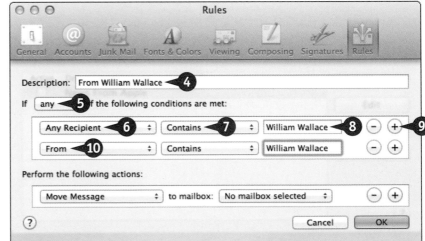

⑫ On the top left **Action** pop-up menu, choose the action you want to happen when the conditions are met.

⑬ On the top right **Action** pop-up menu, choose the result of the action, such as a location or a sound.

⑭ To add another action, click **Add** (⊕).

⑮ Repeat steps **12** and **13** to configure the new action.

⑯ Repeat steps **14** and **15** to add and configure more actions.

⑰ Click **OK**.

Ⓐ The rule is created and appears on the list of rules on the Rules pane.

⑱ Close the Preferences window.

When messages are received that meet the rule's conditions, whatever actions it includes are performed automatically.

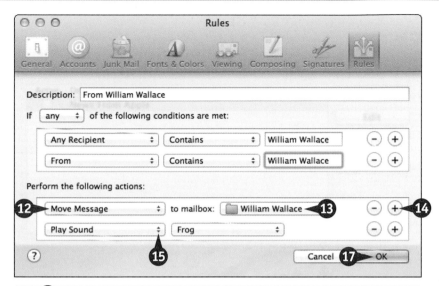

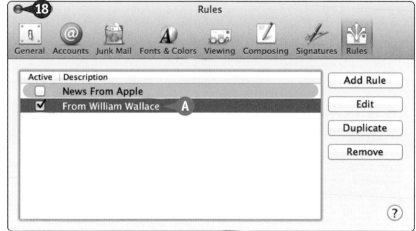

What are some examples of useful actions available for rules?

Move Message moves e-mail messages to specific locations, such as mailboxes that you have created on your MacBook Pro or even the Trash. Forward Message can be useful when you always want to forward messages to another address in specific situations. If you usually reply to a specific person's e-mail, Reply to Message can be useful.

How do I know a rule is working?

Select a message to which the rule should apply, open the **Message** menu, and then select **Apply Rules**. If the actions you expect happen, then the rule is working. You should also select a message to which the rule should not apply and do the same thing. If the rule's actions occur, then the rule is not configured correctly.

Set Mail Preferences

Like most applications, Mail includes a number of preference settings that you can use to configure the way it works to meet your individual preferences. Mail will work fine for many people with the default settings, but as you use the application more, it will be worth your time to explore the options to make it work even better for you.

These include the General, Fonts & Colors, Viewing, and Composing preferences. You use the General tab to set general Mail preferences, such as sound effects, where attachments are stored, and what location to include in searches. You use the Viewing and Composing preferences to configure how you view and write e-mail.

Set Mail Preferences

Set General Preferences

1. Press ⌘+, .

2. Click the **General** tab.

3. Choose how often you want to check for new messages.

4. Choose the sound you want to hear when new messages arrive.

5. To mute sounds for other actions, uncheck the **Play sounds for other mail actions** check box.

6. Choose the mailboxes for which you want the number of unread messages to appear on the Dock icon for Mail.

7. Choose the folder in which attachments should be stored by default.

8. Choose what you want Mail to do with attachments that you have not changed when you delete the associated message.

9. Configure specific areas that should be included in searches.

Set Fonts & Colors Preferences

1. Press ⌘+, .

2. Click the **Fonts & Colors** tab.

3. Click the **Select** button next to the fonts you want to format and use the resulting Fonts panel to configure that font.

4. Click the **Use fixed-width font for plain text messages** check box.

5. Click the **Color quoted text** check box and pop-up menus to set color quoted text.

Set Viewing Preferences

1 Press ⌘+,.

2 Click the **Viewing** tab.

3 Choose the level of information at the top of e-mail messages.

4 If you use Messages, click this check box to show online friends.

5 To add emphasis to unread messages by showing them in bold, check this check box.

6 If you do not want to display images not embedded in messages, uncheck this check box.

7 If you prefer to see e-mail addresses and names, uncheck this check box.

8 Click this check box to set how Mail indicates that messages are part of the same conversation.

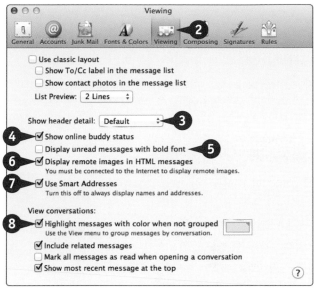

Set Composing Preferences

1 Press ⌘+,.

2 Click the **Composing** tab.

3 Choose the default format for messages.

4 Choose a spell check option.

5 To see the individuals in a group when you address a message to the group, check this check box.

6 If you have more than one e-mail address, choose the default account for new messages.

7 To use the same format as the original message, check this check box.

8 To select the text to be quoted when you reply to a message, select this option.

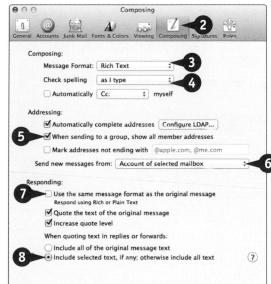

TIP

How else can I use threading?

Threading is a way to identify and group messages on the same topic (that have the same subject line), which is called a conversation in Mail. On the **View** menu, choose **Organize by Conversation** to show these messages in groups that you can collapse or expand. This is a useful way to organize your Inbox because it keeps related messages together as conversations. When you select the parent message in a thread, you see a summary of all the messages that thread contains.

Chat with FaceTime

FaceTime is a great way to communicate because you get to both see and hear the person with whom you are chatting. You can use FaceTime to have a video chat with anyone who uses current versions of Macs, iPhones, iPod touches, or iPads. Using FaceTime is simple, fun, and free. (All you need is an Apple ID, which you can get at no cost if you do not have one already.)

Before you can start having FaceTime chats, you need to do some basic configuration. Once that is in place, conducting FaceTime chats is easy.

Chat with FaceTime

Configure FaceTime

1. Launch FaceTime by clicking its icon ( ) on the Dock.

   The first time you launch FaceTime, it prompts you to type your Apple ID.

2. Type your Apple ID and password.

3. Click **Sign In**.

4. Confirm or update your e-mail address.

Note: People use your e-mail address to request a FaceTime session.

5. Click **Next**.

   Once the address you used is verified, the Contacts section appears in the FaceTime window.

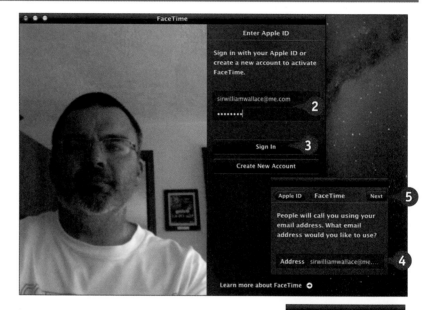

Conduct a FaceTime Chat

1. Click the **Contacts** tab.

   You see the contacts in your Contacts.

Note: For information about using the Contacts, see Chapter 15.

2. Click the contact with whom you want to have a FaceTime session.

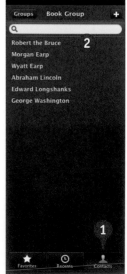

You see the contact's detailed information.

③ Double-click the e-mail address or phone number you want to use for the FaceTime session.

Note: To use a phone number, the person with whom you want to have a FaceTime session must have an iPhone 4 or later.

FaceTime notifies the contact and requests a session.

If the contact accepts your request, the FaceTime session starts and you can hear and see the other party. If the contact declines, is not available, or does not have a FaceTime capable device, you see a "not available" message.

④ Drag the preview window that the other person is seeing to change its location.

Note: If you do not see the buttons on the screen, move the pointer over the window and they appear.

⑤ Mute the audio and darken the video by clicking **Mute** (⬛).

⑥ Click **Full Screen** (⬛) to have a full screen FaceTime window.

⑦ Click **End** to end the FaceTime session.

TIP

Are there easier ways to find someone to have a FaceTime chat with?
Yes. If you click the **Recents** tab at the bottom of the Contacts pane, you can see a list of the people with whom you have had a FaceTime chat recently. You can request a FaceTime session by clicking one of the recent FaceTime chats. You can also save a contact as a favorite by viewing the contact and clicking **Add to Favorites**; you can request a chat from the contact by double-clicking the favorite on the Favorites tab.

Explore Messages

The Messages application is a great way to communicate with other people in real time. Its interface is simple and elegant, but it packs all the features that you need to have great text, audio, and video chats.

After some quick configuration of Messages, you can use it to communicate with people all over the world in any format you choose. Messages can even help when you have computer problems, because you can use it to share the desktop of your MacBook Pro with someone else over the Internet or over a local network, such as a network in your home.

Ⓐ Messages Window

Text conversations appear in the Messages window.

Ⓑ Person You Are Texting

At the top of the window, you see the person with whom you are texting.

Ⓒ Other Person's Last Text

On the left side of the window, you see the last text from the other person involved in the conversation.

Ⓓ Your Recent Comments

On the right side of the window, you see your most recent contributions to the conversation.

Ⓔ Text Box

When you want to add to the conversation, you can type text in the text box.

Ⓕ Emoticon Menu

You can add emoticons to a conversation by selecting them from the menu.

Ⓐ Audio Chat Window

When you audio chat with people, you see a visual representation of the sounds you hear.

Ⓑ How Many People Are Involved

At the top of the window, you see how many people are participating.

Ⓒ Each Person Participating

Participants in the conversation have their own sound bar so that you can see when they speak.

Ⓓ Your Volume Level

The bottom bar represents how loud your speech is.

Ⓔ Add Button

You can click Add (⊞) to add more people to the conversation.

Ⓕ Mute Button

You can click 🎤 to mute your sound.

Ⓖ Volume Slider

You can use this slider to set the volume level of a conversation.

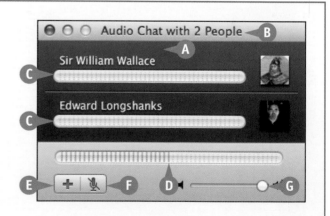

A Video Chat Window

This window shows each of the people with whom you are having a video conference.

B Participant Windows

Each participant gets his own window for the chat.

C Your Window

During a video chat, you see yourself as the other participants see you.

D Effects

You can use the Effects tools to apply a variety of interesting effects to the video.

E Add

You can add up to three other people in a video conference.

F Mute

You can click ⬛ to block sound from your end.

G Full Screen

When you click ▥, the video conference fills the desktop.

A Shared Screen

You can use Messages to view and control another person's computer.

B Your Computer

When you are sharing a desktop, you see a preview of your desktop; you can click it to move back to your computer.

C Shared Applications

When someone shares a screen with you, you can work with applications and documents on her computer just as if you were seated in front of it.

Configure Messages Accounts

Before you start chatting, you need to configure the accounts you are going to use to chat. With an iCloud account, you can have text chats. With an America Online Instant Messenger account (AIM), you can also have audio and video chats. If you have an iCloud account, you also have an AIM account, so if you want to use the audio and video chats, you should set up your account as an AIM account.

To set up chat accounts, you use the Messages Preferences dialog. The type of account you use determines which of the features you can use in Messages.

Configure Messages Accounts

Create Accounts

1. Launch Messages by clicking its icon on the Dock ( ) or by double-clicking its icon in the Applications folder.

Note: The first time you start up Messages, the Setup Assistant walks you through the creation of an account.

2. Click **File** and select Preferences.

3. Click the **Accounts** tab.

4. Click Add (+).

5. From the **Account Type** pop-up menu, choose the type of account you want to use to chat; if you are using an iCloud account/Apple ID, select **AIM**.

6. Type a member, screen, or username for your account; if you are using an Apple ID, include the entire e-mail address.

7. Type the password for your account.

8. Click **Done**.

   Messages creates the account and you see it on the Account list.

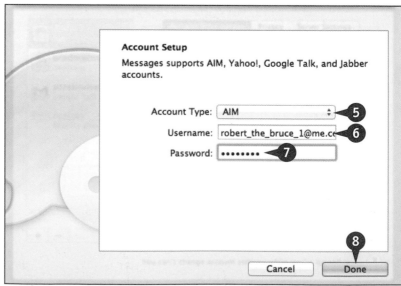

9 To add more accounts, click **Add**
(⊞).

10 Repeat steps **4** to **7**.

Ⓐ You see all the accounts you have
created.

Enable or Disable Accounts

1 Move back to the Accounts
preferences dialog, as described in
steps **1** to **3** in the previous section.

2 Select the account you want to
enable or disable.

3 Deselect the **Enable this account**
check box.

In this example, the account is
disabled and you can no longer use
it to chat.

Note: To re-enable an account, select its
Enable this account check box.

TIPS

How do I change the format of my text messages?
Open the Messages Preferences dialog (press ⌘+,). Click
Messages. On this tab, you can change the fonts and colors
used during text chats along with the background colors.

**What kind of Internet connection do I need to have an audio
and video chat over the Internet?**
Audio and video chats require broadband Internet connections.
As long as you can connect through a Wi-Fi, DSL, cable, or other
fast connection, you can chat with audio and video. Prepare to
be amazed at the quality of both audio and video chatting.

Chat with Text

Text chatting is a great way to have real-time conversations with other people while not consuming all of your and their attention throughout the conversation. Text messaging is a great way to exchange short messages in the format of a conversation. With Messages, you can also include photos and documents in your chats.

While not required if you are only chatting with iCloud users, it is a good idea to set up buddies with whom you will chat. Buddies make starting chats easier.

Chat with Text

Add a Buddy

1. Press ⌘+1.

   The Buddies window opens.

2. At the bottom of the Buddies list, click **Add** (➕).

3. Select **Add Buddy**.

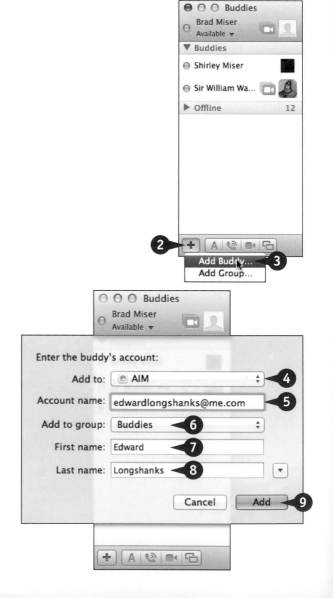

4. Select the account that you want to associate with the buddy.

5. Type the buddy's account name.

6. Select the group in which you want to place the buddy.

7. Type the buddy's first name.

8. Type the buddy's last name.

9. Click **Add**.

   The person is added to your Buddies list.

Start a Text Chat

1 Press ⌘+1.

2 Click the buddy with whom you want to chat.

3 Select **Invite to Chat**.

Ⓐ The Messages window becomes active and you see the buddy with whom you are chatting.

4 Type your message.

5 Press **Return**.

Messages sends your message and adds it to the message log at the top of the window next to your icon.

6 Read the reply.

7 Type your response.

8 To add an emoticon, select one from the pop-up menu.

9 Press **Return**.

Messages sends your response and adds it to the conversation.

Ⓑ You can view images included in the chat.

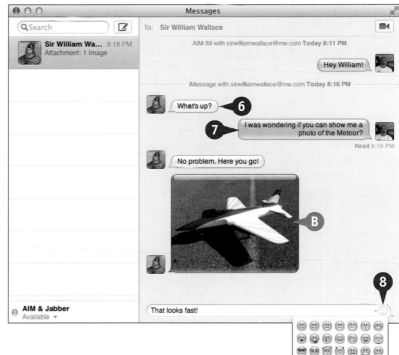

TIPS

How do I respond when someone wants to chat with me?
When someone wants to chat with you, a new message appears in the Message list along the left side of the Messages window and you hear the new message sound. Click the message and read its content. You can then reply to the message.

How can I include documents in a text chat?
Drag an image or other document file from the desktop and drop it into the text box. If you want to send text along with the file, type the text. Press **Return**. Messages sends the text and file to the person with whom you are chatting.

Chat with Audio

Text chatting is great, but being able to talk to someone can be even better. Of course, you can always use the phone, but that can be expensive. Using the Messages audio chat feature, you can have conversations with one or more people at the same time at no cost to you.

Before you start talking, take a moment to set up your MacBook Pro microphone; you can use the built-in microphone or you can use an external microphone, such as a USB or Bluetooth headset. Then you can talk whenever you want.

Chat with Audio

Check the Microphone

1. Open the **Apple** menu (🍎) and select **System Preferences**.

2. Click the **Sound** icon.

3. Click the **Input** tab.

4. Speak normally.

A. As you speak, the input level indicator shows the relative input volume. When you speak normally, the gauge should register toward the center of the range.

5. Drag the **Input volume** slider to the right to increase the level of sound input, or to the left to decrease it.

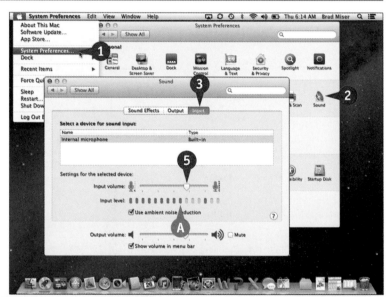

Audio Chat

1. Click the **Messages** icon on the Dock.

2. Press ⌘+1 to open the Buddies window if it is not open already.

3. Click the buddy with whom you want to chat and select **Invite to Audio Chat**.

Note: If the Invite to Audio Chat command is not available, the buddy is not capable of audio chatting with you.

The Audio Chat window opens and Messages attempts to connect to the buddy you selected. If the person is available and accepts your chat request, you are connected and the audio chat begins.

④ Speak to the person and listen as you would on a telephone.

⑤ To change the volume, drag the slider to the left to decrease the volume level, or to the right to increase it.

⑥ To mute your side of the conversation, click **Mute** (🔇) and then click it again to resume your conversation.

⑦ To add another person to the chat, click **Add** (➕) and click the buddy you want to add.

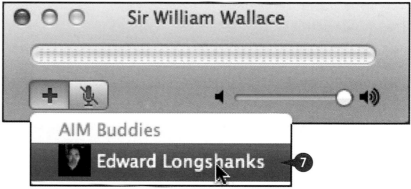

After the second person accepts, all three of you are able to hear each other.

⑧ Repeat step **7** to continue adding people and chatting.

⑨ When you are done, close the chat window.

TIPS

How do I avoid chat requests?
To prevent any chat requests from popping up, you need to quit Messages. If you want to show your status to others, open the **Status** pop-up menu just below your name at the top of the Buddies window. Choose the status you want them to see on their Buddy lists. Select **Offline** if you do not want to chat. To chat again, select **Available** from the menu.

How do I respond to an audio chat request?
When someone wants to have an audio chat, a prompt appears and you hear the invite tone. Click the prompt. Click **Accept** to start the chat, click **Decline** to avoid it, or click **Text Reply** to reply with text. If you decline, the person who requested the chat sees a message saying that you have declined.

Chat with Video

Earlier, you saw how easy using FaceTime is to video chat with someone. You can also use Messages to video chat. Messages has some benefits over FaceTime. One is that you can chat with more than one person at the same time. Another benefit is that the people with whom you chat only need a video chat-capable application, instead of requiring FaceTime.

Conducting a video chat is similar to an audio chat. First, make sure your video and audio are set up correctly. Second, start a chat.

Chat with Video

Check the Camera

① Click **Camera** (▣) next to your name at the top of the Buddies or Bonjour list.

The My FaceTime HD Camera window opens.

② Move your MacBook Pro or yourself until the image is what you want others to see.

③ When you are satisfied with the view, close the window.

Video Chat

① Press ⌘+1 to open the Buddies window if it is not open already.

② Click the buddy with whom you want to chat.

③ Select **Invite to Video Chat**.

Note: If the Invite to Video Chat command is not available, the buddy is not able to video chat with you.

The Video Chat window opens and Messages attempts to connect to the buddy you selected. If the person is available and accepts your chat request, you are connected and the video chat begins.

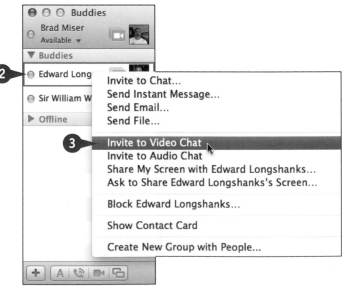

Ⓐ You see the buddy's image in the window.

Ⓑ The inset preview window shows you what the other person is seeing in his chat window.

④ Drag the preview window to where you want it to be on the screen.

Note: See the section, "Add Effects and Backgrounds to Video Chats" to apply interesting effects during your chats.

⑤ To mute your end of the conversation, click **Mute** (🔇); click it again to resume your conversation.

⑥ To make the window fill the desktop, click **Full Screen** (⤢).

⑦ To add another person to the conversation, click **Add** (➕) and click the buddy that you want to add.

Ⓒ When the person accepts your invitation, a third video window appears and you see the second person.

You can see and talk to the other people, and they can see and talk to each other.

⑧ When you are done, close the window.

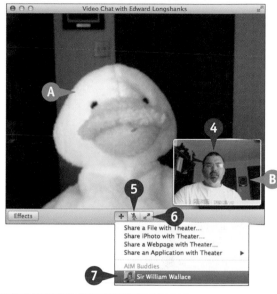

TIPS

How many people can I have in a video or audio conference at the same time?
You can have up to four participants (including yourself) in a single video conference. You can have up to ten people (including yourself) in an audio conference at the same time.

Is Messages compatible with other kinds of video conference systems?
Just one. To use Messages for video conferences, all participants must be using Messages(or the older iChat) or the latest version of AOL Instant Messenger for Windows. (However, do not expect the same quality for Windows users that you experience with Mac users.)

Add Effects and Backgrounds to Video Chats

Having a video chat is both an effective way to communicate with other people, and a lot of fun. And there are ways to make it even more fun. You can apply special effects to the images being shown during a video chat, and you can apply background images or movies to video chats to make them more interesting. With a motion background, it appears as if you are in front of or in whatever the background is; this is like the green screen technique used during weather broadcasts, movies, and so on. A static image as a background can also make it appear that you are somewhere you are not. These do not improve the communication, but they can be a lot of fun.

Add Effects and Backgrounds to Video Chats

1 Start a video chat.

2 Click **Effects**.

3 Click the effect, image, or video that you want to apply.

A Messages applies the effect to your image.

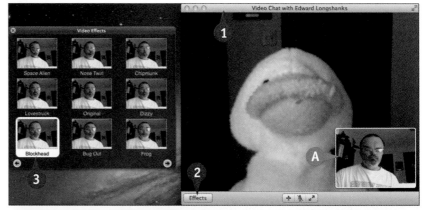

4 Scroll to the right in the Video Effects palette until you see the video backgrounds.

5 Click a video background and move out of the camera view at the prompt.

6 When the prompt disappears, move back into the picture.

B To the other participants, it looks as if you are actually in front of the background image or video.

Present Documents with Theater

Sometimes you want to share documents with other people while you talk about the documents. The obvious case is a presentation that you want to use to convey information to others, but other times you want to "talk" through a document to explain it to someone, such as when you are collaborating with someone on it.

You can use Messages to present documents to other people over the Internet. When you present a document, the other people see the document, as well as see and hear you through a video chat.

Present Documents with Theater

1 Start a video chat.

2 Click **Add** (⊞).

3 Select **Share a File with Theater**.

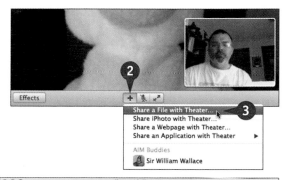

The Share with Theater dialog appears.

4 Navigate to and select the document (such as a presentation) that you want to share.

5 Click **Share**.

A You see the document you are sharing.

B In the lower-left corner of the window, you see a preview window showing the buddy with whom you are chatting.

6 Move through the document and speak to deliver your message to the audience.

7 When you are done, close the Video Chat window.

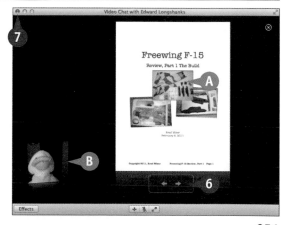

Share Desktops with Others

You can share your desktop so that the people with whom you are chatting can see and control what happens on your computer. When you share someone else's screen, you can see and control his computer. Sharing screens is a great way to collaborate on projects or to share information.

Screen sharing is especially useful when troubleshooting problems. The person who is having a problem can share his desktop with the person helping so that she can see what is happening, which is much easier than trying to describe a problem. She can also take control of the computer to actually solve the problem.

Share Desktops with Others

Share Your Desktop

1 Press ⌘+**1** to open the Buddies window if it is not open already.

2 Click the buddy with whom you want to share your screen.

3 Click **Share My Screen with buddyname**, where *buddyname* is the name of the buddy you selected.

A When the buddy accepts your invitation, he can control your MacBook Pro. Do not be surprised when the pointer moves and commands are activated, such as opening applications, without you doing anything. The buddy also sees what you do on your desktop.

While screens are being shared, you can audio chat. It is good practice for the person controlling the computer to explain what she is doing as she does it.

4 To end screen sharing, open the **Buddies** menu and select **End Screen Sharing**.

The sharing connection ends and your computer returns to your control.

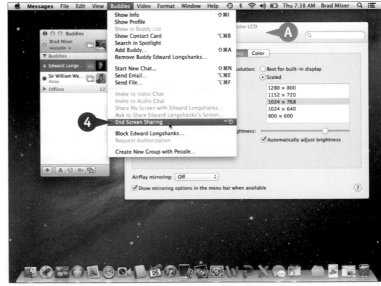

Share a Desktop Belonging to Someone Else

1 Press ⌘+**1** to open the Buddies window if it is not open already.

2 Click the buddy with whom you want to share your screen.

3 Click **Ask to Share** *buddyname*'s **Screen**, where *buddyname* is the name of the buddy you selected.

Messages sends a share request to the buddy. When he accepts, you see two windows on your screen.

B One window is the buddy's desktop, which is the larger window by default.

C The other window is a preview of your desktop, which is labeled My Computer.

Note: You can move the preview window around the screen if it blocks the part of the shared desktop that you want to see.

4 You can work with the buddy's computer just as if you were sitting in front of it.

5 To move back to your desktop, click in the My Computer window.

The two windows flip-flop so that your desktop is now the larger window.

6 When you are done sharing, click **Close** (⊠) on the My Computer window.

TIPS

How do I know when someone wants to share his screen with me?

You receive a screen-sharing invitation in Messages. When you click the invitation, you have the following options: Accept to start screen sharing, Decline to prevent it, or Text Reply to send back a text message. If you choose to share the person's screen, you are able to see and control that person's computer.

How do I share a screen that is on the same local network as my MacBook Pro?

Open the Sharing pane of the System Preferences application and select the **Screen Sharing** check box to turn it on. Use the Allow Access For tool to configure share permissions for specific user accounts or for all users. On a different Mac on the local network, select the computer whose screen you want to share. Click **Connect** and log in under a user account that has permission to share the screen. Once you are logged in, click **Share Screen**.

Communicate with Twitter

Twitter is a popular way to communicate in very short (140 characters or fewer) messages called tweets. You can follow someone on Twitter, which means you can see any messages they post to their Twitter account. You can respond to tweets on someone's account. You can also post messages on your account, and people who follow you can read them.

To use Twitter, you need a Twitter account and an application. A Twitter account is free, as are many Twitter applications.

Communicate with Twitter

Set Up Your Twitter Account

Note: To obtain a Twitter account, visit http://twitter.com.

1. Click the **Apple** menu (![]) and select **System Preferences**.

2. Click **Mail, Contacts & Calendars**.

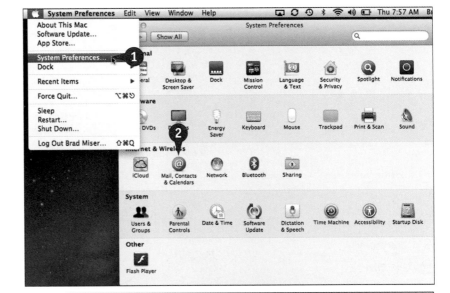

3. Click **Twitter**.

4. Type your Twitter username.

5. Type your Twitter password.

6. Click **Sign In**.

   You return to the Mail, Contacts & Calendars window and see your Twitter account information.

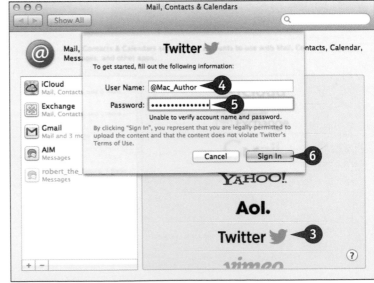

Send and Read Twitter Messages

1 Open your Twitter application and sign in to your Twitter account if required.

Note: You can also use Twitter by visiting http://twitter.com.

A You see the messages from people you are following.

2 Scroll the window to read all the tweets.

3 To tweet a message to your followers, click ✏.

4 Type your tweet.

5 Click **Tweet**.

Anyone who follows you can see the message in his Twitter feed.

TIPS

How do I find and install a Twitter application?
Open the App Store application. In the Search box, type **Twitter**. There are a number of Twitter applications. Click the **Install** button for the application you want to use. It is downloaded and installed on your MacBook Pro.

How else can I use Twitter?
You can share photos and other content on Twitter. To do so, select the item you want to send via Twitter, click the **Share** button, and choose **Twitter**. The item you selected is sent in a tweet.

PART IV

Going Further with MacBook Pro

Your MacBook Pro can help you get things done, such as printing and managing your contacts and calendars. To keep it working well, you should know how to maintain it and troubleshoot problems. Use iTunes to enjoy audio and video. If you have an iOS device, you want to keep that device in sync with your MacBook Pro.

Chapter 14: Printing on Paper or Electronically 258

Chapter 15: Managing Contacts 268

Chapter 16: Managing Calendars 284

Chapter 17: Maintaining a MacBook Pro
and Solving Problems 300

Chapter 18: Enjoying Music and Video with iTunes 322

Chapter 19: Using a MacBook Pro with iPhones,
iPods, and iPads 352

Understanding Printers

Although we live in an electronic world, printing is an important part of using a MacBook Pro. Many types of printers are available along with different options for how your MacBook Pro communicates with them. The two most common types of printers are inkjet printers and laser printers. You can connect a printer to your MacBook Pro using a USB or Ethernet cable, or you can print wirelessly either over a network to a printer connected to an AirPort base station, Time Capsule, or other hub, or directly between the computer and a wireless printer. You should understand a number of concepts as you build a printing system for your MacBook Pro and the network it is on.

Inkjet Printers

Inkjet printers create text and graphics by spraying droplets of ink on paper in various combinations. Inkjet printers produce high-quality output, especially when using the appropriate paper. These printers are inexpensive and many offer features such as scanning and faxing. Inkjet printers are usually less expensive than laser printers initially, but they consume large amounts of ink, which is expensive. You can expect to pay a significant portion of the purchase price of the printer each time you replace one or more ink cartridges; in some cases, you may pay more for new cartridges than you do for a new printer. Still, for many people, inkjet printers make a lot of sense.

Laser Printers

Laser printers use a laser, mirrors, and an imaging drum to transfer toner onto paper. Laser printers produce very high quality output and are fast relative to inkjet printers. Although a laser printer is typically more expensive than an inkjet printer, the cost per page of a laser printer can actually be significantly less than that of an inkjet printer. Like inkjet printers, many laser printers print in color. With some careful shopping, you can often get a color laser printer for not much more than an inkjet printer.

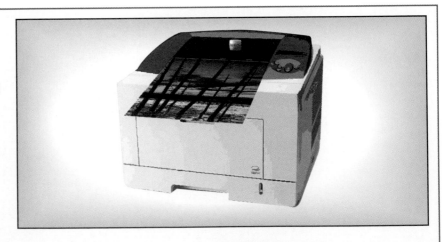

Printer Connections

Your MacBook Pro needs to communicate with a printer to print. You can connect a MacBook Pro to a printer in three ways. First, some printers use USB to communicate. Second, networkable printers have an Ethernet port that you can use to connect your MacBook Pro directly to the printer, or more likely, to connect the printer to your network. The third, and most convenient, way to connect is wirelessly. Some printers support wireless connections directly; however, you can connect a printer to an AirPort Extreme Base Station, AirPort

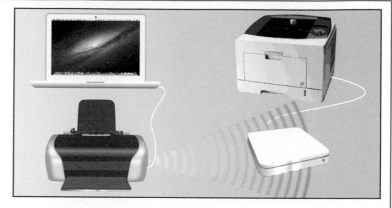

Express Base Station, or Time Capsule by using an Ethernet port or its USB port to print to it wirelessly.

Printer Sharing

If you have more than one computer, you can share the same printer with all the computers over a local network (wired, wireless, or both). You can connect the shared printer directly to a Mac through USB or Ethernet, or connect it to an AirPort Base Station or Time Capsule (which is the best option because it does not depend on the Mac running for the printer to be available on the network). See Chapter 7 for information about setting up a wireless network.

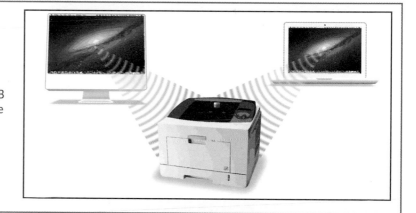

PDF

Adobe invented the Portable Document Format (PDF) as a means to share and print documents that do not depend on the specific applications or fonts installed on a computer. PDF is the standard format for electronic documents, no matter how they are distributed. This is good news for Mac users because support for PDF documents is built into OS X. You can read PDF documents using the Preview application, but more importantly for this chapter, you can also print any document to the PDF format so that you can easily share it with others through e-mail or over the web.

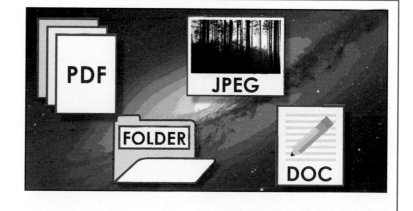

Install and Configure a USB Printer

Connecting a USB printer directly to a MacBook Pro is simple, and almost all inkjet printers, as well as some laser printers, support USB connections. After you have connected the printer to your MacBook Pro, you need to configure your computer to use it.

To print to a specific printer, your MacBook Pro must have that printer's driver software installed on it. In most cases, OS X downloads the printer's current software and installs the appropriate software automatically as soon as you add the printer to your computer.

Install and Configure a USB Printer

1. Connect the printer to a power source and turn it on.

2. Connect the printer to the MacBook Pro using a USB cable.

3. Click **Apple** (🍎) and select **System Preferences**.

4. Click the **Print & Scan** icon.

5. Click **Add** (➕).

6. Select **Add Printer or Scanner**.

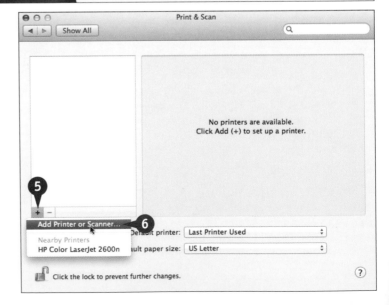

⑦ Click the printer you connected with the USB cable.

Note: If you are prompted to download and install software, you can click **Install** to do so now or click **Not Now** and the software will be installed after step **8**.

⑧ Click **Add**.

Your MacBook Pro downloads and installs any necessary software. This process can take several minutes.

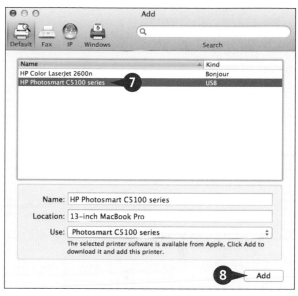

Ⓐ You return to the Print & Scan window and see the printer you added.

⑨ If you want the printer to be the default, select it from the **Default printer** pop-up menu.

⑩ Select the default paper size from the **Default paper size** pop-up menu.

The printer is ready to use.

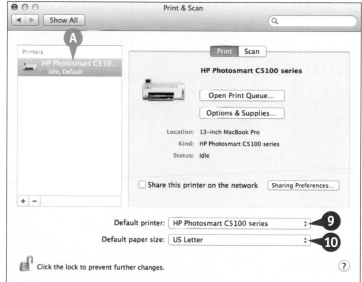

TIPS

Can I use any printer with a MacBook Pro?
It depends. A compatible printer must support a connection technology that MacBook Pro supports (which is true for almost all printers). More importantly, a printer must have Mac-compatible drivers; most printers do have Mac drivers available, and OS X either includes them or downloads them for you automatically.

How do I install printer software if it does not install automatically?
Go to the manufacturer's website, look for the Support page, and then look for the Downloads section; there you can search for a Mac driver for the printer. When you find it, you can download and install it. (You may need to change your Gatekeeper setting as explained in Chapter 9.) Then, add the printer again. This time, you will be able to select the appropriate driver.

Install and Configure a Network Printer

Your MacBook Pro is wireless so you do not have to use a cable to print. Fortunately, many printers are designed to connect to a network so that any computer that can connect to that network can use the printer. This is especially useful when a hub provides a wireless network.

One way to connect a printer to a network is by using Ethernet. This provides fast and trouble-free connections. The only downside is that the printer has to be within cable range of a hub, such as an AirPort Extreme Base Station or an Ethernet hub, on the network.

Install and Configure a Network Printer

1. Connect the printer to a power source and turn it on.

2. Connect the printer to a hub using an Ethernet cable.

3. Connect the MacBook Pro to the same network using Wi-Fi or an Ethernet cable.

4. Click **Apple** (🍎) and select **System Preferences**.

5. Click the **Print & Scan** icon.

The Print & Scan pane appears.

6. Click **Add** (➕).

7. Select the printer you want to use.

OS X downloads and installs the software for the printer, if necessary.

8 Configure any options for the printer if prompted and then click **OK**.

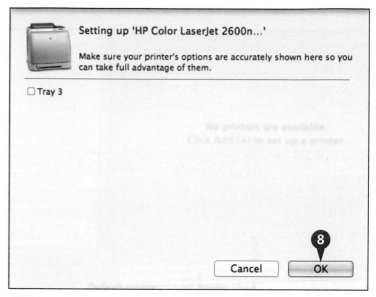

Setting up 'HP Color LaserJet 2600n...'

Make sure your printer's options are accurately shown here so you can take full advantage of them.

☐ Tray 3

Cancel   OK

A You return to the Print & Scan window and see the printer you added.

9 If you want the printer to be the default, select it from the **Default printer** pop-up menu.

10 Select the default paper size from the **Default paper size** pop-up menu.

The printer is now ready to use.

Print & Scan

Show All

Printers

HP Color LaserJet 2600n
Idle, Default

HP Color LaserJet 2600n

Open Print Queue...

Options & Supplies...

Location:
Kind: HP Color LaserJet 2600, 1.3.0.261
Status: Idle

☐ Share this printer on the network   Sharing Preferences...

Default printer: HP Color LaserJet 2600n

Default paper size: US Letter

Click the lock to prevent further changes.

TIP

What is Bonjour?
Bonjour is the OS X network discovery technology. When a device can use Bonjour, it broadcasts its identity on the network. When you connect to that network to search for a device, such as a printer, Bonjour devices are discovered automatically and you do not have to search for them or deal with their network addresses. You simply select the device you want to access and connect to it.

If you do not print very often or you mostly print photos, an inkjet printer might be your best option. However, if you print a lot or print mostly text documents, a laser printer will save you money over the long run. For the ultimate in printing, get a color laser printer, which is not as expensive as it sounds.

Print to Paper

With at least one printer connected to your MacBook Pro, you are ready to print. The steps to start the print process are the same, regardless of what type of printer you are using. However, each printer offers its own set of options, so the configuration for your print job will depend on your type of printer.

After you print to a printer the first time, you will often use the same settings, so you can just skip the configuration of options.

Print to Paper

Select Pages

1. With a document you want to print open, click **File** and select **Print**.

A The Print sheet appears and you see a preview of the document.

2. Select the printer you want to use from the **Printer** menu; if you want to use the current printer, skip this step.

3. Set the number of copies.

4. Use the **Pages** menu to select the number of pages you want to print (see the first Tip for details).

5. If you are ready to print, click **Print** and skip the rest of these steps.

6. To select more printing options, click **Show Details**.

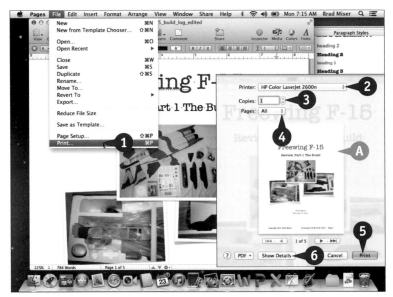

Cover Page Options

Note: The details and options you see depend on the specific printer you are using. This example shows an HP Color LaserJet 2600n. Explore the menus and options for your printer to see what is available to you.

7. To preview the document, click **Forward** (▶) or **Back** (◀).

8. To print specific pages, click **From** and type the starting and ending pages in the boxes.

9. Click the arrows and select the option you want to configure from the pop-up menu.

10. Configure the cover page options.

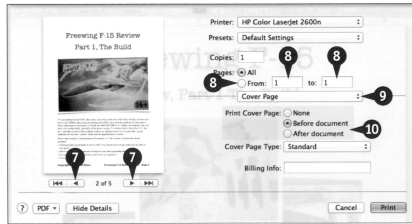

Paper Handling Options

11 Repeat steps **9** and **10** to select any other options you want to configure, such as Paper Handling.

12 Configure the paper handling options.

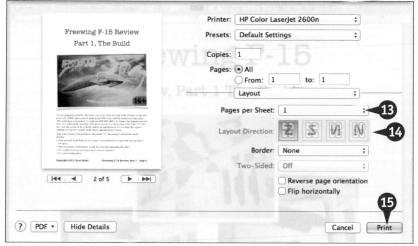

Layout Options

13 Click the arrows and select the **Layout**.

14 Configure the layout options.

15 Click **Print**.

The document prints to the selected printer using the options you configured.

TIPS

How do I print only specific pages?
In the Print sheet, open the **Pages** menu and select **Range**. The range boxes appear. In the first box, type the page at which you want to start printing. In the second box, type the page at which you want to stop printing. Complete the rest of the print process; only the pages in the range you selected will print.

How can I monitor and control printing?
When you print, an application with the name of the printer you are using opens. In this application, you can see the status of all the print jobs sent to the printer. You can also select a print job and click **Pause** to stop it, **Delete** to remove it, and so on.

Print to PDF

The Portable Document Format, or PDF, is a great way to distribute documents you create to other people. This is because PDF files appear correctly on any computer equipped with a PDF reader application, regardless of the fonts installed on it, and people cannot easily change PDF documents you create.

Support for creating PDF documents is built into OS X so that you can create a PDF file from any file you work with. The filename extension for PDFs is .pdf. It is added automatically, so you just need to make sure you do not change it.

Print to PDF

1 Open the document from which you want to create a PDF file.

2 Click **File** and select **Print**.

3 Click the **PDF** down arrow.

4 Select **Save as PDF** from the drop-down list.

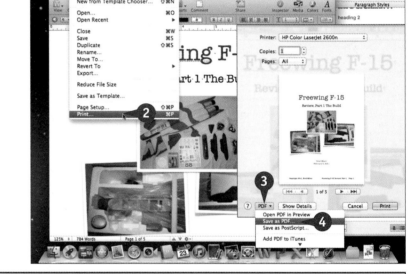

5 Type a name for the PDF file you are creating.

6 Choose the location in which you want to save the PDF file from the **Where** pop-up menu.

7 Type a title for the PDF file.

8 Type the author's name.

9 Type an additional subject.

10 Type keywords used during Spotlight and other searches, in the Keywords field, using commas to separate the keywords.

11 To set passwords for the PDF file, click **Security Options**.

12 To require a password to open the PDF file, click the **Require password to open document** check box and type the password in the Password and Verify fields.

13 To require a password to copy content from the document, click the **Require password to copy text, images and other content** check box and then type the password in the Password and Verify fields.

14 To require a password to print a document, click the **Require password to print document** check box and type the password in the Password and Verify fields.

15 Click **OK**.

16 Click **Save**.

The application creates the PDF file.

PDF Security Options

12 ☑ Require password to open document

Password: •••••••••

Verify: •••••••••

13 ☑ Require password to copy text, images and other content

14 ☑ Require password to print document

Password: •••••••••

Verify: •••••••••

(?) Cancel OK **15**

Save As: FW-15_build_log ▼

Where: 📄 Documents ⬍

Title: FW-15_build_log

Author: Brad Miser

Subject: Free Wing F-15

Keywords: (RC) (F-15) (Build Log) EDF

Security Options...

Cancel Save **16**

TIPS

What applications can open a PDF document?
By default, PDF documents open in the OS X Preview application, which provides the basic set of tools you need to view and print them. A number of other applications can open PDF files as well, most notably the free Adobe Reader application, available at http://www.adobe.com. Reader offers many features for viewing and working with PDF documents.

What if I want to configure or change a PDF document?
If you want to change a PDF or to create more sophisticated PDFs with features such as tables of contents, hyperlinks, and combinations of PDF documents in different formats, you can use Adobe Acrobat. Acrobat is also available on the Adobe website at http://www.adobe.com, but it requires a license fee to use.

Explore the Contacts Window

Contacts is both a powerful and easy to use contact information manager. You can quickly build your contact information and then use that information in many ways.

You can open Contacts by clicking its Dock icon, which is a book with the @ symbol on its cover, or by double-clicking its icon in the Applications folder. Before you start using Address Book Contacts, check out a few important concepts to help you master your contacts quickly and easily.

A Toolbar

Provides the View buttons and other controls.

B Groups

Shows the groups in which your contacts are organized.

C List

Shows the contacts in the group you are currently browsing.

D Search Bar

Enables you to search for contacts.

E Selected Group

You can select a group to browse the contacts it contains.

F Selected Card

The highlight shows the card selected on the List.

G Card

Shows the detailed contact information for the card selected on the List.

H Add Card

Enables you to add cards (new contacts).

I Edit

Use this button to change the information on the card being shown.

J Share

Use this button to send the current card to someone via e-mail.

Cards

Each contact is represented by a card. Like Rolodex cards of old, Contacts cards contain contact information. Unlike physical cards, Contacts cards are virtual cards, or *vCards*, making them flexible because you can store a variety of information on each card. You can also store different information for various contacts.

Wyatt Earp
"Lawdawg"
Dodge City Marshall

Contact Information

Each card in Contacts can hold many physical addresses, phone numbers, e-mail addresses, URL addresses, and so on. Because vCards are flexible, you do not have to include each kind of information; you include only the information appropriate for each contact. Contacts displays only fields that have data in them so that cards are not cluttered up with empty fields.

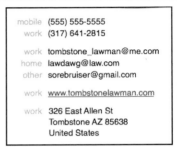

mobile	(555) 555-5555
work	(317) 641-2815
work	tombstone_lawman@me.com
home	lawdawg@law.com
other	sorebruiser@gmail.com
work	www.tombstonelawman.com
work	326 East Allen St Tombstone AZ 85638 United States

Groups

Groups are collections of cards. They are useful because you can do something once with a group and the action affects all the cards in that group. For example, you can create a group containing family members whom you regularly e-mail. Then, you can address a message to the one group instead of addressing each person individually.

All Contacts

On My Mac
All on My Mac

iCloud
All iCloud
Book Group

Smart Groups

Smart Groups are also collections of cards for which you define criteria and cards are added to the group automatically. For example, suppose you want a group for people with a specific last name. You can simply create a Smart Group with that criterion, and Contacts adds all the people with that last name to the group automatically.

Contacts Actions

In addition to using information stored on cards indirectly — for example, looking at a phone number to dial it — you can use some data to perform an action by clicking on the information's label and choosing an action. Some of the most useful actions are sending e-mails, visiting websites, and looking up an address on a map.

Add a Contact Manually

Before you can work with contacts, you need to create a card for the contacts you want to manage. You can capture contact information on cards in Contacts in several ways.

One way is to manually create a card and add contact information to it. This is easy to do and you can choose the specific information you add for a new contact. You can add new fields to cards as needed so that there is practically no limit to the amount of information you can store on a card. In many cases, you start a new card from another application, such as Mail, and add information to it by editing the card, which works similarly to creating a new card.

Add a Contact Manually

1 Click **Add Card** (⊞).

A new, empty card appears in the Card pane.

2 Type the contact's first name in the First field, which is highlighted.

3 Press **Tab**.

4 Type the contact's last name in the Last field.

5 Press **Tab**.

6 Type the contact's company or organization in the Company field.

If the card is for a company, check the **Company** check box and type the company name.

7 Press **Tab**.

8 Click the pop-up menu (▯) next to the first field (Work, by default).

9 Select the type of contact information you want to enter.

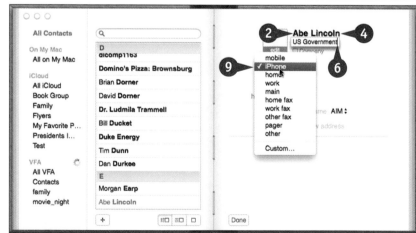

10 Type the selected information in the field, such as a phone number or e-mail address.

11 Repeat steps **7** to **10** to enter information into each field to which you want to add information.

12 To remove a field from the card, click **Delete** (⊟).

13 To add another field of the same type to a card, use the Add New field that appears when you have filled in all the existing fields of that type.

14 To add an image to the card, drag it from the desktop and drop it onto the image well.

A sheet that enables you to resize and place the image appears.

15 Drag the slider to the left to make the image smaller, or to the right to make it larger.

16 Drag the image so that the part you want to appear on the card is contained within the box.

17 Repeat steps **15** and **16** until the image is sized and placed as you want it.

18 Click **Done**.

The image is saved, the sheet closes, and you return to the card.

19 Click **Done**.

The card is saved and only fields containing information are shown.

TIPS

What if the information I want to enter is not available on a pop-up menu?
If the information you want to enter is not shown in the pop-up menu, click the menu arrow and select **Custom**. Type the label for the field you want to add and then click **OK**. You return to the card, and the custom label appears on the card. Enter the information for that field. The custom field is added to the card.

How can I configure the default information that appears on new cards?
Open the **Contacts** menu and choose **Preferences**. Click **Template**. Remove fields you do not want to appear by default by clicking **Delete** (⊟). Add more fields of an existing type by clicking **Add** (⊕) next to that type. Add fields that do not appear at all by clicking **Add Field** and then choosing the field you want to add to the template. Close the Preferences dialog.

Work with vCards

Many applications, including Contacts, use vCards to store contact information. One of the most common ways to receive vCards is through e-mail as attachments. You can simply drag the vCard from the e-mail onto your desktop. vCard files have .vcf as their filename extension.

You can add contact information to Contacts using vCards other people send to you; once you have added these cards, you can use them just like those you create in Contacts manually. You can also create a vCard for yourself to send to others so they can easily add your data to their contact information.

Work with vCards

Add Contacts with vCards

1 Drag the vCard file onto your desktop.

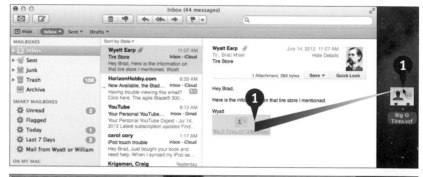

2 Drag the vCard file from the desktop onto the List pane of the Contacts window.

A sheet appears, confirming that you are adding a new card.

3 Click **Add**.

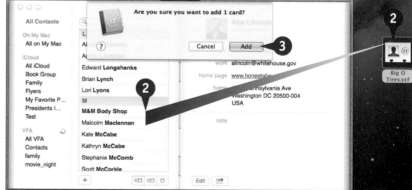

Ⓐ The vCard is added to Contacts; you can work with it just like cards you create within Contacts.

Create vCards from Contacts Cards

❶ Search or browse for the cards for which you want to create vCards.

Note: To quickly find your card, open the Card menu and choose Go to My Card. Your card, which is marked with a silhouette icon, appears in the Card pane.

❷ Drag the card from Contacts onto your desktop.

Note: The filename of the vCard is the name of the contact.

The vCard is created, and you can provide it to other people. They can then add its contact information to their contact manager.

Ⓑ You can easily e-mail a card by clicking its **Share** button. A new e-mail message with the card attached is created.

TIP

How can I add contact information to Contacts from e-mails when a vCard is not attached?
When you receive an e-mail in Mail, you can add the sender's name and e-mail address to Contacts. Position the pointer over an address and when the address becomes highlighted, click the trackpad button to open the action menu. Choose **Add to Contacts**. A new card is created with as much information as Contacts can extract, usually the first and last name along with an e-mail address. Using Contacts, you can add other information to the card as needed.

Find Contact Information

The whole point of having contact information is being able to find and use the information you need. Contacts makes it simple to quickly find information you are interested in.

You can find information by browsing your contacts. Or, you can search for specific contact information. Browsing is most useful when you do not have many contacts or if you have them organized into groups containing a relatively small number of contacts, browsing is fast and easy to do. Searching is usually the fastest way to find a contact because you can quickly get to any contact in the Contacts application; searching is also simple.

Find Contact Information

Browse for a Contact

1. Press ⌘+1 to move to the Groups view.

2. Select the group that you want to browse.

   A. To browse all your contacts, click **All Contacts**.

   B. The cards in the selected group appear on the List.

3. Scroll to browse up and down the list of names.

4. Click the card containing the contact information you want to view or to use, such as someone to whom you want to send an e-mail.

   The card's information appears on the card pane of the Contacts window.

5. To focus on the card only, press ⌘+3.

   C. Contacts moves into the Card Only view.

6. To move among the cards in the current group, click the forward or back buttons.

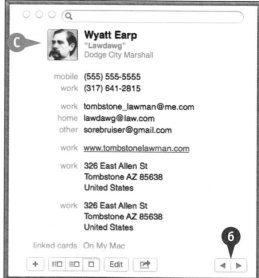

274

Search for a Contact

1 Select the group that you want to search.

Note: You can search in any view. When you search in Groups or List and Card view, you search in the selected group. When you search in Card Only view, you search the All Contacts group.

All the cards in the selected group appear in the Name pane.

2 Type search text in the Search bar.

Note: Contacts searches all the fields at the same time, so you do not need to define what you are searching for, such as a name instead of an address.

Ⓓ As you type, Contacts reduces those shown to only those that match your search.

3 Continue typing in the Search bar until the card you want appears in the Name pane.

4 Click the card to view its information.

Ⓔ The part of the card that matches your search is highlighted in gray.

5 Clear the Search bar by clicking **Stop Search** (Ⓧ).

All the cards in the selected group appear again.

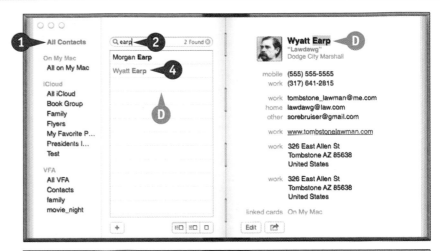

Can I search for contact information by phone number or e-mail address?
When you perform a search, Contacts searches all the fields on all cards simultaneously. If it finds a match in any of these fields, a card is included in the search results shown in the Name pane. For example, if you enter text, it looks for matches in any fields that include text. Likewise, if you type numbers, Contacts searches any fields containing numbers.

Can I browse or search in multiple groups at the same time?
You cannot browse the cards in multiple groups at the same time; you can browse only one group at a time by selecting the group you want to browse. You get the best search results if you search only with the All Contacts group selected.

Create an Address Group

A group is useful because it enables you to store many cards within it. Then you can take an action on the group and it affects all the cards included in the group. Groups make working with multiple cards at the same time easier and faster.

For example, when you want to send an e-mail to everyone in a group, you can do so easily and quickly by sending one message to the group rather than adding each person's e-mail address individually. You can also create a group for contacts that you use frequently to make finding contacts by browsing faster.

Create an Address Group

1 Point to the area to the right of the location where you want to store the group, such as iCloud if you want to keep the group in your iCloud account.

2 Click **Add** (⊕).

A new group appears in the Group pane with its name ready to be edited.

3 Type a name for the group.

4 Press **Return**.

The group is created and is ready for you to add cards to it.

5 Click **All Contacts**.

All the cards in Contacts are shown in the Name pane.

6 Browse or search for the first card you want to add to the group.

Note: See the previous section, "Find Contact Information," for the steps to browse and search.

276

7 Drag the card onto the group to which you want to add it; when the group is highlighted, release the trackpad button.

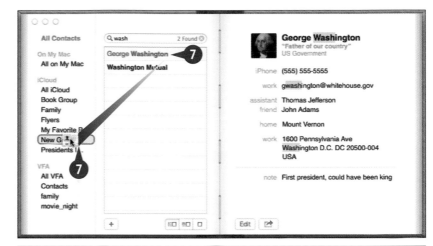

8 Select the group to which you added cards.

Ⓐ The cards included in the group are shown.

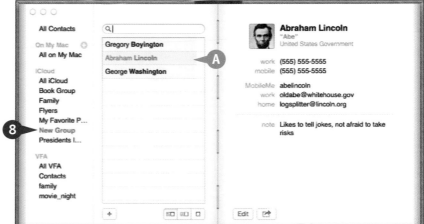

Can I add more than one card to a group at the same time?
Yes. To add multiple cards to a group at the same time, press and hold ⌘ while you click each card that you want to add to the group. Then you can drag all the cards you have selected onto the group at the same time.

How do I create a Smart Group?
Open the **File** menu and choose **New Smart Group**. Type the name of the group. Use the pop-up menus and other controls to configure the first criterion, such as "Name includes Smith." Click **Add** (⊕) to create more criteria. Choose **all** if you require that all the criteria be met, or **any** if you want only one criterion to be required. Click **OK**.

Use Address Cards and Groups

After you have added all that great contact information, Contacts helps you use your contacts in many ways. For example, you can quickly create and address a new e-mail address using a contact's card. Or, you can see a physical address on a map and visit a website just with a couple of clicks on a contact's card. Unlike physical contact information, such as a Rolodex, contacts in the Contacts application can be used directly to perform tasks. Check out the following tricks that Contacts can do for you. While these are not all you can do with contacts, they will get you started.

Use Address Cards and Groups

Address E-Mail

1. Find the card for the person you want to e-mail.

2. Click the label for the e-mail address, such as **work** if you want to send an e-mail to the work e-mail address.

   The contextual menu appears.

3. Choose **Send Email**.

   Your default e-mail application opens, and a new message to the address you selected in step **2** is created.

Visit Websites

1. Find a card with a home page or other web page URL on it.

2. Click the label next to the URL you want to visit.

Note: If the URL is in blue, you can click it to go to the related website.

3. Choose **Open URL**.

   Your default web application takes you to the URL you clicked.

Map a Physical Address

1 Find the card containing the address you want to map.

2 Click the label of the address you want to see on a map.

The contextual menu appears.

3 Choose **Map this Address**.

Your default web application takes you to a Google map showing the address you clicked.

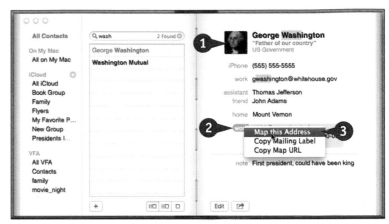

Print an Envelope or Mailing Label

1 Find the card containing the address for which you want a mailing label.

2 Click the label of the address you want to place on an envelope or label.

The contextual menu appears.

3 Choose **Copy Mailing Label**.

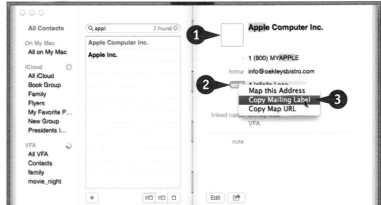

4 Open the application you use to print envelopes or labels.

This example uses a widget called Easy Envelopes from Ambrosia Software.

5 If the address is not inserted automatically, open the **Edit** menu and then select **Paste**, or press ⌘+V to insert the address.

A Once the address is in the application, use the application's printing feature to print the envelope or label.

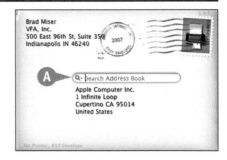

TIP

How can I share my Contacts with other people?
You can easily share your Contacts. Move to the card you want to share. Click the **Share** button ( ). On the resulting menu, choose **Email Card** to send it via an e-mail message, **Message Card** to send it via a Messages message, or **AirDrop Card** to send the card to another Mac user via AirDrop.

Change or Delete Address Cards or Groups

Over time, you will need to update your Contacts by adding new information, changing existing information, or removing information you no longer need. Fortunately, with Contacts, all these tasks are simple.

You can change information for cards or groups that you want to continue to use. You can add new information to a card using steps similar to those used when you create a new card manually. You can also remove information for a card or change existing information. When you decide you do not want a card or group anymore, you can delete it. When you delete a group, the cards it contained remain in the Contacts application.

Change or Delete Address Cards or Groups

Change Address Cards

1. Search or browse for the card you want to change.

2. Click **Edit**.

   Existing fields become editable and Delete buttons (⊖) appear.

3. Click the information you want to change.

4. Make changes to that information.

Note: You move between fields on a card by pressing `Return` or `Tab`.

5. To delete information from the card, click ⊖.

   The field clears; after you exit Edit mode, that field no longer appears on the card.

6. To add information to the card, enter it in an existing field, or if all the current fields are full, enter it in the add new field section for the type of information you want to add.

7. Choose a label for the new field on the pop-up menu.

8 Type information into the new field.

9 After you have made all the changes to the card, click **Done**.

The changes you made to the card are saved.

Delete Cards from Address Groups

1 Select the group you want to change.

2 Select a card you want to remove from the group.

3 Press **Delete**.

A warning sheet appears.

4 Click **Remove from Group**.

If you started with a manually created group, the card is removed from the group, but remains in Contacts. If you started with a Smart Group, the card is deleted from Contacts, so be careful not to delete a card from a Smart Group that you want to keep.

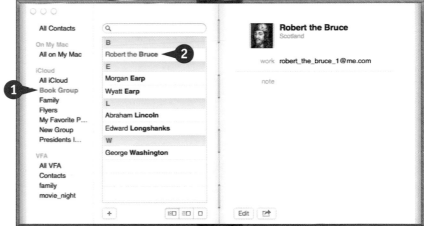

TIPS

How do I delete a card I do not need anymore?
Select the card you want to remove and press **Delete**. Click **Delete** in the confirmation sheet. The card is removed from Contacts.

How do I delete a group I do not need?
Select the group you want to delete and press **Delete**. Click **Delete** in the confirmation sheet. The group is removed from Contacts; however, the cards in that group remain in Contacts.

Print Envelopes and Contact Lists

While many of the benefits of the Contacts application are because it is digital, it is useful to be able to apply the information in Contacts in the physical world. Contacts enables you print your contact information a number of ways, including mailing labels, envelopes, contact lists, and a pocket address book. The details of each of these tasks are slightly different, but the general process is the same so once you have printed one type, you can print the others as easily.

Printing envelopes takes the tedium out of addressing envelopes and makes envelopes look better. Contact lists are a good way to carry contact information with you when you do not have your MacBook Pro handy.

Print Envelopes and Contact Lists

Print Envelopes

1. Select the cards for which you want to print envelopes.

2. Press ⌘+P.

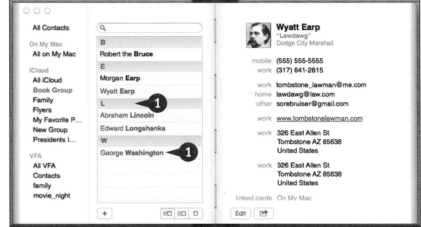

3. Choose **Envelopes** on the **Style** pop-up menu.

Note: If you do not see these options, click Show Details.

4. Click the **Label** tab.

5. On the **Print my address** pop-up menu, choose which of your addresses you want to print as the return address on the envelope.

6. On the **Addresses** pop-up menu, choose the addresses for the contacts to which you want to address the envelopes, such as work or home.

7. Use the **Print in** pop-up menu to determine the order in which the envelopes print.

8. Check the check boxes for additional information you want to include on the envelope, such as **Company** or **Country**.

9. Use the color button to set the color of the text printed on the envelopes.

10. Click **Print**.

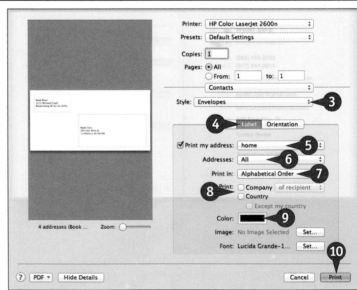

Print Contact Lists

1 Select the cards you want to include on the list; to include everyone in a group on the list, click the group.

2 Press ⌘+P.

3 Click the **Style** arrows and select **Lists** from the pop-up menu.

4 Click the **Orientation** buttons to set the orientation of the list (portrait or landscape).

5 Click the check box for each kind of information you want to include for the contacts on the printed list.

6 Click the **Font Size** arrows and select the list font from the pop-up menu.

7 Click **Print**.

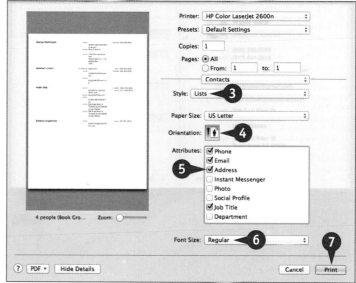

TIPS

What is a pocket address book?

A pocket address book is a smaller version of a contact list designed to be carried more easily than a list. A pocket address book can be printed in a couple of formats, including Index, which shows contacts by alphabetical order, or Compact, which uses a compressed format.

How can I print addresses on standard mailing labels, such as those produced by Avery?

On the **Style** pop-up menu, choose **Mailing Labels**. Click the **Layout** tab. On the **Page** pop-up menu, choose the brand of labels you use and then choose the specific type on the related pop-up menu. This creates a format for the addresses that will fit onto the selected label when you print.

Explore Calendar

Calendar is OS X's calendar application. As you can probably guess, you can use it to track calendar events; however, Calendar goes beyond these basics.

One of the best things about Calendar is that you can share your calendars on the web so that other people can work with them. By subscribing to other people's calendars, you can see what they are up to, which makes coordinating events among a group of people much easier. You can also use Calendar to directly coordinate events with other people, such as inviting people to a meeting you are hosting.

Ⓐ Back and Forward Buttons

Click these buttons to move back or forward in the calendar; these work when you are viewing the calendar by day, week, month, or year.

Ⓑ View Selection Buttons

Use these buttons to determine whether you view the calendar by day, week, month, or year.

Ⓒ Search Bar

Enables you to search events on your calendars.

Ⓓ Calendars

Enables you to manage the calendars with which you are working.

Ⓔ Create Quick Event

Enables you to create an event with basic information.

Ⓕ Events

Colored blocks represent events; the color indicates the calendar on which those events are stored.

Ⓖ All-Day Events

At the top of each day, you see the events that are scheduled across the entire day.

Ⓗ Accounts

Calendars are associated with specific accounts, such as iCloud, Exchange, and so on.

Create a Calendar

In Calendar, you store events and reminders on a calendar. You can have as many calendars as you want. For example, you might want one calendar for work information and another for family events.

You can configure a calendar so its events appear in the Calendar window or are hidden. In addition, each calendar can have its own color so that you can see what events and reminders are associated with it. You can create calendars for online accounts, such as iCloud or Exchange. This is useful because you can then access your calendars from other devices, such as an iPhone.

Create a Calendar

1 Launch Calendar by clicking its icon on the Dock.

The Calendar window opens.

2 Click **File**, click **New Calendar,** and then click the account on which you want to store the calendar, such as **iCloud**.

The new calendar appears on the list. Its name is ready to edit.

3 Type the name of the calendar and press **Return** to save it.

4 Perform a secondary click on the new calendar.

5 Select **Get Info**.

The calendar's Info sheet appears.

6 Type a description of the calendar in the Description field.

7 If you want alarms on the calendar to be ignored, check the **Ignore alerts** check box.

8 Select the color you want to associate with the calendar on the color pop-up menu.

9 If you do not want events on the calendar to affect your availability for events, uncheck the **Events affect availability**.

10 Click **OK**.

The sheet closes and the new calendar is ready to use.

Add an Event to a Calendar

An event in Calendar is a period of time for which you want to plan, such as a meeting, recurring activity, vacation, or other happening that is important to you. Events are associated with a specific time period on a calendar within Calendar. They can also have lots of other information, including file attachments and web addresses.

You can create events on a calendar and then configure them in many ways, such as the time, date, and alarms. You can drag to create events when viewing the calendar by Day or Week. You can double-click a date in Month view to create an event. You cannot create events in Year view.

Add an Event to a Calendar

1 Move to the calendar and to the date on which you want to create an event.

2 Drag over the time period for the event; drag across multiple days if the event extends beyond one day.

3 Release the trackpad button when you reach the end of the event.

The new event is created and its name is highlighted.

4 Type the name of the event.

5 Press **Return** to save it.

6 Double-click the event.

A A summary of the event appears.

7 Click **Edit**.

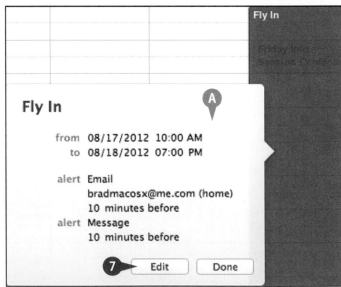

The event's Info window appears. Here you can edit and add to the event's information.

8 Edit the name, if needed.

9 Enter a location for the event.

10 If needed, change the event's dates and times using the date and time tools.

11 If the event repeats, select the frequency of the event on the **repeat** pop-up menu, and set the last date on which the event should be scheduled on the **end** pop-up menu.

12 Use the **show as** pop-up menu to select how your availability appears to others if they try to schedule you for an event.

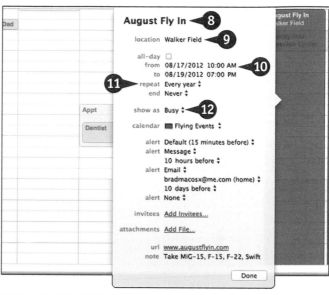

13 To change the calendar with which the event is associated, select a different calendar on the **calendar** pop-up menu.

14 To set alerts for the event, select the kind of alert on the **alert** pop-up menu, and then configure it using the controls that appear (these are based on the kind of alert you select).

15 To store a file on the event, click **Add File** and select the file you want to attach.

16 To include a URL with the event, type it in the **url** field.

17 Type notes for the event in the **note** field.

18 Click **Done**.

The event is saved on the calendar.

Note: To delete an event, select it and press `Delete`.

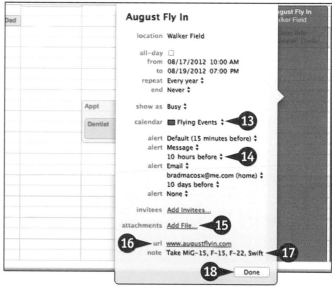

TIPS

What does the Create Quick Event button do?

When you click **Create Quick Event** (⊞), a sheet pops up. Type the name or other information about the event in the sheet and press `Return`. Calendar attempts to interpret what you type, such as dates, and creates an event accordingly. The event's Info window appears, showing the info Calendar entered automatically. You can configure the event using the same steps as in this section.

How can I be alerted to an event?

You can associate alerts with your events; an event can have multiple alerts. Alert options include Message that displays a message about the event; Message with Sound that displays a message and plays a sound; Email that sends an email about the event; or Open file that causes a file to open. If you do not want to be alerted about an event, select **None**.

Schedule and Manage Events with Other People

Many of the events you manage in Calendar involve other people, such as meetings you want to have, group activities, and so on. You can include other people in events by inviting them.

Each invitee receives an e-mail containing information about the event with a calendar item as an attachment. If the invitees also use Calendar or another compatible calendar application, they can accept or decline your invitation. When you open the event's Info window, you see the status of each invitation, such as a question mark when the invitee has not responded.

Schedule and Manage Events with Other People

Schedule an Event with Other People

1 Create an event as described in the previous section.

2 Click **Add Invitees**.

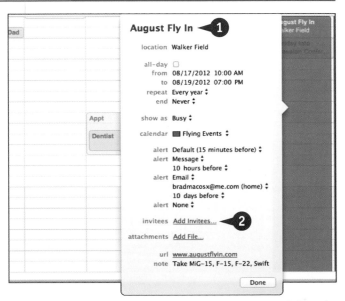

3 Enter the e-mail address of the first invitee.

Note: If possible, Calendar replaces the e-mail address with the person's name.

4 Press **Tab**.

Note: If Calendar presents the address you want to use, click it or select it and press @ret.

5 Repeat steps **3** and **4** until you have entered addresses for all the invitees.

6 Click **Send**.

Each person you invited receives a notification about the event. They can accept the event to add it to their calendar or they can decline.

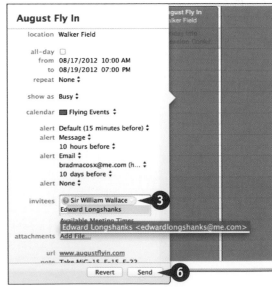

Accept or Decline Invitations

1 When you see the invitation badge on the Calendar icon or when a number appears in the Invitation button (⬇1), click it.

You see information about the event.

Note: To see the event on the calendar, click the event information box. The calendar scrolls so that you can see the event you are potentially adding to your calendar.

2 To add the event to your calendar, click **Accept**; to decline it, click **Decline**; or to indicate you are considering it, click **Maybe**.

The person who invited you to the event receives a notification about your decision.

Manage Events that Involve Other People

1 Open an event to which you have invited others.

Ⓐ The icon next to each name indicates the status of the person's attendance. For example, if the person has accepted the event, the icon is a check mark in a green circle (⊘).

2 When you finish viewing the status information, click **Done**.

Note: If you perform a secondary click on a person's name, you can choose from a number of actions, such as sending an e-mail, inviting again, and so on.

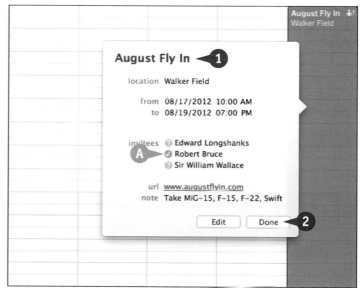

TIPS

How do I invite someone to an existing event?
Open the event and enter the e-mail address of the person you want to add to the event. Click **Send**. At the prompt, select if you want everyone to be updated or only the person you added to the event.

What if someone I invite does not use Calendar?
People who do not use Calendar or a compatible application receive an e-mail with information about the event and with the event as an attachment. If the person has a calendar application that is not compatible, he may be able to double-click the attachment to add the event to his calendar. If someone does not use Calendar, the status information for that person in Calendar may not be accurate.

Share Calendars

Calendar makes sharing your calendars with other people fast and easy. You can publish your calendars to the web so that people can view your calendars in a web browser or subscribe to them so that they can see them in their Calendar application. Calendars that you publish like this cannot be changed by the people who view them.

You can also share your calendar with other Calendar users. This enables calendar collaboration; for example, the other person can add or change events on the shared calendar. You should share a calendar only when you are comfortable that the recipient is trustworthy with your sensitive calendar information.

Share Calendars

Publish Calendars

1. Perform a secondary click on the calendar you want to publish and select **Share Calendar**.

The Publish calendar sheet appears.

2. Type the name of the published version of the calendar in the **Share calendar as** field if you do not want to use the default name.

3. Click **Everyone**.

4. Click **Share**.

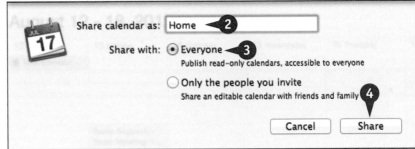

5. Perform a secondary click on the calendar you published and select **Resend Invitations**.

A new e-mail message is created; the message contains a link someone can use to subscribe to the calendar within Calendar (this is shown in the next section).

Note: To view the calendar in a web browser, select Copy URL to Clipboard, move into a web browser, and paste the URL in the address bar. You can also provide the URL to others so they can view the published calendar on the web.

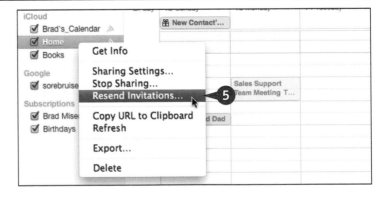

Share a Calendar with Others

1 Perform a secondary click on the calendar you want to publish and select **Share Calendar**.

The Publish calendar sheet appears.

2 Type the name of the published version of the calendar in the **Share calendar as** field if you do not want to use the default name.

3 Click **Only the people you invite**.

4 Click **Add** (⊞).

5 Type the name or e-mail address of the person with whom you want to share the calendar.

6 Select the permission the person will have for the calendar; select **Read & Write** if you want the person to be able to change the calendar or **Read only** if you do not.

7 Repeat steps **4** to **6** to share the calendar with other people.

8 Click **Share**.

Calendar starts sharing the calendar.

A When the people with whom you shared the calendar open Calendar and click the **Invitation** button (⬇1), they can choose to join the calendar, which adds it to Calendar, and they can start using it according to the permission you gave them.

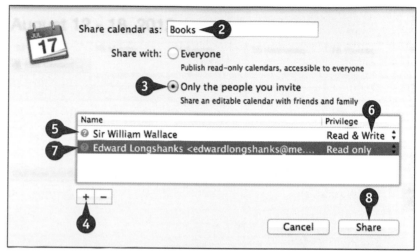

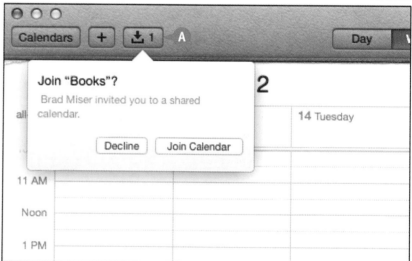

How do I stop publishing or sharing a calendar?
Perform a secondary click on the shared or published calendar. Select **Stop Sharing**. Click **Stop Sharing** at the prompt. The calendar is no longer available to others.

How can I tell if someone has accepted my calendar?
When someone accepts your calendar, you see a notification informing you about it. You can also perform a secondary click on the calendar and select **Sharing Settings**. You see the accepted icon (✓) next to people who have accepted the calendar.

Working with Shared Calendars

Other people who use Calendar can publish their calendars as easily as you can publish yours. When someone sends his calendar information to you, you can subscribe to the calendar or visit it on the web. If you subscribe to the calendar, you can only view its information.

When you subscribe to a calendar, it is added as a calendar to Calendar, and you can use Calendar's tools to view it (you cannot make changes to someone else's calendar). When you visit a calendar on the web, you view it through a web browser, such as Safari.

Working with Shared Calendars

Subscribe to Calendars

1 Open an e-mail message containing calendar subscription information.

2 Click the link in the message.

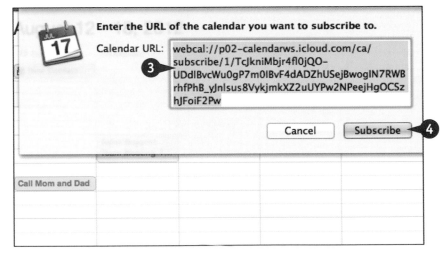

Calendar becomes active and the subscribe sheet appears.

3 Review the URL for the calendar to make sure you want to subscribe to it.

4 If so, click **Subscribe**.

Calendar downloads the calendar information, and you see the calendar's Info sheet.

5 If you want to change the name of the calendar as it appears in your Calendar application, edit the name in the Name field.

6 Use the color pop-up menu to associate a color with the calendar.

7 Choose where you want to store the calendar on the **Location** menu.

8 If you do not want alerts, attachments, or reminders removed, uncheck the respective **Remove** check boxes.

9 On the **Auto-refresh** pop-up menu, choose how often you want the calendar's information updated.

10 Click **OK**.

The calendar is added to Calendar in the Subscriptions section.

Work with a Shared Calendar

1 Open an e-mail containing the **Join Calendar** button.

Your default web browser opens your iCloud website.

2 Select the **Email me when this calendar changes** check box.

3 Click **OK**.

The calendar is added to Calendar.

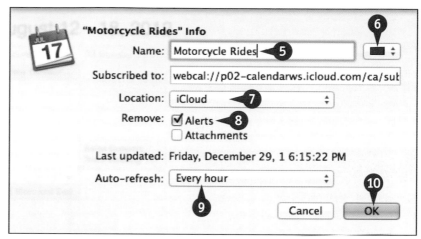

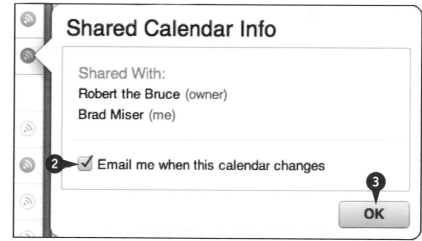

How do I know when people have changed a shared calendar?

When changes are made to a shared calendar, you receive notifications informing you about the change.

How can I keep track of birthdays?

If you keep birthday information for your contacts in the Contacts application, you can enable the Birthdays calendar in Calendar (see the next section). This creates an event for every birthday stored in Contacts. Set the reminders for the birthdays and you will always have a handle on birthdays that are important to you.

Configure Calendar Preferences

You can further tailor how Calendar works by changing its preferences. For example, on the General tab, you can determine whether weeks are five or seven days long and when days start. You can also configure the start and end time for the "working" part of the day. You do not have to make any changes to these settings for Calendar to work well for you, but it is a good idea to become familiar with the options to make it work even better for you. On the Advanced tab, you can determine how reminders are managed and control alarms for all Calendar events and reminders.

Configure Calendar Preferences

Configure Calendar Preferences

1 Press ⌘+,.

The Calendar Preferences dialog opens.

2 Click the **General** tab.

3 On the **Days per week** pop-up menu, select **5** if you want weeks to be shown as the five workdays, or **7** if you want to see all seven days.

4 On the **Start week on** pop-up menu, select the first day of the week.

5 On the **Scroll in week view by** pop-up menu, select how you want the calendar to scroll in this view, either by **Week** or **Day**.

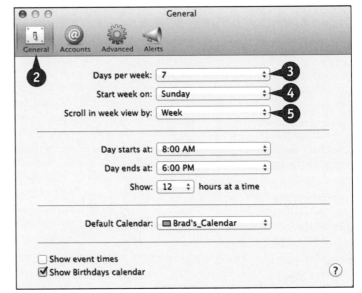

6 Use the **Day starts at** and **Day ends at** pop-up menus to define the times at which "work" days start and end.

Note: This setting controls the unshaded amount of each day on the calendar, indicating when you are "working."

7 On the **Show** pop-up menu, determine how many hours Calendar shows at once.

8 Choose the calendar you want to be selected by default when you create a new event.

9 If you want event times to be shown next to their titles, check the **Show event times** check box.

10 If you want the Birthdays calendar in Calendar to be shown, check the **Show Birthdays calendar** check box.

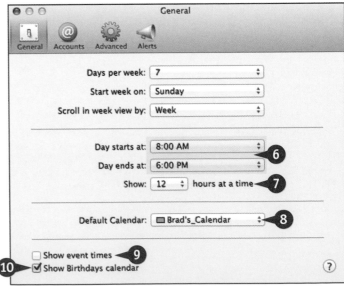

Configure Advanced Calendar Preferences

1 Press ⌘+,.

The Calendar Preferences dialog opens.

2 Click the **Advanced** tab.

3 If you want to be able to manage events in different time zones, check the **Turn on time zone support** check box.

4 If you want events to be shown when you are using the Year view, select the **Show events in year view** check box.

5 To show each week's number, select the **Show week numbers** check box.

6 If you want events to open in a separate window when you edit them instead of in the "floating" window, check the **Open events in separate windows** check box.

7 When you change an event, you can choose to be prompted before sending the event to its invitees by checking the **Ask before sending changes to events** check box.

8 If you want Mail to automatically retrieve event invitations you receive, check the bottom check box.

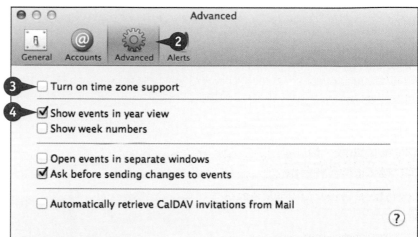

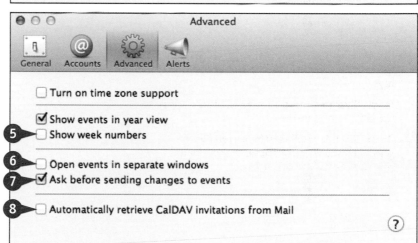

TIP

How does time zone support work?

When you enable time zone support, Calendar can help you manage the often confusing situation when you are managing events across multiple time zones. When you create an event, you can associate it with a specific time zone. When viewing your calendars, you can set the current Calendar time zone using the Time Zone pop-up menu located in the upper-right corner of the Calendar window. When you set this, all events are shifted according to the relationship between their specific time zones and Calendar's so that you see all events according to the current time zone. To see an event in a specific time zone (such as when you travel there), select that time zone on the pop-up menu.

Print Calendars

Although using an electronic calendar is convenient and more powerful than a paper-based calendar, sometimes you might want a paper calendar to carry with you for those situations in which you do not have your MacBook Pro with you for various reasons. You can use Calendar to print calendars in various formats and with specific options. There are quite a few options so it is a good idea to explore them for yourself to see which might be useful for you. Printed calendars can mimic Calendar's Day, Week, or Month view, or you can print a calendar list, which is an efficient way to print information for many events.

Print Calendars

Print Day, Week, or Month View

1. Open the **File** menu and select **Print**.

   The Print dialog appears.

2. On the **View** pop-up menu, select **Day**, **Week**, or **Month**.

   A. The preview of the calendar shown in the left pane of the dialog changes to reflect your selection.

3. Use the pop-up menus and boxes in the Time range section to determine how much calendar time is represented in the printed version.

4. Check the check boxes for the calendars you want included on the printed version; uncheck the check boxes for those calendars you do not want to include.

5. Use the Options check boxes to configure various options for the printed calendar, such as whether all-day events are shown or if the mini-calendar appears at the top of each page.

6. Use the **Text size** pop-up menu to set the relative size of the font used on the printed calendar.

7. Click **Continue**.

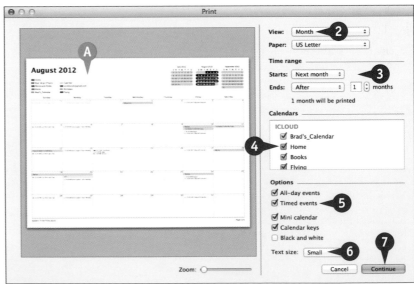

8 Use the printer's options to configure the print job; these are specific to the type of printer you are using.

9 Click **Print**.

The calendar prints according to your settings.

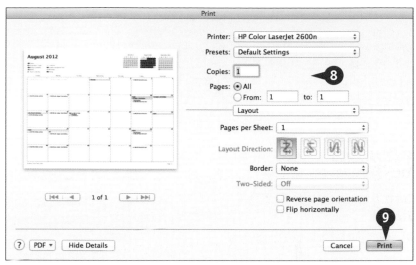

Print a Calendar List

1 Press ⌘+P.

The Print dialog appears.

2 Select **List** on the **View** pop-up menu.

B Calendar events and reminders are formatted in a list format, which makes them more compact than a calendar view.

3 Use the Time range tools to set the number of days included on the printed list.

4 Use the rest of the controls to set various options for the printed list, such as what calendars are included, whether timed events are included, and so on.

5 Click **Continue**.

6 Use the Print dialog to configure and print the list.

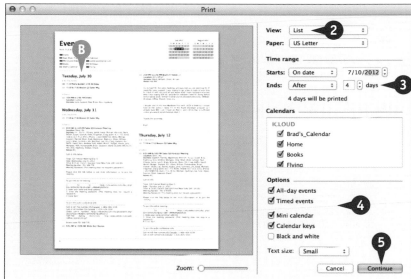

How can I access my calendars when I am away from my MacBook Pro?

When you use a calendar stored on an online account, such as iCloud, Google, or Exchange, you can access that calendar from any device that has web browser access by logging in to your iCloud website and using its Calendar application. You can also set up your accounts on iPhones, iPod touches, and iPads so that your calendars are available on those devices too.

How can I tell if someone is available for a meeting?

When you add invitees to an event, click the **Available Meeting Times** link. A window opens that shows each person you have invited; shading on the calendar indicates each person's status. Click **Next Available Time** to find a time when each person is available. Click **Done** to close the window.

Explore Reminders

The Reminders application does just what its name implies: It reminds you about "things." You can use it to remind you of anything that you want to be reminded of, such as items you have to do, things you want to pick up at the store, and so on. Reminders can have alerts associated with them so that you do not have to look at your reminder list to know when you are supposed to remember something.

Ⓐ Reminder Lists

You can create and manage multiple lists of reminders, such as a list for work and one for a hobby.

Ⓑ Current List

When you select a list, you see the reminders it contains.

Ⓒ Complete Reminders

When you mark a reminder as complete, it disappears from the list, but is still available by clicking the Completed link.

Ⓓ Priority

You can associate an importance level with your reminders; this is indicated by the exclamation marks.

Ⓔ Due Dates

You can assign a due date to reminders, or you can leave them without a date.

Ⓕ Complete Check Box

Check a reminder's check box to mark it as complete.

Ⓖ Show Calendar

When you click this, a mini-calendar appears in the lower left corner of the Reminders window.

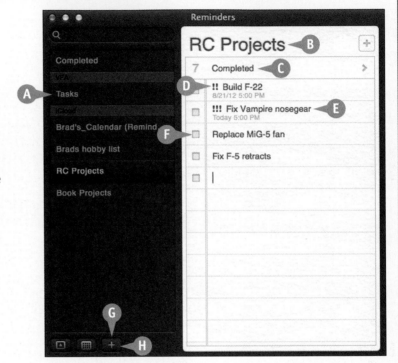

Ⓗ Add List

Click this and select a location in which to create a new list.

Create a Reminder

Whereas events are periods of time for which you want to plan and that you want to manage, reminders are specific actions that you want to perform or are something you want to remember. Reminders can contain basic information about something, such as a description, along with information to associate it with a date. Reminders are very useful to help you remember just about anything you want to remember, such as things you need to pick up at a store, something you need to take with you when you leave, and so on. You can configure reminders with alerts, a priority, and related information.

Create a Reminder

1 Select the list to which you want to add a reminder.

2 Click **Add** (⊞).

A new empty reminder is added to the list.

3 Type the title of the reminder.

4 Point to the right side of the window and click the **Info** button (ⓘ).

5 To set an alert for the reminder, select the **On a Day** check box.

6 Use the date and time tool to set when you want to be alerted.

7 Set the priority of the reminder.

8 Enter notes about the reminder.

9 Click **Done**.

The reminder is saved and appears on the selected list.

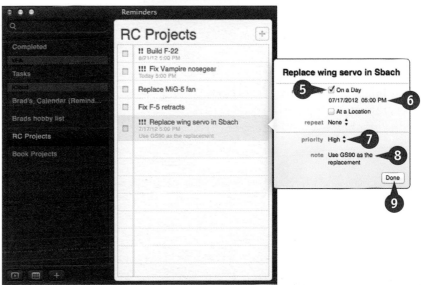

Keep App Store Software Current

Software developers regularly update their applications to improve them and to solve bugs. Apple is no different; it issues updates to its applications, but more importantly, to OS X and the other system software that makes a MacBook Pro work.

It is important that you keep your applications and system software current to ensure that your computer works as well as it can, to limit security issues, and so on. In addition to enabling you to obtain and download software, the App Store application can also help you keep your software up-to-date.

Keep App Store Software Current

Update App Store Software Manually

1 Click **Apple** (![apple]) and select **Software Update**.

The App Store application opens to the Updates tab and checks for updates to the software you have downloaded from the store. If updates are available, you see them listed.

Note: If there are not any updates, your software is current and you can click File and then select Quit to quit the App Store application.

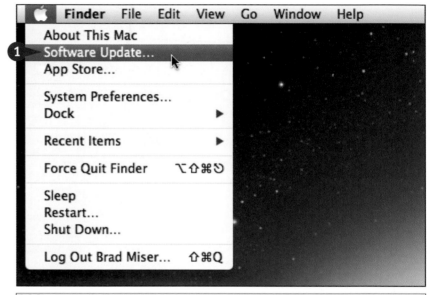

2 Click **Update** for the application you want to update.

Your MacBook Pro downloads and installs the update.

Note: Some updates require you to restart your MacBook Pro; click Restart at the prompt.

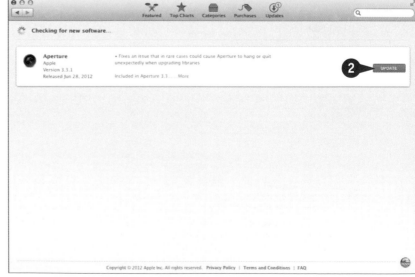

Update Apple Software Automatically

1 Click **Apple** and (![]) and select **System Preferences**.

2 Click the **Software Update** icon.

3 Check the **Automatically check for updates** check box.

4 Check the **Download newly available updates in the background** check box.

5 Check the **Install system data files and security updates** check box.

6 If you have more than one Mac and want all the apps you download on your other Macs to be downloaded to your MacBook Pro, check the **Automatically download apps purchased on other Macs** check box.

7 Quit the System Preferences application.

OS X automatically checks for updates and notifies you when they are available. It also downloads and installs important system and security files automatically.

TIPS

Should I really install all updates to my software?

Yes, you should generally install all updates as they become available. In rare situations, an update actually causes more problems than it solves; however, in such cases the problematic update is usually followed by one that quickly corrects these problems. You can simplify the update process by configuring your MacBook Pro for automatic updates.

How do I manually install all updates at the same time?

When more than one update is available, you see the UPDATE ALL button at the top of the Updates tab of the App Store application. Click that button to download and install all the updates that are available for your software.

Maintain and Update Applications Not from the App Store

You may have applications installed that you did not obtain from the App Store, such as those you have installed from the web or from a disc. Even though you cannot use the App Store to update these applications, you also need to keep them current.

Most applications support manual and automatic updates. Typically, you will find a Check for Updates command on the *Application* menu (where *Application* is the name of the application you are using) or Help menu. Most applications also support automatic checks for updates; one example is Snapz Pro X from Ambrosia Software.

Maintain and Update Applications Not from the App Store

Manually Update Apps

1. Open the application.

2. Click **Help**.

   Note: the Check for Updates command, and even what it is called, depend on the specific application you are working with. Check the Help menu first; if you do not see it there, check the user documentation.

3. Click **Check for Updates**.

   If updates are available, the application prompts you to download and install them; follow the onscreen instructions to complete the update. If updates are not available, you see a message saying so.

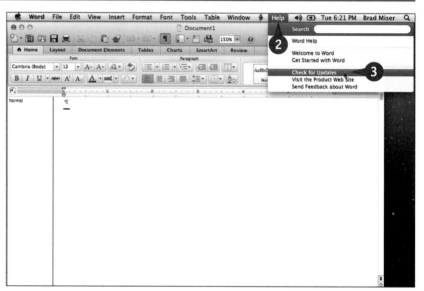

Automatically Update Apps

1. After launching the application, open its Preferences tools.

2. Select the option to check for updates automatically.

Note: This command may use different wording for different applications.

   Each time you launch the application, it checks for newer versions. When it finds one, it prompts you to download and install the newer version. Follow the onscreen instructions to complete the update.

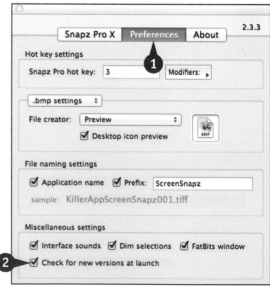

Profile Your MacBook Pro

Your MacBook Pro includes a lot of hardware and software components. Each of these components has a specific version and set of capabilities. Most of the time, you do not need to worry about these details.

However, sometimes they can be very important, especially when you are trying to troubleshoot and solve problems. Keeping a current profile of your MacBook Pro is a good idea so that you have detailed information about it should you need to solve a problem or evaluate your MacBook Pro capabilities.

Profile Your MacBook Pro

1 Click **Apple** (🍎) and select **About This Mac**.

The About This Mac window appears.

2 Click **More Info**.

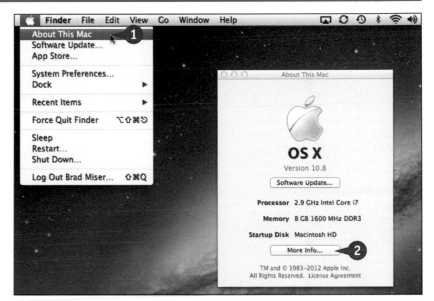

The System Information application appears.

Ⓐ At the top of the window, you see various categories of information about your MacBook Pro, such as hardware components.

3 Click the tab of an area for which you want detailed information.

Ⓑ The details appear in the bottom pane of the window.

4 Continue to select other areas to get details about them.

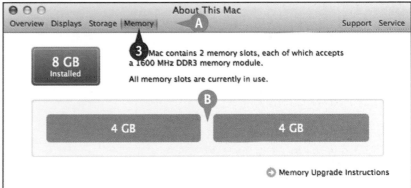

Monitor Your MacBook Pro Activity

You cannot always tell what is happening with a MacBook Pro just by looking at its screen or observing how applications are performing. Being able to identify what is happening on your MacBook Pro in detail is useful, especially when you are troubleshooting a problem.

With the Activity Monitor application, you can see the status of your MacBook Pro in a very detailed way. For example, you can see how much processing power specific applications are using, which can often tell you when an application is having a problem.

Monitor Your MacBook Pro Activity

1 Press ⌘+Shift+U to open the Utilities folder within the Applications folder.

2 Double-click the **Activity Monitor** icon.

The Activity Monitor application opens.

3 Click the **CPU** tab.

A In the upper part of the window, you see a list of all the processes running on the MacBook Pro.

B At the bottom of the window, you see a graphical representation of the activity of various MacBook Pro processes.

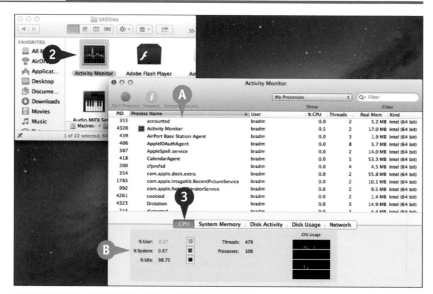

4 Click the **Disk Activity** tab.

C At the bottom of the window, you see how data is being read from and written to the disk.

5 Click the **% CPU** column heading to sort the list of processes by the amount of processor activity being used for each process.

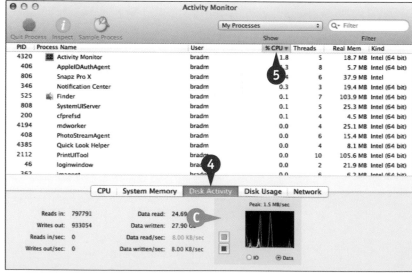

Note: You can limit the processes shown in the window to be just for applications, which can make the window's information easier to interpret.

6 From the pop-up menu at the top of the window, select **Windowed Processes**.

D The list now includes only processes associated with applications that have windows open on the desktop.

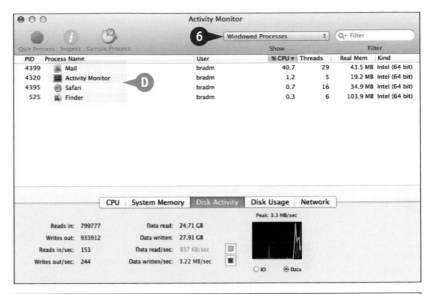

7 Click the **Disk Usage** tab.

8 Click the arrows and select the disk you want information about from the pop-up menu.

E The information at the bottom of the window shows how much of the disk is being used.

TIP

How do I deal with a process that is using a lot of CPU resources for a long period of time?

This often indicates that an application is *hung*, meaning that its processes are having a problem. Switch to the application and try to quit it. If it does not quit, the application is hung. Go back to Activity Monitor, select the process, and click the **Quit Process** button. Click **Force Quit**; the process is stopped. Forcing an application to quit loses any unsaved data that it contains, so make sure the application is really hung before doing this (wait several minutes to be sure that it is not busy working on a task). Save your work in other open applications, and then restart your MacBook Pro.

Maintain or Repair the Drive on Your MacBook Pro

If the drive on your MacBook Pro is not performing optimally, your MacBook Pro is not at its best either. You can do a lot for the drive by applying good housekeeping practices to it to keep as much free space available as possible (see the tip at the end of this section).

You cannot repair a disk while your MacBook Pro is started up from it, but you can start up from the Recovery HD volume and then use the OS X Disk Utility application to maintain the MacBook Pro drive and to solve some problems if they occur.

Maintain or Repair the Drive on Your MacBook Pro

1 Shut down your MacBook Pro.

2 Restart your MacBook Pro while pressing and holding **Option**.

Ⓐ You see the startup drives available to you.

3 Click the Recovery disk icon.

4 Click the arrow underneath the Recovery disk icon.

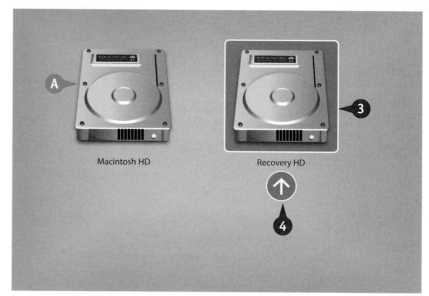

Macintosh HD   Recovery HD

The MacBook Pro starts up from the Recovery HD volume and the OS X Utilities window appears.

5 Click **Disk Utility**.

6 Click **Continue**.

Disk Utility opens.

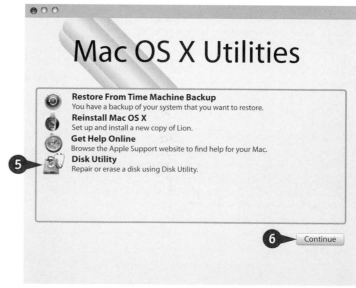

Mac OS X Utilities

Restore From Time Machine Backup
You have a backup of your system that you want to restore.

Reinstall Mac OS X
Set up and install a new copy of Lion.

Get Help Online
Browse the Apple Support website to find help for your Mac.

Disk Utility
Repair or erase a disk using Disk Utility.

Continue

7 Select the disk you want to maintain or repair, such as the internal disk on the MacBook Pro.

8 Click **Repair Disk**.

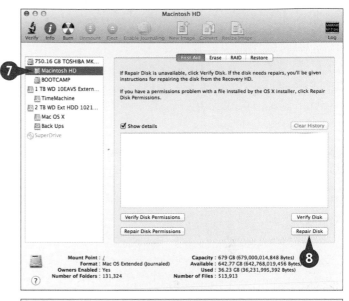

B Disk Utility checks the drive for problems and repairs any that it finds. The progress appears at the bottom of the window.

Note: If Disk Utility finds and repairs any problems, your disk returns to good operating condition.

9 Click **Repair Disk Permissions**.

Disk Utility corrects problems associated with file and folder permissions on the disk. You can monitor the progress of the process in the bottom part of the window.

10 When complete, restart the MacBook Pro (it restarts from the internal drive automatically).

TIP

What other housekeeping practices can I use to optimize my MacBook Pro?
When you are done with folders or files, move them off the internal drive. You can do this by deleting them if you are sure you will not need them again, or by archiving them by burning them onto a CD or DVD and then deleting them from the hard drive. You should try to keep your folders and files well organized so that you have a better idea of what you have stored on the hard drive. You should also make sure that you keep a good backup for all the important files on your internal drive.

Back Up with Time Machine and an External Hard Drive

If something really bad happens to your MacBook Pro, you can lose all the files it contains. This includes data you create, such as your photos, movies, and documents. Much of this data simply cannot be replaced at any cost.

The way to minimize this risk is to back up consistently. The OS X Time Machine application is designed to make it easy for you to do this so you can recover important files when you need to. All you need is an external hard drive on which to store your backups. (Time Machine can actually back up your files on your internal drive too, but you do not want to rely on that as your sole protection against data loss.)

Back Up with Time Machine and an External Hard Drive

1 With an external hard drive that you will use for backups connected to the MacBook Pro, click **Apple** (🍎) and select **System Preferences**.

Note: See Chapter 8 for information about connecting your MacBook Pro to an external hard disk. You should use a disk with a large storage capacity for this purpose to provide the longest period of protection possible.

2 Click the **Time Machine** icon.

The Time Machine pane opens.

3 Drag the slider to the **On** position.

Ⓐ If you have used Time Machine before, click Select Disk.

Time Machine activates.

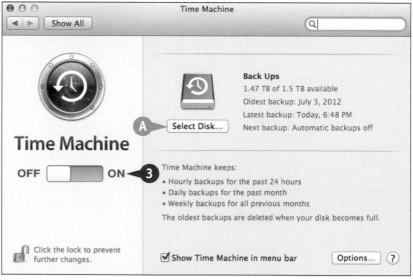

The Select Drive sheet appears.

④ Select the drive on which you want to store the backed-up information.

Ⓑ If you want the backed-up data encrypted, click the **Encrypt backups** check box. This prevents the data from being used without the encryption passcode.

Note: If you select this option, make sure you never lose the password.

⑤ Click **Use Disk**.

The sheet closes and you return to the Time Machine pane.

Ⓒ The drive you selected is shown at the top of the pane along with status information about the backup process.

⑥ Click **Options**.

The Exclude sheet appears, where you can exclude files from the backup process. This is useful because you can exclude files that do not need to be backed up to make your backups smaller.

TIP

Why would I exclude files from my backups?
Backing up files requires disk space, just as storing them does. The more and larger files you back up, the more room each backup consumes on your backup disk, resulting in fewer backups being stored. This reduces how far you can move "back in time" to restore files from the backup. By excluding files, you make your backups smaller, which means you can go farther back in time to restore files. You have to trade off the total amount of data you back up versus the number of backups you want to maintain.

continued ▶

Time Machine makes it very easy to create a backup system, and after a few minutes of setup time, backing up is automatic. Unfortunately, many Mac users do not create a backup system. If you do not back up your files, you will eventually lose data. It is not a question of "If," but "When."

At some point, you will lose files that you either have to pay to get again or cannot re-create at all, such as your iPhoto collection. With a backup system in place, recovering these files is a simple exercise. Without one, it might be impossible.

Back Up with Time Machine and an External Hard Drive (continued)

⑦ To prevent backups when your MacBook Pro is running on battery power, uncheck the **Back up while on battery power** check box.

⑧ If you want to be notified when old backups are deleted, check the **Notify after old backups are deleted** check box.

⑨ Click **Add** (⊞).

The select sheet appears.

⑩ Navigate to and select the folders or files you want to exclude from the backup.

⑪ Click **Exclude**.

⑫ If you selected system files, click **Exclude System Folder Only** to exclude only files in the System folder, or click **Exclude All System Files** to exclude system files no matter where they are stored.

Note: Exclude All System Files is usually the better option.

You return to the Exclude sheet and see the files you have excluded from the backup.

⑬ Click **Save**.

You return to the Time Machine pane, and Time Machine starts a countdown to the backup process. When the timer reaches 0, the backup process starts.

Time Machine automatically backs up your data every hour.

Note: After you disconnect the external hard drive so you can move the MacBook Pro around, the next backup is made the next time you reconnect the external hard drive. You should connect the backup drive frequently to ensure your backups are current.

TIPS

How long is my data protected?
Time Machine backs up your data for as long as it can until the backup hard drive is full. It stores hourly backups for the past 24 hours. It stores daily backups for the past month. It stores monthly backups until the backup disk is full. To protect yourself as long as possible, use the largest hard drive you can afford, and exclude files that you do not need to back up.

How can I tell when the last backup was made?
At the top of the Time Machine pane, you see status information about your backups, such as the time and date of the most current backup.

Back Up Wirelessly with a Time Capsule

The Apple Time Capsule device combines an AirPort Extreme Base Station with a hard drive. This makes wireless backups simple because the Time Capsule provides the wireless network you use, so that any computer on the network can also access the Time Capsule's hard drive to back up data.

This makes backing up even more convenient because you do not even have to tether your MacBook Pro to a drive; you can back up from wherever you are. To start backing up wirelessly, install a Time Capsule on your network. Then, configure Time Machine on your MacBook Pro to back up to it.

Back Up Wirelessly with a Time Capsule

① Install a Time Capsule on your network.

Note: See Chapter 9 for details on Time Capsule.

② Click **Apple** (🍎) and select **System Preferences**.

③ Click the **Time Machine** icon.

The Time Machine pane opens.

④ Drag the slider to the **On** position.

The Select Drive sheet appears.

5 Select the Time Capsule.

6 Click **Use Disk**.

7 Type the Time Machine password.

8 Click **Connect**.

You return to the Time Machine and a countdown to the backup process starts. When the timer reaches 0, the backup process starts.

Time Machine automatically backs up your data every hour.

TIPS

How can I maximize the length of time my files are protected?
You should eliminate files that you do not really need to back up because they are protected in some other way, such as system files that you can always re-install. To do this, click the Time Capsule and then click Options. Use the resulting sheet to exclude files. The details are explained in the section, "Back Up with Time Machine and an External Hard Drive."

How can I protect my files even better?
Online backup services, such as www.carbonite.com, are ideal for this because you can back up any time you are connected to the Internet. And, your files are even safer because they are stored in a completely different location than your computer, providing extra protection.

Restore Files with Time Machine

If you use Time Machine to keep your important data backed up, losing data from your MacBook Pro is not a big deal. (If you do not have your data backed up, it can be a very, very big deal.)

You can use Time Machine to restore files that are included in your backups. You can restore files and folders from the Finder, and you can recover individual items from within some applications (such as photos from within iPhoto). Even if you have not actually lost files, you should try restoring files regularly to make sure your backup system is working correctly.

Restore Files with Time Machine

1. Open a Finder window showing the location where the files you want to recover were stored.

2. Click Go.

3. Click Applications.

4. Double-click the **Time Machine** icon.

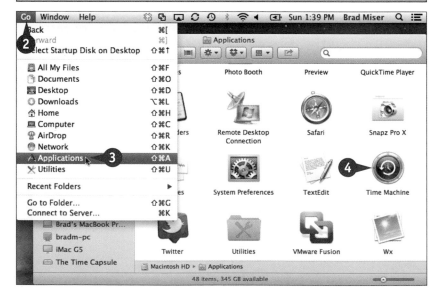

The desktop disappears and the Time Machine window fills the entire space.

Ⓐ The Finder window appears in the center of the screen. Behind it, you see all the versions of the window stored in your backup from the current version as far back in time as the backups go.

Ⓑ Along the right side of the window, you see the timeline for your backups. Backups in magenta are stored on your backup drive, while those shown in gray are stored on your internal drive. You can restore files from either location.

⑤ Click the date and time on the timeline when the version of the files you need were available.

⑥ When you reach the files or folders you want to restore, select them.

⑦ Click **Restore**.

The files and folders you selected are returned to their prior locations.

Note: To restore all of the files in the front-most window, click Restore All.

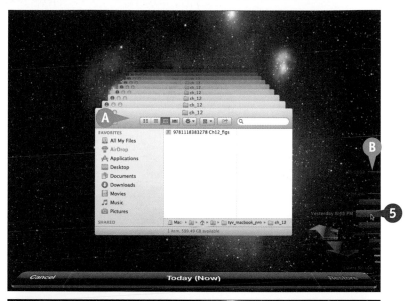

TIPS

How else can I move back in time using Time Machine?
In addition to using the timeline to move back in time, you can also click the windows behind the front-most window; each time you click a window, it moves to the front and becomes the active window. You can also click the large backward and forward arrows in the lower-right corner of the Time Machine window to move back or forward in time, respectively.

How can I restore individual files for an application that supports Time Machine?
Some applications, such as iPhoto, support Time Machine directly. To restore files to such applications, open the application and move to the location where the file was previously stored. Launch Time Machine. Move back in time, select the files you want to restore, and click **Restore**. The files are returned to the application.

Troubleshoot and Solve MacBook Pro Problems

Once in a while, your MacBook Pro is not going to cooperate with you. You might experience applications that hang (they stop doing anything while displaying the spinning color wheel icon) or quit unexpectedly; or, something odd might happen. In the most extreme case, you might not be able to get your MacBook Pro to start up at all.

The first step in solving any problem is understanding when and how it happens. Part of this is determining if the problem is general or related to a specific user account. Once you have some idea of how and when the problem occurs, you can try to solve it.

Troubleshoot and Solve MacBook Pro Problems

Find the Cause

1 Restart your MacBook Pro by clicking **Apple** (🍎) and selecting **Restart**.

Note: If your MacBook Pro does not respond to any commands or keys, press and hold the Power button until the MacBook Pro shuts off. Press the Power button again to restart it. This causes all unsaved data to be lost, so only use this option when necessary.

2 To restore your most current window, click the **Reopen windows when logging back in** check box in the Restart prompt that appears.

3 Click **Restart**.

The MacBook Pro restarts.

4 Try to replicate the problem by doing the same things you did when it first occurred.

5 If you cannot cause the problem to happen again, assume it was solved by the restart and continue working.

6 If you can cause the problem to happen again, use Activity Monitor to see if any applications or processes appear to be consuming large amounts of resources, such as more than 90 percent of CPU activity. If they are, you have found a likely source of the problem.

Note: For more information, see the section, "Monitor Your MacBook Pro Activity."

7 In the Activity Monitor window, check if the hard drive is too full. Remove files to make more space available on the drive.

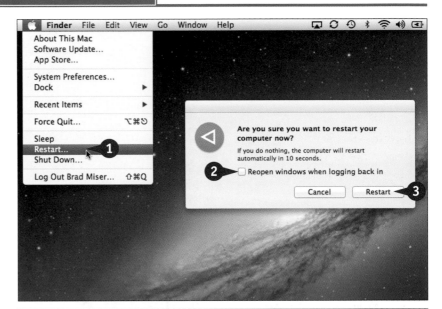

8 To see if your problem might have to do with newly installed software, click the **System Report** button in the System Information application to get detailed information about your MacBook Pro profile.

Note: For more information, see the section, "Profile Your MacBook Pro."

9 Click the **Applications** category.

10 Click the **Last Modified** down arrow to sort the window by the last modified date so the most recent date is at the top of the window.

11 Look for any applications you installed just before you started having problems.

The detailed information you collected should give you an idea of the cause of the problem.

Determine if a Problem Is System-wide or User-Specific

1 Log in to your troubleshooting user account.

Note: Create a user account that you use only when you are trying to solve problems (see Chapter 6).

2 Try to replicate the problem under the new account.

If you can repeat the problem, it is systemic instead of being specific to a user account.

If you cannot repeat the problem, it is likely related to an issue with your user account. In most cases, the issue is related to a preference file that has been corrupted. The next steps explain how to remove preference files.

TIPS

If I cannot find the cause of the problem, can I still fix it?
Yes. Restarting your MacBook Pro is almost always the first thing you should try when you encounter a problem. A simple restart will solve a lot of issues, and because it is so easy to do, you should give it a try when you run into an issue. If it solves the problem, you do not need to think about it anymore.

How do I best prepare myself to solve problems?
Many different problems are possible, but you are likely to experience only a few. There is really no way to provide a comprehensive list of problems in a short section like this one. If you can understand how to describe a problem and know where to go for help (see the last section in this chapter), then you will be able to solve most problems you encounter.

continued ▶

When it comes to effective troubleshooting and problem solving, a cool, calm state is your best friend. Unfortunately, problems tend to be very frustrating, especially when you are working. Stress and frustration can lead to you being unable to take your time and logically approach problem solving. And, an emotional state can lead to rash actions that can make problems worse.

Sometimes, the most important step in troubleshooting is taking a break. Getting away from a problem for a while can clear your head and make a solution come much more quickly than just continuing to work through it.

Troubleshoot and Solve MacBook Pro Problems (continued)

3 Press **Option**, click **Go**, and then select **Library**.

4 Open the **Preferences** folder.

5 Delete the preference files for the application you are having trouble with. The application's name is part of the preference's filename.

6 Try to replicate the problem.

If you cannot repeat the problem, you have likely solved it.

Hung Application Problem

1 Identify the hung application by the spinning color wheel remaining on the screen for several minutes.

2 Press ⌘ + **Option** + **Esc**.

Note: When you force an application to quit, you lose any unsaved changes in its open documents. So, make sure the application is truly hung by letting it sit for a couple of minutes before you force it to quit.

3 In the Force Quit Applications window, select the hung application.

4 Click **Force Quit**.

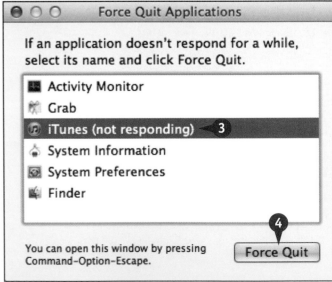

⑤ At the prompt, click **Force Quit**.

OS X forces the application to shut down.

⑥ Restart your MacBook Pro.

If the application works normally, the problem is solved. If the application continues to hang, you should update it.

Start Up Problem

① Make sure your MacBook Pro either is connected to power or has a full battery.

Note: If you see a not symbol (circle with a slash through it) when you start up your MacBook Pro, you have to start up from an alternate disk or from the Recovery HD volume.

② Restart from the Recovery HD volume.

Ⓐ Your MacBook Pro starts up from the Recovery HD and you see the OS X Utilities window.

If MacBook starts up, you know the problem is with the system software installed on the primary startup disk.

③ Try repairing the startup drive.

If the problem does not recur, you are done. If the problem does recur, you need to reinstall OS X.

④ Restart from the Recovery HD volume.

⑤ Launch the Reinstall OS X application.

⑥ Follow the on-screen steps to reinstall or repair the system software on the primary startup disk.

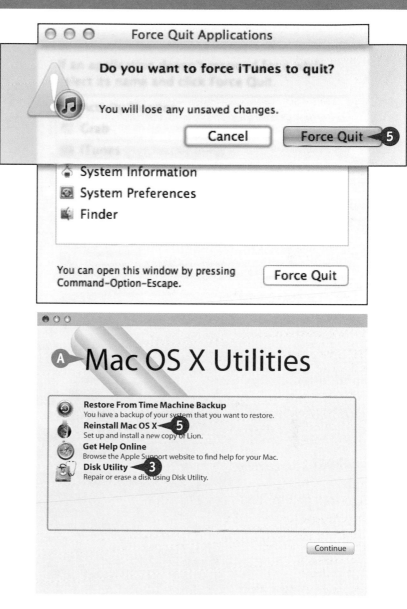

TIP

How can I limit damage resulting from MacBook Pro problems?
Back up your data. You should always have current backups of your data because losing data is the most severe consequence of any MacBook Pro problem you might encounter. Losing data is not just something that might happen to you; it will happen to you at some point. In addition to knowing how to start up from the recovery drive, you should also keep good backups of your data. If something happens to the system software on your MacBook Pro, you can restart from this drive and hopefully solve the problem you are having. You should also keep a record of important usernames and passwords, such as your Apple ID, so that you will be able to recover content, such as applications, should you need to.

Capture a Screenshot

When you experience a problem, capturing a screenshot is a great way to describe and document the problem for yourself. Asking for help is even more useful because you can give the screenshots to the person who is helping you.

OS X has two built-in ways to capture a screenshot. You can use keyboard shortcuts, or for more sophisticated shots, you can use the Grab application. This application enables you to capture the full screen, a specific window, or even just a portion of the screen.

Capture a Screenshot

Capture a Screenshot with a Keyboard Shortcut

1. Open the window that you want to capture.

2. To capture the entire desktop, press ⌘ + **Shift** + **3** and skip steps **3** and **4**.

3. To capture a portion of the screen, press ⌘ + **Shift** + **4**.

4. Drag over the area of the screen you want to capture; release the trackpad button when the area you want to capture is highlighted.

5. Double-click the image file.

Ⓐ Preview opens and you see the screenshot.

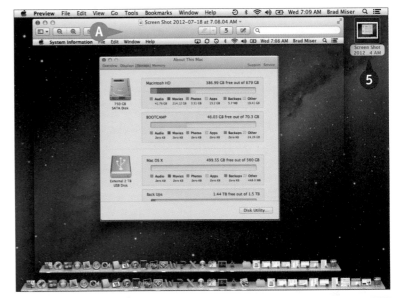

Capture a Timed Screenshot with Grab

1. Open the Grab application from Utilities in the Applications folder.

2. Open the window that you want to capture.

3. Switch back to Grab.

4. Press **Shift** + ⌘ + **Z**.

5. In the Timed Screen Grab dialog, click **Start Timer**.

6. During the countdown, arrange the screen exactly as you want to capture it.

   When the timer ends, OS X takes the screenshot and opens it in Grab.

7. Save the screenshot.

Get Help with MacBook Pro Problems

None of us knows all the solutions to all, or even most of, the problems you may encounter while using your MacBook Pro. Fortunately, you do not need to because there is a lot of useful information that you can take advantage of to help solve problems.

One of the most important troubleshooting skills is to be able to know where to get help and be able to ask for it clearly so that you are more likely to get help you need. Many problems you encounter have been experienced and solved by someone else already.

Get Help with MacBook Pro Problems

1 If the problem is related to Apple hardware or software, visit www.apple.com/support.

2 Search for the problem you are having.

3 Browse the information on the Search Results page to locate the problem and its solution.

Note: If you purchased AppleCare, you can use that technical support service. See your documentation for contact information.

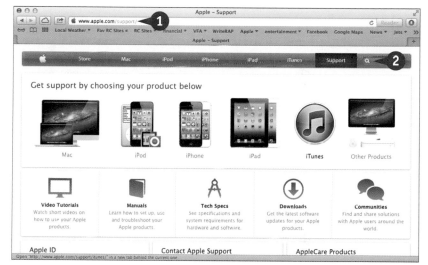

4 If you do not find what you need, open Safari and type the problem you are having in the Address bar.

5 Press **Return** to search for the problem you are experiencing.

6 Browse the results of the search to find the information you need.

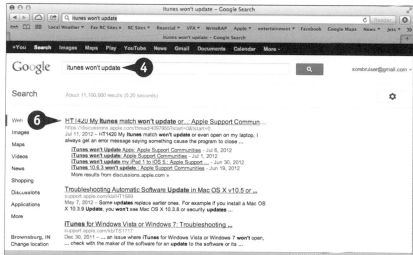

Explore iTunes

iTunes enables you to organize and enjoy music, video, books, and more on Macs, Windows PCs, iPods, iPads, or iPhones. With the integration of iTunes to the iTunes Store, it is easy to add great audio, video, books, and apps for mobile devices to your iTunes library whenever you want.

In addition to being incredibly powerful, iTunes is also very well designed and therefore easy to use. In fact, the application is so well designed that a number of its interface elements have been adopted in other applications, including the OS X Finder application that manages the desktop on your MacBook Pro.

A Source Pane

Shows all the sources of content available to you.

B Library

Stores and organizes all the content you manage in iTunes.

C Categories

Allow you to organize your library into different types of content.

D Cover Flow View

Shows content in the selected source as album covers that you can flip through.

E View Buttons

Allow you to change views.

F Search Bar

Enables you to search the selected source.

G Source Information

Shows information about the source you have selected, including how long the content will play and how much disk space it consumes.

H Content Pane

Shows detailed information about the content of the selected source.

I Artwork/Video Viewer

Shows album art when you select or listen to audio, or video when you play video content.

Ⓐ List View

Presents content in the selected source in a list.

Ⓑ Column Browser

Enables you to browse the selected source quickly.

Ⓒ Playback Controls

Allow you to control playback of audio and video content.

Ⓓ Browse Path

Highlighted items show the path to the content you are browsing.

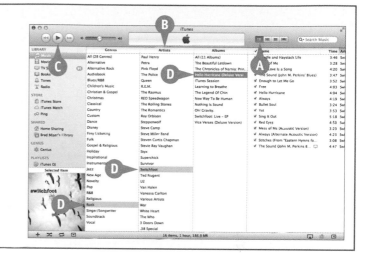

Ⓐ Grid View

Shows content in the selected source, organized in a grid.

Ⓑ Album Grid View

Shows the content organized by album.

Ⓒ Information Window

Displays information about what you are listening to, syncing, and so on.

Ⓓ Show/Hide iTunes Sidebar

Opens or closes the iTunes sidebar.

Ⓔ Start Genius

Starts the iTunes Genius feature.

Ⓕ Output Options

A menu that enables you to choose where you want iTunes output to play.

Ⓖ Show/Hide Artwork/Video Viewer

Opens or closes the Artwork/Video Viewer window.

Ⓗ Repeat

Causes content in the selected source to repeat.

Ⓘ Shuffle

Tells iTunes to play content in the selected source in random order.

Ⓙ Create Playlist

Enables you to create playlists and Smart Playlists.

Explore the iTunes Store

The iTunes Store makes it easy to add music, movies, TV shows, books, and other content to your iTunes library. Because the iTunes Store is integrated within the iTunes application, moving between the store and your own content is seamless.

You can browse for content just by clicking any of the text or graphics you see. You can also search for specific content in the store and preview items of interest. When you are ready to download content, making the purchase is just a matter of a couple of clicks.

Ⓐ iTunes Store Home Page

Links take you directly to specific content as well as to categories.

Ⓑ Albums

Album covers and titles are links to those albums.

Ⓒ Categories

These links take you to the homepages for categories of content.

Ⓓ Quick Links

These links take you to tools such as the Power Search tool or Browser.

Ⓔ Current Account

When you are logged in to an iTunes Store account, you see your username.

Ⓕ Return to iTunes

Clicking this icon exits the iTunes Store and returns you to iTunes.

Ⓐ Content Page

This section displays information about a specific item.

Ⓑ Buy Album Button

You can buy an album by clicking its **Buy** button.

Ⓒ Like

You can let others know you like specific content by clicking this button.

Ⓓ Tracks

The contents of the current item are shown in the bottom of the window.

Ⓔ Buy Button

You can use a track's **Buy** button to buy only that track.

Ⓕ Artist Link

You can click the artist name to see all content by that artist.

Ⓖ Preview

You can click this button to hear or watch a preview.

Obtain an iTunes Store Account

The iTunes Store features music, movies, TV shows, podcasts, e-books, and other content that you can browse, preview (except e-books), and then purchase. You can also rent content, including movies. Content you buy or rent from the iTunes Store is immediately downloaded and ready for you to use.

To be able to purchase or rent content from the iTunes Store, you need to have an iTunes account and be logged in to it. (You can browse, search, and preview content without being logged into an account.) You can get an account from within iTunes.

Obtain an iTunes Store Account

Note: If you already have an Apple ID, such as one you use to make purchases from the online Apple Store or your iCloud account, you can skip these steps because your Apple ID enables you to use the store.

① Click **iTunes Store** on the Source list.

iTunes connects to the iTunes Store and you see the home page.

② Click **Sign In**.

The Sign In dialog appears.

③ Click **Create Apple ID**.

The Welcome to the iTunes Store screen appears.

④ Follow the on-screen instructions to create your account.

When you have created your account, you have an Apple ID and password. This enables you to log in to your account on the iTunes Store and purchase content from it.

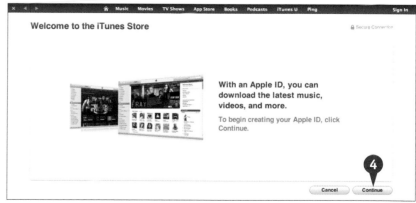

Understanding the iTunes Library

The iTunes library is where you store all of your content, including music, movies, TV shows, books, and ringtones. Before you can enjoy content in iTunes, it has to be available there; you can add content from many sources, including ripping music from CDs you already own and downloading content from the iTunes Store. Once content is stored in your iTunes library, you can use iTunes tools to keep that content organized so that you can easily access it, and of course, do all sorts of great things with it.

Categories

The content in your library is organized automatically by categories, including Music, Movies, TV Shows, and Books. Within the library source, you see an icon for each category. When you select a category, the content it includes appears in the right part of the iTunes window where you browse and search it. When you find the content you want, you can listen to it, view it, create playlists, burn it to disc, and so on.

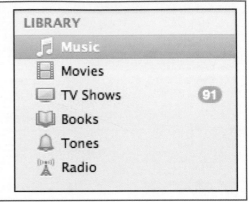

Devices

iTunes considers sources of content stored outside of its database to be *devices*. If you use an iPod, iPad, or iPhone with iTunes, they appear in the Devices section when connected to your MacBook Pro. Devices also include audio CDs. Like other sources, you select a device to work with it. For example, to configure the content on an iPod, you select its icon, and its settings tools appear in the right part of the window.

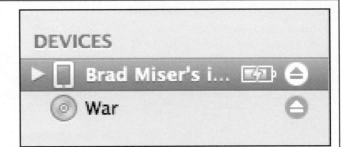

Tracks

Although it is easy to think of tracks as the songs on a CD, iTunes considers everything that you listen to or watch to be a track. So, each episode in a season of a TV series you download from the iTunes Store is a track, as is each section of an audiobook. Tracks are what you see in each row in the Content pane.

✔	Name		Time	Artist
✔	Roll Me Away		4:40	Bob Seger
✔	Night Moves	⊙	5:26	Bob Seger
✔	Turn The Page		5:04	Bob Seger

Tags

A lot of information is associated with the content in the iTunes library. This includes artist, track name, track number, album, genre, and rating. Each of these data elements is called a *tag*. Each tag can appear in a column in the Content pane, and you can view all

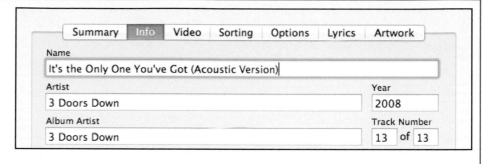

the tags for a track in the Info window. Tags are important because they enable you to identify and organize content. Fortunately, iTunes automatically tags most of the content you work with, but you can also add or change tags when you need to.

Playlists

One of the best things about iTunes is that you can create custom collections of content you want to listen to or watch. These collections are called *playlists*. Playlists can include any combination of content organized in any way. There are two kinds of playlists. You manually place content into a playlist, or when you create a Smart Playlist, you define criteria for content and iTunes automatically places the appropriate content into it. After you have created a playlist, you can listen to it, burn it to disc, or move it to an iPad or iPhone.

The iTunes Way

Although iTunes enables you to work with a lot of different kinds of content (such as music, audiobooks, movies, and music videos), it uses a consistent process

to work with any kind of content. First, you select the source of the content you want to work with; this can be a library category, device, or playlist. Second, you browse or search for content you want within the selected source if the content is not ready for you immediately. Third, you select the specific track you want. Fourth, you use the iTunes controls to play the content. This process is consistent regardless of the type of content, and so once you get the hang of it, you can quickly enjoy any content you want.

Browse or Search for iTunes Content

Before you can enjoy audio or video content, you need to find that content so that you can select it. You can find content in two ways: by browsing or by searching.

Browsing is a good way to find something when you are not quite sure what you want to listen to or watch. Searching is useful when you know exactly what you want, but are not quite sure where it is. The iTunes window has several views; this section assumes that you are using the List view, but you can browse or search in any of the views in a similar way (other views are covered later in this chapter).

Browse or Search for iTunes Content

Browse for iTunes Content

1 In the Source pane, select the source of content you want to browse, such as **Music**.

Note: If the Browser does not appear, open the View menu, select Column Browser, and then select Show Column Browser.

2 Open the **View** menu and select **Column Browser**.

3 Select the columns you want to see, such as **Genres**, **Artists**, and **Albums**.

4 Select **On Top** or select **On Left**.

5 In the Genres column, select the genre you want to browse.

6 Select the artist whose music you want to browse.

7 Select the album you want to browse; click **All** to see all the artist's albums in the selected genre.

A The tracks on that album appear.

8 Select the track you want to hear.

9 Use the playback controls to play the track.

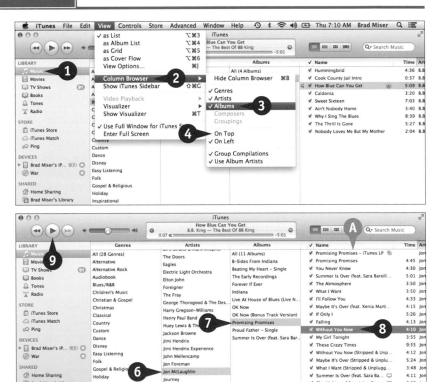

Search for iTunes Content

1 In the Source pane, select the source of content you want to search, such as **TV Shows**.

2 Type the text or numbers for which you want to search in the Search bar.

B As you type, only content that meets your search criteria appears in the Content pane, and you see what you are searching for at the top of the pane.

3 To make your search more specific, open the **Search** menu.

4 Select the tag by which you want to limit the search.

5 Select the content you want to listen to or watch.

6 Use the playback controls to play the content.

How can I make a column wider to see all of its information?
Point to the line at the right edge of the column. When ▐ changes to ⊞, drag to the right to make the column wider or to the left to make it narrower.

How can I show the Column Browser when it sometimes disappears?
The Column Browser is not all that useful for some sources, such as an audio CD, because you can usually see all the content on the source in the Content pane, and most content is from the same genre and artist. When you select such a source, the Column Browser is hidden. You can show it again by clicking **View**, clicking **Column Browser**, and then selecting **Show Column Browser**.

Browse the Library with Cover Flow View

The List view is very functional and efficient, but it is not all that pretty, nor is it that exciting to browse. The Cover Flow view allows you to browse for music similar to flipping through a stack of CDs (only easier). You view content by its cover art, and you can flip through the content available to you until you see something that you like. You can work with individual tracks as you can in the List view because the current content appears in the List view at the bottom of the window.

Browse the Library with Cover Flow View

1 Select the source you want to browse, such as **Music**.

2 Click **Cover Flow View** (▦).

3 To change the size of the Cover Flow pane, drag the **Resize** handle (▦) up or down.

4 To move through the content quickly, drag the scroll bar to the left or right.

As you drag, the covers flip quickly.

Ⓐ The content in the album directly facing you appears on the content list, where you can listen to or watch it.

5 To browse in full-screen mode, click **Full Screen** (▣).

The Cover Flow pane fills the desktop.

6 Browse the content by using the scroll bar or clicking to the left or right of the artwork facing you.

7 Control the content with the playback controls.

8 To return to the iTunes window, click **Full Screen** (▣).

330

Browse the Library with Grid View

G rid view collects the content you are browsing into a grid with thumbnails for the collections you are viewing. What a collection includes depends upon the type of content you are browsing. For example, when you browse the Music source, the thumbnails can represent genres, albums, artists, or composers; when you select TV Shows, the thumbnails represent seasons of a show or the genres of shows you have.

You move into a collection by double-clicking a thumbnail, whereupon you see content organized by collections, such as albums.

Browse the Library with Grid View

1 Select the source you want to browse, such as **Music**.

2 Click **Grid View** (⊞).

3 Select what you want the grids to represent, such as clicking **Genres** to have each box represent the content in its genres.

Ⓐ In the Content pane, you see the collections for the type of content you selected.

4 Double-click a genre.

Ⓑ The content of the selected genre appears in List view, grouped by album or collection.

5 Browse the genre.

6 Click a column heading to change how the list is sorted.

7 Select the content you want to play.

8 Use the playback controls to play it.

Listen to Audio Content

If you have used any type of audio player before, you should be able to quickly listen to audio content in iTunes. iTunes uses playback controls that will likely look familiar to you even if you have never used the application before.

Of course, whereas most audio players give you just basic controls, iTunes really lets you fine-tune your audio experience by choosing exactly how you want to listen. You can quickly choose and play any of your content and control the playback with just a few mouse clicks.

Listen to Audio Content

① Browse or search for the audio content you want to hear.

② Select the first track you want to hear.

③ Click **Play** (▶).

The audio content begins to play.

Ⓐ In the Information pane, you see information about what is playing, such as the track name, artist, and a timeline.

Ⓑ The track currently playing is highlighted and marked with a blue speaker icon (🔊).

④ Click **Pause** (⏸ changes to ▶) or press `Spacebar` to pause the audio.

⑤ Click **Previous** (⏮) to jump back to the previous track.

⑥ Click **Next** (⏭) to jump to the next track.

⑦ Set the volume level by dragging the slider.

Watch Movies and TV Shows

Tunes works as well for video content as it does for audio content. You can watch movies, TV shows, music videos, and video podcasts within the iTunes window, in the Artwork/Video viewer, or in full-screen mode. You can easily switch between modes to suit your preference.

Watching video content works according to the iTunes pattern: Find the content you want to view, select it, and use the iTunes controls to play the content. Like audio, the playback controls will likely look very familiar to you.

Watch Movies and TV Shows

1 Browse or search for the video content you want to watch.

2 Select the first video track you want to see.

3 Click **Play** (▶) or press Spacebar.

A The video begins to play.

4 Position the pointer over the video image.

B The video controls appear.

5 Use the controls to play the video.

6 To stop the video and move back into iTunes, click **Close** (⊗).

Add Audio CD Content to the iTunes Library

It is likely that you already have music on CD. And even though the iTunes Store has a huge music collection, some music you want may only be available on CD. You can add music from CDs to iTunes by importing that music. Once imported, this music becomes part of your iTunes library and you can listen to it, add it to playlists, put it on custom CDs you burn, and so on. If your MacBook Pro does not have an internal DVD drive, you will need to use an external one.

First, you need to do a one-time configuration of iTunes to import audio. Then you can import CDs to build up your iTunes library.

Add Audio CD Content to the iTunes Library

Prepare iTunes to Import Audio CDs

1 Press ⌘+, to open the Preferences dialog.

2 Click the **General** tab.

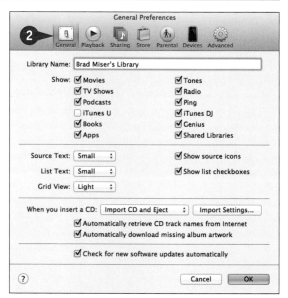

3 From the **When you insert a CD** pop-up menu, select **Import CD and Eject**.

4 Check the **Automatically retrieve CD track names from Internet** check box.

5 Check the **Automatically download missing album artwork** check box.

Note: You must be signed into the iTunes Store to complete step **5**.

6 Click **OK**.

Note: By default, iTunes encodes all audio content using the AAC (Advanced Audio Coding) format. If you want to use a different format, click Import Settings and use the resulting dialog to choose and configure the format you want to use.

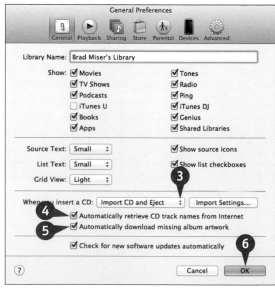

Import Audio CDs to the iTunes Library

1 Insert an audio CD.

Ⓐ iTunes connects to the Internet and identifies the CD you inserted.

The import process starts.

Ⓑ The song currently being imported is marked with an orange circle (⊚).

Ⓒ You see information about the import process in the Information pane.

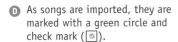

Ⓓ As songs are imported, they are marked with a green circle and check mark (⊘).

When iTunes has imported all the tracks on the disc, it ejects the disc.

The tracks on the CD are now part of your iTunes library.

TIPS

How does iTunes know what is on an audio CD?
When you insert an audio CD, iTunes connects to the Internet and looks up the CD in an online CD database. When it finds the CD, iTunes adds tags for the album including name, artist, and track titles. It also retrieves album art for any music in the iTunes Store. iTunes remembers CDs so that the next time you insert them, the information iTunes looked up is there automatically.

How should I encode music from audio CDs?
AAC is the best option for most people because it provides good sound quality in relatively small files. That is a good thing because you can store more content in your iTunes library and on iPods, iPads, or iPhones. If you demand the absolute highest audio quality, you can use the Apple Lossless format, which produces significantly larger files with slightly better sound quality.

Buy Music, TV, Movies, and More from the iTunes Store

The iTunes Store has a lot of great content that you can easily preview, purchase (some is free), and download to your MacBook Pro, where it is added to your iTunes library automatically. When you are interested in content, you can preview it to decide whether you want it. Buying something you want is just a matter of clicking the related Buy button.

One of the nice things about the iTunes Store is that you can buy individual tracks so if you just like one or two songs on an album, you can buy just those songs instead of paying for the entire CD from which they come.

Buy Music, TV, Movies, and More from the iTunes Store

Log In to Your iTunes Store Account

1 Select **iTunes Store** on the Source list.

2 Click **Sign In**.

3 Type your Apple ID.

4 Type your password.

5 Click **Sign In**.

You enter the store and see the Home page.

Browse the iTunes Store

1 Click the **iTunes Store** link on the Source list.

2 Click the **Browse** link.

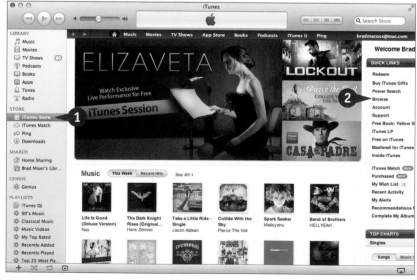

336

The Store Browser appears.

3 Click a content category.

Note: This example uses Music; different types of content have other categories to browse.

4 Select a genre.

5 Select a subgenre.

6 Select an artist.

7 Select an album.

A The contents of the selected album appear in the bottom pane of the window. This pane works just like the Content pane when you browse your iTunes library.

You are ready to preview and purchase content.

Search the iTunes Store

1 Move into the iTunes Store.

2 Type information you want to search for in the Search bar.

B As you type, iTunes attempts to match what you are typing and presents the matches on a pop-up menu.

3 If a match appears, click it on the pop-up menu to perform the search; if not, continue typing until you have typed all the text you want to search for and press **Return**.

C The results of your search appear.

4 Review the results of the search.

5 To see the results in a specific category, click the **See All** link for that category.

6 To get more information for a specific album, click its cover.

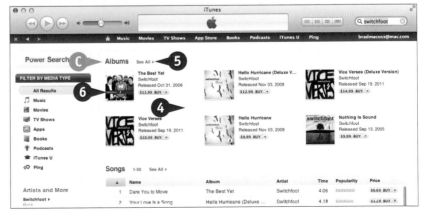

continued ▶

Y ou can move around the iTunes Store in many ways. Just about every object on the screen is linked to more specific information about something, until you get down to the individual items that you purchase, such as songs, movies, or TV shows. Browsing and searching are both useful techniques for finding great content.

In addition to previewing content, you can read reviews to find out what other people think about the content in which you are interested. You can also read details about items, including the iTunes reviews.

Buy Music, TV, Movies, and More from the iTunes Store (continued)

Ⓐ The album's page appears.

❼ Read the full text associated with the album by clicking **More** in the iTunes Review section.

The text expands.

❽ Read the information about the album.

❾ To read other people's feedback about the album, scroll down the screen and read the customer reviews and ratings.

Preview iTunes Store Content

❶ Hover over the item you want to preview.

❷ Click **Preview** (🔘).

A preview plays. If the content is audio, you hear it. If it includes video, you also see the video.

You can control previews with the same controls you use to play content in your iTunes library.

Buy and Download Content from the iTunes Store

1 Preview the content you are interested in.

2 Click the **Buy** button for the content you want to purchase.

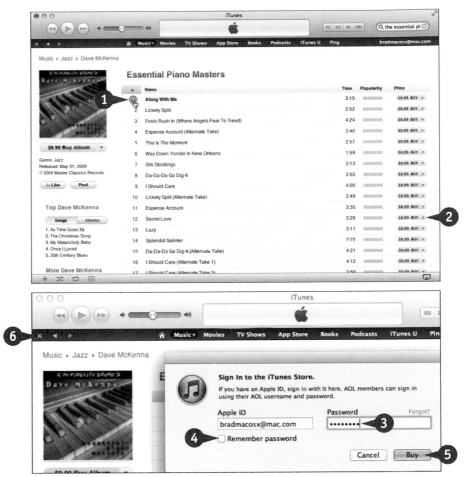

3 Type your account's password.

4 To have iTunes remember your password for more purchases during this shopping session, check the **Remember password** check box.

5 Click **Buy**.

iTunes immediately downloads the content to your library.

6 Click **Exit iTunes Store** (✕).

TIP

How can I use content I purchase from the iTunes Store?
Audio content you purchase from the iTunes Store is not restricted by any limitations. Video content does have some limitations, including the number of computers it can be played on; each computer has to be authorized with your iTunes Store user account to be able to play it. Rented video content can be played on only one device at a time and is deleted automatically after 30 days or after 24 hours of when it is first played (48 hours outside of the US).

continued ▶

You can buy items individually, such as songs or episodes of TV shows, from the iTunes Store. You can also buy collections, including albums or seasons of TV shows. You can even pre-purchase some kinds of content. For example, you can purchase a season pass for a current TV show; as new episodes are added to the iTunes Store, they download to your iTunes library automatically. You can also preorder music; as soon as it is released, the music downloads to your computer. You can also collect items you are interested in on your Wish List, from which you can buy them at a later time.

Buy Music, TV, Movies, and More from the iTunes Store (continued)

7 Click **Downloads** on the Source list.

A iTunes displays the items that it downloads. You see the download progress for each item.

Note: Items that you purchase from the iTunes Store automatically appear in the Purchased playlist. To see your purchased content, select that source.

Add Content to Your Wish List

1 View content you want to save in your Wish List.

2 Open the menu at the right end of the Buy button and select **Add to Wish List**.

iTunes adds the item to your Wish List.

3 Click the menu at the right end of
your iTunes account.

4 Select **Wish List**.

B Your Wish List opens. You
can browse your list, preview
items, and purchase them as
you can from other pages in
the iTunes Store.

Note: If you configure iTunes to
remember your password, then
iTunes purchases the content as
soon as you click a Buy button.
You can use your Wish List to
store items you are thinking about
buying so you have a buffer
between being interested and
actually buying.

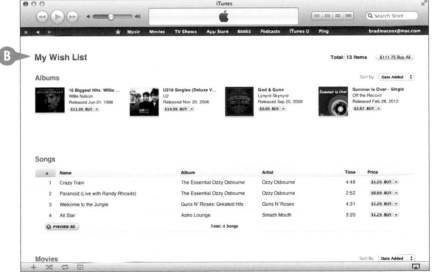

TIP

What about content I purchased previously that was restricted through Digital Rights Management (DRM)?
Previously, there were two kinds of content on the iTunes Store: iTunes Plus and protected. iTunes Plus content had no restrictions.
You could use protected content on up to five computers at the same time, and you could burn unique playlists to a disc up to seven
times. If you previously purchased protected content from the iTunes Store, you can convert that content into unprotected content
by clicking the iTunes Plus link in your section on the iTunes Store home page. You have to pay a fee for each item you convert, but
this cost is significantly less than that of purchasing the content.

Subscribe and Listen to Podcasts

Podcasts are episodic audio or video programs that you can listen to or watch. Podcasts are often like radio shows, and in fact, many *are* radio shows. Most radio shows offer podcast versions that you can download to your MacBook Pro and copy to an iPod or other device. Podcasts go way beyond just radio shows, however; you can find podcasts on many different topics.

You can subscribe to many different podcasts in the iTunes Store. Once you have subscribed, iTunes automatically downloads episodes for you so that they are available for you to listen to or watch, which you do in the same way as with other content in the library.

Subscribe and Listen to Podcasts

Find Podcasts

① Enter the iTunes Store.

② Click **Podcasts**.

③ Search for a podcast that interests you.

Note: You can also browse for podcasts.

The search results appear.

④ Click a podcast to get more information.

The podcast's home page appears.

⑤ To play an episode, select it and double-click the trackpad.

Note: Because most podcasts are free, the entire episode plays instead of just a preview.

⑥ Read about the podcast.

⑦ To subscribe to a podcast, click its **Subscribe** button.

⑧ Click **Subscribe**.

iTunes adds available episodes of the podcast to your library, and some of the recent episodes download to your computer.

Listen to Podcasts

1 Click **Podcasts** in the Source list.

Ⓐ You see all the podcasts to which you have subscribed.

2 Click a podcast's triangle to expand it so you see all the episodes you have of that show.

3 Select and play an episode of a podcast just like other content.

Ⓑ iTunes marks podcasts you have not played with a blue dot (●).

4 If an episode you want to listen to has not been downloaded yet, click **Get**.

5 Click **Get All** to get all episodes.

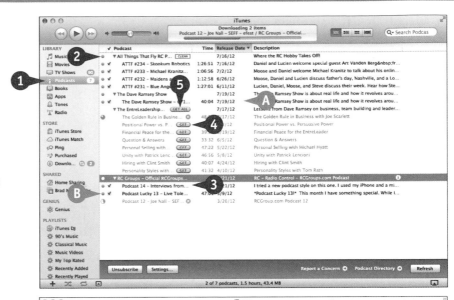

Configure Podcast Settings

1 Click **Podcasts** in the Source list.

2 Click **Settings**.

3 In the Podcast Settings dialog, select **Podcast Defaults** from the **Settings for** menu.

Note: You can configure different settings for a podcast by selecting it from the Settings for menu.

4 Select how often iTunes looks for new episodes.

5 On the **When new episodes are available** menu, select what you want iTunes to do.

6 Select how you want iTunes to keep episodes.

7 Click **OK**.

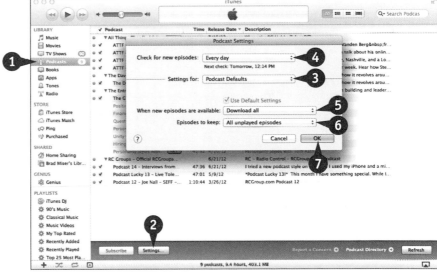

TIPS

How do I subscribe to a podcast when it is not available in the iTunes Store?

Some websites provide a URL to a podcast subscription; copy this URL, click **Advanced**, click **Subscribe to Podcast**, paste the URL in the dialog, and click **OK**. Other sites provide podcasts as MP3 files that you can download and add to the iTunes library; you work with these files just like tracks from a CD.

How do I use the podcast application for a radio show I am interested in?

When shows offer podcasts as MP3 files that you have to access for a fee, they often provide an application that downloads the files automatically. After you install and configure such an application, it downloads the show's MP3 files to the location you specify. Add them to the iTunes library by dragging them there or by clicking **File** and then clicking **Add to Library**.

Copy iTunes Content from Other Computers onto Your MacBook Pro

If you have another computer with iTunes content on it, you can use the Home Sharing feature to copy content you have purchased from the iTunes Store and any other iTunes content on your MacBook Pro to build up your iTunes library. This is a fast and simple way to fill your iTunes library with a lot of audio and video content that you can enjoy.

This process has two steps. The first is to configure Home Sharing on the computer from which you will copy content. The second is to access the sharing computer and import its content into the MacBook Pro iTunes library.

Copy iTunes Content from Other Computers onto Your MacBook Pro

Configure Home Sharing

1. In iTunes on the computer receiving content, open the **Advanced** menu and select **Turn On Home Sharing**.

2. On the Home Sharing setup screen, type the Apple ID under which the content was purchased.

3. Type the password for the Apple ID.

4. Click **Create Home Share**.

   Home Sharing starts and you see its information window.

5. Click **Done**.

Note: You can set up shares on multiple computers at the same time.

Import New Content to the iTunes Library

1 Expand the shared source by clicking its triangle.

2 Select the type of content to add.

3 Use the Search bar or browser to find specific content you want to add to your library.

4 Select the content you want to add.

5 Click **Import**.

iTunes copies the content you selected into the iTunes library.

TIPS

How can I automatically add new content?
To import content automatically into iTunes, click the **Settings** button, check the check box for each type of content you want iTunes to automatically copy, and click **OK**.

How else can I share content?
Open the **Sharing** pane of the iTunes Preferences dialog. Check the **Share my library on my local network** check box. Check **Share entire library**. Other iTunes users on your network will be able to listen to music in your library.

Create a Genius Playlist

ⁱTunes Genius is a feature that tries to select music for you based on a specific song; it places similar music into a Genius playlist that you can listen to, put on an iPod, iPad, or iPhone, or burn to a disc. How Genius picks songs based on other songs is a bit of a mystery, but you may be amazed at how well this feature works.

You can create as many Genius playlists as you want. All you need to do is to turn on the Genius feature, select a song, and tell Genius to get to work.

Create a Genius Playlist

Start Genius

1 On the **Store** menu, select **Turn On Genius**.

2 Click **Genius**.

3 Click **Turn On Genius**.

4 At the prompt, type your account password.

5 Click **Continue** and follow the on-screen instructions to complete the Genius configuration, which includes agreeing to terms and conditions.

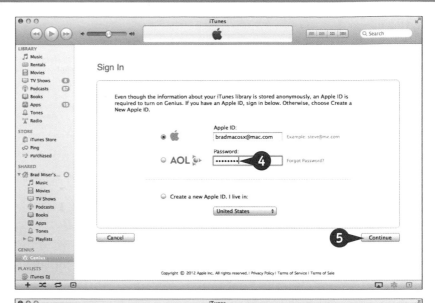

Create a Genius Playlist

1 Select the song that you want Genius to base the playlist on.

2 Click **Genius** ().

The Genius builds the playlist and you see its contents. You can play the playlist just like other playlists.

TIPS

How can I save a Genius playlist?

To save the playlist permanently, click **Save Playlist**. To have Genius update its contents, click **Refresh**.

How else can I use the Genius?

Click the Music source or a playlist. From the menu bar, click **View** and then click **Show iTunes Sidebar**. The iTunes Sidebar appears. Click a song. In the Sidebar, you see a number of sections. The specific sections depend on what you have selected. In the Genius Recommendations sections, you see album and songs in the iTunes Store that are similar to what you have selected. You can preview or download these.

Create a Standard Playlist

Playlists enable you to create your own custom content collections (such as music, audiobooks, and video) that you can then play, burn to disc, or move to an iPod, iPad, or iPhone. You can create as many playlists as you want, and they are completely customizable; you can include as many tracks as you want in the order you want them. You can even include the same track in a playlist multiple times for those tracks you just have to hear over and over again. A standard playlist is one in which you manually place and organize songs.

Create a Standard Playlist

1 Click **Create Playlist** (⊞).

iTunes creates a new playlist, and its name is ready for you to edit.

2 Type a name for the new playlist and press **Return**.

The playlist moves to a location on the Source list based on the title you gave it (iTunes sorts playlists alphabetically).

3 Double-click the playlist.

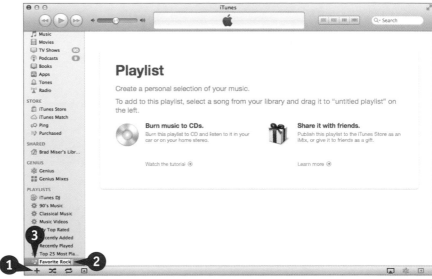

A The playlist opens in a separate window, making it much easier to add songs to it.

4 Position and size the playlist window so you can see it and the iTunes window at the same time.

5 Click the iTunes window.

6 Select the category of content you want to add.

7 Browse or search for content you want to add to the playlist.

8 Drag tracks from the Content pane onto the playlist's window.

iTunes adds the tracks to the playlist.

9 Repeat steps **6** to **8** until you have added all the tracks you want to include in the playlist.

10 Click the playlist's window.

B Its contents appear in the Content pane.

11 Drag tracks up and down the playlist until they are in the order in which you want them to play.

As with other sources, when you play in order, tracks play from the top of the window to the bottom.

12 Close the playlist's window.

TIPS

Can I sort the contents of a playlist?
You can sort a playlist that you create by clicking the column heading by which you want to sort it. When you sort a playlist you have organized manually so that the tracks play in a specific order, that order is lost.

How can I create a playlist for an album I just downloaded from the iTunes Store?
Select all the tracks on the album. Click **File**, and then select **New Playlist from Selection**. iTunes creates a new playlist containing all the tracks you selected. If the tracks are all from the same album, the name of the playlist is the name of the album.

Create a Smart Playlist

Standard playlists are great because you can easily create custom content collections, but you need to do some work to create and fill them. Why not let iTunes do the work for you? That is where a Smart Playlist comes in.

Instead of placing content into a playlist manually, you define the criteria for content and iTunes grabs the appropriate content from the library and places it into the Smart Playlist for you automatically.

Create a Smart Playlist

1. Open the **File** menu and select **New Smart Playlist**.

   The Smart Playlist dialog appears.

2. Select the first tag on which you want the Smart Playlist to be based in the Tag menu.

   For example, to include genre in the condition, select **Genre**.

3. Select the operator you want to use from the Operator menu, such as **is**, **is not**, or **contains**.

4. Type the condition you want to match in the Condition field.

   Your condition can include text or numbers.

5. To add another condition to the Smart Playlist, click **Add Condition** (⊕).

   A new, empty condition appears.

6. Select a second tag.

7. Select an operator.

8. Type a condition you want to match in the Condition field.

9. Repeat steps **5** to **8** until you have added all the conditions you want to include.

10. Select **all** from the pop-up menu at the top of the dialog if all the conditions must be met for a track to be included in the Smart Playlist, or select **any** if only one of them must be met.

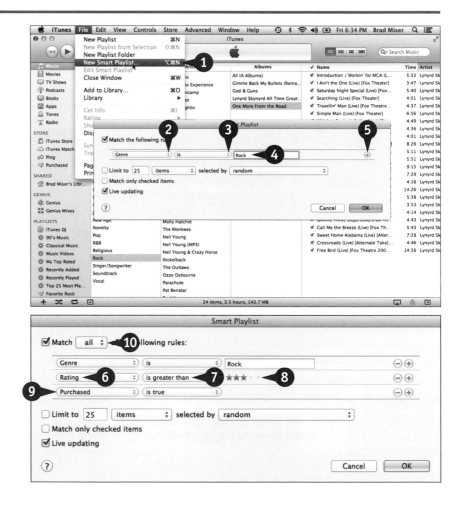

11 If you want to limit the size of the playlist, check the **Limit to** check box; if not, skip to step **15**.

12 Select the parameter by which you want to limit the playlist in the first menu, such as **items**.

13 Type an appropriate amount for the limit you specified in the Limit to field, such as the number of hours.

14 Select how you want iTunes to choose the songs it includes based on the limit in the **selected by** menu.

15 To include only tracks whose check box in the Content pane is selected, check the **Match only checked items** check box.

16 If you want iTunes to update its contents over time, check the **Live updating** check box.

17 Click **OK**.

A iTunes adds the Smart Playlist to the Source list, the tracks that meet the playlist's conditions are added to it, and its name is ready for you to edit.

18 Type the playlist's name and press **Return**.

The playlist is complete.

TIPS

How do I change the contents of a Smart Playlist?
If you want to change the contents of a Smart Playlist, you have to change the criteria for the list. To do so, click it again and select **Edit Smart Playlist**. Use the resulting Smart Playlist dialog to change the conditions; this changes the playlist's content. These playlists also change as content changes so it meets or no longer meets the criteria.

How can I drag the contents of a Smart Playlist onto another playlist to move it there?
The Smart Playlist does not actually contain the content you see or even pointers to that content, and so you cannot move tracks from a Smart Playlist to another playlist nor can you delete tracks.

Understanding How iOS Devices Work with a MacBook Pro

Apple iOS devices — iPhones, iPads, and iPod touches — are incredibly popular, and for good reason. They offer amazing functionality in small, extremely mobile devices. An iOS device (or two) makes an ideal companion for your MacBook Pro because you can easily share content that is stored on your MacBook Pro on an iOS device. For example, you can access the same e-mail messages using Mail on a MacBook Pro and the Mail app on an iOS device. You can think of an iOS device as an extension of your MacBook Pro.

iOS

iOS is the name of the software that runs iPads, iPhones, and iPod touches. It was the first major operating system that you control solely by using finger gestures on the screen. Since the iPhone was released, other manufacturers have imitated the iOS software because it has proven to be so well designed. A number of features of iOS have been incorporated into the OS X system software that runs your MacBook Pro, such as the trackpad gestures.

Synchronization

Synchronization keeps information on each device consistent with the most current version of that information. For example, when you add an event to the Calendar application on your MacBook Pro, you also want that event to appear in the Calendar app on an iOS device. There are a couple of ways to synchronize: using iTunes or through an online account, such as iCloud.

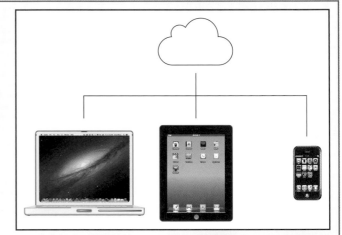

iTunes

In addition to all the great audio and video functionality that iTunes offers (as explained in Chapter 18), iTunes also enables you to work with iOS devices. You can use iTunes to synchronize information between your MacBook Pro and iOS devices. You can also use iTunes to maintain an iOS device through updates of the iOS software or to correct problems by restoring that software. And, connecting an iOS device to your MacBook Pro charges the device's battery.

iCloud

iCloud also works with iOS devices. The "cloud" provides online storage of information, documents, photos, and more that you can access with your MacBook Pro and iOS devices. This enables you to synchronize your computer and your iOS devices. The benefit of using iCloud for synchronization is that it is wireless so that you can use iCloud whenever you have an Internet connection. For more information about iCloud, see Chapter 10.

Other Online Services

iCloud is one of several online services that you can use with your MacBook Pro and an iOS device. Other services work similarly. For example, Microsoft Exchange is the most widely used e-mail and calendar system among businesses and large organizations. You can configure an Exchange account in the Mail application on your

MacBook Pro and iOS devices so that you can access your Exchange data from each one. Google offers similar features, including e-mail, calendar, and contacts.

Device Management

In addition to keeping information synchronized on iOS devices, you can also use your MacBook Pro and the iTunes application to manage your device. This includes keeping the

Version	
Check for Update	Your iPad software is up to date. iTunes will automatically check for an update again on 7/25/12.
Restore	If you are experiencing problems with your iPad, you can restore its original settings by clicking Restore.

operating system software current by updating it, solving problems on the device by restoring the software, and keeping the device's battery charged. You can also use iTunes to configure the Home screens and install and update the apps on an iOS device.

Use iTunes to Move Music onto an iPhone, iPod, or iPad

One of the great things about an iOS device and the iPods is that you can carry music with you and enjoy it wherever you go. Chapter 18 explains how to create a music library in iTunes on your MacBook Pro. You can move any music in your library onto an iOS device or iPod. Once there, you can use the device's Music app to listen to it. You can configure the specific music that you move onto an iOS device or iPod by choosing your entire library or by selecting playlists, artists, albums, and genres.

Use iTunes to Move Music onto an iPhone, iPod, or iPad

1 Connect your device to your MacBook Pro.

If iTunes is not open already, it launches after you connect the device.

2 In iTunes, select the device on the Source list.

3 Click the **Music** tab.

4 Select the **Sync Music** check box.

5 To move all of your music onto the device, select the **Entire music library** option and skip to step **13**; to choose specific content to copy, continue to step **6**.

Note: To move music videos in your collection or voice memos you have recorded onto the device, click the **Include music videos** and **Include voice memos** check boxes.

6 Select the **Selected playlists, artists, albums, and genres** option.

7 To have iTunes fill up any empty space on the device with music, click the **Automatically fill free space with songs** check box.

8 Click the check boxes for any playlists you want to move onto the device.

9 Click the check boxes for any artists whose music you want to move onto the device.

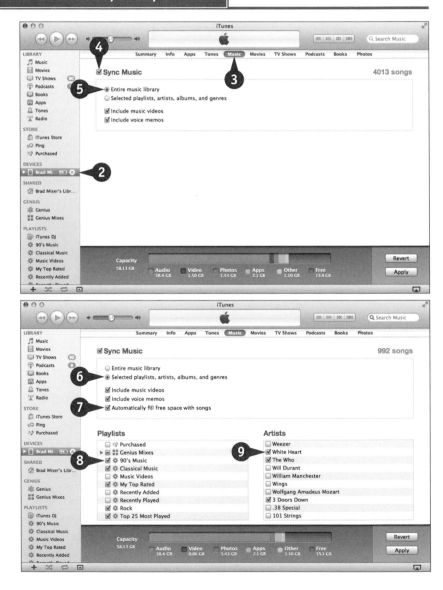

10 Scroll down the screen.

11 Click the check boxes for any genres whose music you want to copy onto the device.

12 Click the check boxes for any albums you want to copy onto the device.

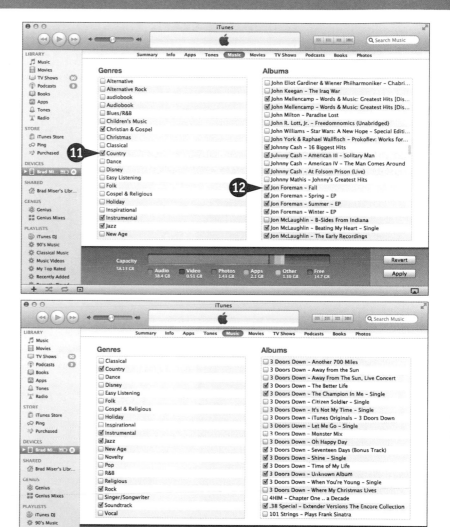

13 Click **Apply**.

iTunes copies the music you selected onto the device and you can use that device to listen to it.

Note: Every time you connect the device to your MacBook Pro, it will sync using the current settings.

How do I handle a message saying there is not enough space?
If you select more content than there is space on the device to store that content, you see a message saying so when you try to sync the device. If you selected your entire music library, choose the **Selected playlists, artists, albums, and genres** option and select less content. You can click the device's memory option at the bottom of the iTunes window.

How can I add music to my device over Wi-Fi?
You can sync an iOS device wirelessly by clicking the **Sync with this device over Wi-Fi** check box on the Summary tab and then clicking **Apply**. To sync the device, you can select it on the Source list and click **Sync**. You can also open the Settings app on the device, tap **General**, tap **iTunes Wi-Fi Sync**, and then tap **Sync Now**.

Use iTunes to Manage Apps and Home Screens on an iOS Device

One of the reasons iOS devices are so useful is the incredible amount and diversity of apps that you can run on them. You can use iTunes to download apps from the iTunes Store similarly to how you can download music and other content. After you have downloaded the apps to your MacBook Pro, you can copy them onto the device through the sync process. You can also use iTunes to update apps; the next time you sync the device, iTunes copies the updated apps onto the device.

Use iTunes to Manage Apps and Home Screens on an iOS Device

Use iTunes to Install Apps

1 Connect your iOS device to your MacBook Pro.

If iTunes is not open already, it launches after you connect the device.

2 In iTunes, select the iOS device on the Devices list.

3 Click the **Apps** tab.

On the left side of the window, you see the apps that are included in your iTunes library.

4 Select the **Sync Apps** check box.

5 Click the arrows and choose how you want iTunes to list the apps from the menu, such as **Sort by Kind**, **Sort by Name**, and so on.

6 Select the check boxes for the apps you want to install on the device.

7 Deselect the check boxes for the apps you do not want to install on the device.

8 Click **Apply**.

iTunes installs the apps you selected onto the device.

Use iTunes to Configure Home Screens

1 Connect your iOS device to your MacBook Pro.

If iTunes is not open already, it launches after you connect the device.

2 In iTunes, select the iOS device on the Devices list.

3 Click the **Apps** tab.

On the right part of the screen, you see the Home screen on the iOS device.

4 Select the **Sync Apps** check box.

5 To move an app onto a different screen, drag its icon from the screen where it is currently located onto the thumbnail of the screen where you want to place it.

6 When you have placed the icon on the correct screen, drop it.

7 To change the location of an app on a screen, drag its icon to its new location.

8 Click **Apply**.

The iOS device arranges the Home screens as you configured them to be.

TIPS

How do I create app folders?

To create a folder, drag one app icon on top of another and drop it. A new folder appears and opens; edit the default name of the folder if you want. Click outside the folder to close it. Drop more app icons onto the folder to add them to it.

How do I use iTunes to update my apps?

When updates are available for apps in your Library, you see the number available as a badge on the Apps icon on the Source list. Select **Apps**. Click the **xx Updates Available** link at the bottom of the window, where **xx** is the number of updates available. Click the **Download All Free Updates** link. The next time you sync the device, iTunes installs the update apps onto it.

Use Photo Stream to Synchronize Photos on iOS Devices

Current iOS devices have cameras, which is great because you almost always have a device with you and so you always have a camera. You can use iCloud Photo Stream to automatically upload photos you take on an iOS device to the cloud. From there, they can automatically download to other devices, including your MacBook Pro.

Chapter 10 provides the steps to set up your MacBook Pro to use Photo Stream. In addition to uploading photos you take on the device to the cloud, you can also download photos from your photo stream onto the iOS device.

Use Photo Stream to Synchronize Photos on iOS Devices

1 Tap **Settings** to open the Settings app.

2 Tap **iCloud**.

3 Tap **Photo Stream**.

4 Tap the **My Photo Stream** slider so its status is **ON**.

5 To enable share photo streams, set the **Shared Photo Streams** slider to **ON**.

Many of the apps available for iOS devices enable you to work with documents and data. You can use iCloud to synchronize documents and data to the cloud from where other devices can access those documents and data. Chapter 10 explains how to use iCloud to sync documents on your MacBook Pro.

Using iCloud to synchronize documents is useful because you always have the current versions of your documents available to you on all of your devices. This enables you to work on documents regardless of which device you happen to be using.

Use iCloud to Synchronize Documents on iOS Devices

1 Tap **Settings** to open the Settings app.

2 Tap **iCloud**.

3 Tap **Documents & Data**.

4 Tap the **Documents & Data** slider so its status is **ON**.

5 If you want to be able to move documents and data while the device is connected to a cellular network, set the **Use Cellular Data** slider to **ON**.

Note: Most cellular data plans have a limit on how much data you can transfer over the cellular network before incurring additional fees. If your account allows a limited amount of data, set **Use Cellular Data** to **OFF** so that you can only transfer documents and data when you are on a Wi-Fi network.

Index

A

AAC (Advanced Audio Coding) format, 334–335
access points, defined, 122
account mailbox folders, Mail, 216
Action pop-up menu, Finder windows, 34
Activity Monitor app, 304, 316
Administrator accounts, 9, 108
Adobe Acrobat app, 267
Adobe Reader app, 267
Advanced Audio Coding (AAC) format, 334–335
AIM (America Online Instant Messenger) accounts, 242
AirDrop feature, 136–137, 279
AirPlay, 153, 159
AirPort Express Base Station, 129, 164–165
AirPort Extreme Base Station, 121–122, 126–130, 134, 144
AirPort Utility, 121, 127–130, 164–165
alert notifications, 52, 55
aliases, defined, 69
Alternate function key, 5
America Online Instant Messenger (AIM) accounts, 242
analog/digital audio in/out ports, 6–7
antivirus apps, 131
Aperture, 185
App Exposé feature, 47, 89
App Store, 74, 300–301
Apple ID, 74, 111, 178, 242, 325
Apple Lossless format, 335
Apple Magic Mouse, 155
Apple MagSafe Airline Adapter, 169
Apple menu, 11
Apple Support website, 145, 321
Apple TV, 152–153, 159
application folders, 81, 357
Application icons, Dock, 13, 27
application installation discs, 71
Application Switcher, 47, 82
application windows
    displaying all open, 46
    expanding to Full Screen mode, 88
    managing multiple, 89
    minimizing, 82
    overview, 10, 25, 73
applications
    adding to desktops, 45
    configuring on Dock, 81
    disappearance from Dock after quitting, 81
    forcibly quitting hung, 83, 305, 318–319

    hiding, 82
    installing, 74–76
    Internet, 123
    launching, 45, 78–81
    managing through iTunes, 353, 356–357
    menus, 73
    overview, 72
    preferences for, 73
    quitting, 83
    reinstalling, 79
    removing, 79
    switching, 82–83
    updating, 75, 300–302, 357
attachments, e-mail, 217, 224–225, 236
audible notifications, 54–55, 106
audio
    adding audio CD content to iTunes, 334–335
    analog/digital audio in/out ports, 6–7
    Calendar event alerts, 287
    digital audio support, 159
    e-mail notification, 236
    from iTunes Store, converting protected (DRM) content, 341
    listening to via iTunes, 332
    muting sound, 5, 107, 236, 239–241, 247, 249
    podcasts, 342–343
    sound effects, 106
    sound input/output, 106–107
    streaming, 179
    syncing iOS devices, 354–355
    system volume, 107
    volume control, 5, 106–107, 159, 208, 240, 246–247
audio chat, Messages, 240, 246–247, 249, 252
Auto-Click folders, 207
AutoFill feature, Safari, 209
Avery mailing labels, 283

B

backing up data, 308–313
badge notifications, 54–55
balance, audio, 106
banner notifications, 52, 55
battery. *See* power management
Battery Status lights, 7
birthday information, displaying in Calendar, 293–294
Bluetooth
    keyboards, 156–157
    mice, 21, 154–155

Bonjour technology, 263
bookmarks
    changing location of in Bookmarks bar, 201
    creating, 200
    displaying address, 191
    navigating to websites via, 191–192
    one-click bookmark folders, 206
    organizing in folders, 201–203
    rearranging folders, 201–203
    storing in Bookmarks bar, 201
    temporary, 203
Bookmarks bar, Safari, 188, 191, 201, 207, 214
Bookmarks mode, Safari, 189, 192, 206
Browse mode, Safari, 188
burn folders, creating and organizing, 68–69
burning discs, 68–69

C

cable Internet connections, 122, 124–125
caching, 192
Calendar app
    accessing from other devices, 297
    accounts, 116–117
    birthday information, 293–294
    creating calendars, 285
    displaying calendars in web browser, 290, 292
    events, 286–289
    iCloud online storage, 177
    meeting availability, 297
    overview, 284
    preferences for, 294–295
    printing calendars, 296–297
    publishing calendars, 291
    sharing calendars, 290–293
camera (webcam), 4, 110, 248
Carbonite, 313
CDs. *See* optical discs
cellular broadband wireless modems, 166–167
Character Viewer, displaying in menu bar, 18
chat, 238–239. *See also* Messages app
clock, 11, 98–100
Collections feature, Safari, 189
color pickers, 27, 94–95
Column Browser, iTunes, 328–329
Column view, Finder windows, 30–31, 56
compressing files and folders, 59

Contacts app
    accounts, 116–117
    adding contacts, 270–273
    birthday information, 293
    browsing for contacts, 274
    changing cards, 280–281
    creating vCards, 273
    e-mail addresses, 223, 278
    groups, 269, 276–277, 281
    iCloud online storage, 177
    mapping physical addresses, 279
    overview, 268
    pocket address books, 283
    printing, 279, 282
    searching for contacts, 275
    sharing Contacts, 279
    visiting websites from, 278
contextual menus, 15, 38
Cover Flow view
    Finder windows, 32
    iTunes, 322, 330
    Safari, 189
CPU, monitoring, 304, 316

D

Dashboard
    accessing via Mission Control, 41–42
    configuring, 49
    opening, 48
    overview, 37
    widgets, 50–51
dates
    of received e-mail messages, 217
    relative, 28
    setting, 100–101
desktops
    adding apps to, 45
    background picture, 96–97
    configuring, 45
    creating, 43
    Dashboard, 37, 48–51
    defined, 37
    deleting, 43
    Dock, 13, 36, 38–39
    Finder windows, 11–12
    how many to use, 43
    installing apps from, 76

desktops *(continued)*
    launching apps from, 45, 80–81
    Launchpad, 37
    layout of, 10
    Mission Control, 36, 40–42, 44
    moving to locations, 56–57
    notifications, 52–55
    overview, 37
    Sidebar, 13
    switching, 44
    windows management, 46
Devices category, Sidebar, 13
dial-up Internet connections, 122, 125
Digital Rights Management (DRM) media, converting, 341
Digital Subscriber Line (DSL) Internet connections, 122, 124–125
disc drive, location of, 4
disk image files (.dmg), 196–197
Disk Utility app, 71, 146–149, 306–307
display
    brightness, 5, 102, 105
    color profile, 105, 151
    dimming when on battery power, 102
    external, 150–151
    overview, 4
    putting to sleep when inactive, 102–103
    resolution, 104–105
    screenshots, 320
    sharing screens, 142–143, 241, 252–253
.dmg (disk image files), 196–197
Dock
    adding folders to, 57
    applications that disappear from Dock after quitting, 81
    configuring apps on, 81
    defined, 13
    launching apps from, 80
    overview, 13, 36
Dock icons, 39
document windows, 10, 25
documents. *See also* printing
    deleting versioned, 87
    including in Messages text chat, 245
    launching apps from, 81
    overview, 72
    presenting through Messages app Theater feature, 251
    recovering, 85
    saving, 84–85
    storing online, 186–187

syncing, 359
    versioning, 84, 86–87
downloading files from web, 196–197
Downloads folder, 196–197
drives, 10, 16. *See also* hard drive
DRM (Digital Rights Management) media, converting, 341
DSL (Digital Subscriber Line) Internet connections, 122, 124–125
DVDs. *See* optical discs

E

Easy Envelopes widget, 279
Edit menu, 11
Eject icon, 13
ejecting discs, 5
e-mail
    accounts, 116–117, 218–219
    addressing from Contacts app, 278
    attachments, 224–225
    creating Contact cards from received, 273
    Dock icon, 216
    iCloud, 177
    organizing messages, 226–227
    overview, 216–218
    preferences for, 236–237
    reading messages, 220
    replying to messages, 221
    rules, 234–235
    searching for messages, 228–229
    sending contents of web pages, 211
    sending links to web pages, 210–211
    sending messages, 222–223
    sharing Contacts via, 273, 279
    signatures, 232–233
    spam, 230–231
    threading, 237
emoticons, Messages, 240
encrypting data, 170–171, 309
envelopes, printing, 279, 282
erasable discs, 69
Ethernet, defined, 121. *See also* wired networks
Ethernet port, 7, 121
expanding compressed files and folders, 59
external displays, 150–151
external hard drives
    backing up data to, 308–311
    compatible, 147
    connecting and powering, 146

connecting to, 10

formatting and partitioning, 146–149

interfaces, 147

external speakers, 107, 158–159

F

Fast User Switching, 11, 115

Favorites category, Sidebar, 13

Fetch app, 197

File Transfer Protocol (FTP), 193, 197

filename extensions, 58, 85, 91

files

compressing, 59

defined, 17

Dock icons for, 13

downloading from web, 196–197

expanding compressed, 59

in Finder windows, 11, 31, 56

finding, 60–62

getting information about, 66–67

icons for, 27

labels, 90–91

overview, 10, 17

renaming, 58

sharing, 141

storing on optical discs, 68–69

FileVault, 170–171

filtering searches, 60–61

Find My Mac feature, 177, 179

Finder app

colors, 94

finding files and folders with, 60–61

menu bar and menus, 11

preferences for, 90–91

Finder menu, 11

Finder windows

Action pop-up menu, 34

choosing start folder for, 91

layout of, 12, 24

overview, 10, 24

Quick Look command, 34

Sidebar configuration, 33

toolbar configuration, 35

views, 26–32

firewalls, 131, 173

FireWire 800 port, 7, 147

folders

accessing apps in, 79

adding to Dock, 39, 57

compressing, 59

defined, 17

Dock icons for, 13

expanding compressed, 59

expanding within window, 29

in Finder windows, 12, 31, 56

finding, 60–62

getting information about, 66–67

labels, 90–91

location of, displaying, 29

organizing bookmarks in, 201–203, 206, 207

organizing Launchpad with, 79

overview, 10, 17

renaming, 58

returning to recent, 57

sharing permissions, 139

sizes of, displaying, 28

Smart Folders, 64–65

spring-loaded, 90

storing on optical discs, 68–69

font smoothing, 94–95

forcibly quitting hung apps, 83, 305, 318–319

formatting external hard drives, 146–149

FTP (File Transfer Protocol), 193, 197

Full Screen mode

application windows, 88

FaceTime sessions, 239

iTunes Cover Flow view, 330

Messages video chat, 241

Quick Look window, 34

function keys, 18

G

Gatekeeper, 51

Genius playlists, iTunes, 346–347

gestures, 14–15, 20–21, 40, 44

Gmail, 219

Go menu, 11, 57

Google, 353

Grab app, 320

Grid view, iTunes, 323, 331

grouping Finder window items, 26–28, 30–31

Guest accounts, 9

H

hard drive
    available storage on, 305, 316
    external, 10, 146–149, 308–311
    maintaining or repairing, 306–307
    monitoring, 304–305
    recovering documents after crashes, 85
HDMI (High-Definition Multimedia Interface) port, 6
headphones, 158
Help menu, 11, 63
help resources, 63, 321
High-Definition Multimedia Interface (HDMI) port, 6
History feature, Safari, 192
Home Sharing feature, iTunes, 344–345
hot corners, 42, 71, 99
HTTP (Hyper Text Transfer Protocol), 193
HTTPS (Hyper Text Transfer Protocol Secure), 193
hubs, 122, 126, 160

I

iCloud accounts
    adding disk space to, 181
    configuring, 179
    e-mail, 219
    Messages app, 242
    obtaining, 178
    overview, 176
    sharing screen, 143
iCloud online services
    calendar storage, 177
    contact storage, 177
    document storage, 186–187
    e-mail, 177
    Find My Mac feature, 177
    overview, 176, 353
    Photo Stream feature, 184–185
    syncing via, 182–183, 359
    website, 176, 180–181
    Windows PCs and, 177
Icon view, Finder windows, 26–27
images
    in Contact cards, 271
    deleting from Photo Stream, 185
    as desktop backgrounds, 41
    of e-mail message senders, 217
    in e-mail signatures, 233
    as Finder window background, 27

including in Messages text chat, 245
    screenshots, 320
    sharing via Twitter, 255
    syncing, 358–359
    for user accounts, 110
Info window, 66–67
inkjet printers, 258, 263
installers, installing apps with, 76
Internet, defined, 120. *See also* wired networks; wireless networks
Internet accounts, defined, 122
Internet connections. *See* networking and Internet connections
Internet Protocol (IP) addresses, 123
Internet Service Providers (ISPs), 122
iOS devices (iPods, iPads, iPhones)
    accessing Calendar from, 297
    creating application folders on, 357
    iCloud, 187
    insufficient storage space on, 355
    iTunes, 326, 352–357
    overview, 352
    syncing to, 183, 191, 352, 354–355, 358–359
    third-party services, 353
IP (Internet Protocol) addresses, 123
iPhoto app, 71, 97, 184–185
ISPs (Internet Service Providers), 122
iTunes app
    application management, 353, 356–357
    audio content, 332, 334–335
    automatic retrieval of album information and cover art, 335
    browsing for content, 328
    burning optical discs from, 71
    categories, 326
    columns, widening, 329
    devices, 326
    Home Sharing feature, 344–345
    importing content automatically, 345
    overview, 322–323, 352
    playlists, 327, 346–351
    podcasts, 342–343
    searching for content, 329
    sharing library on local area networks, 345
    shortcut keys, 5
    syncing audio to iOS devices, 354–355
    tags, 327
    tracks, 326
    video content, viewing, 333
    views, 330–331

iTunes Match service, 179

iTunes Store

adding content to Wish List, 340–341

browsing for content, 336–337

creating playlists from downloaded content, 349

logging in to account, 336

obtaining accounts, 325

overview, 324

podcasts, finding, 342

previewing content, 338

purchasing and downloading content, 339–340

searching for content, 337–338

J

junk e-mail, 219, 230–231

K

key repeat preferences, 18

Keyboard Viewer, 18

keyboards

backlight brightness, 5, 18

Bluetooth, 156–157

layout of, 5

overview, 4

settings for, 18

shortcut configuration, 18–19

wired external, 157

L

LANs. *See* local area networks

laser printers, 258, 263

Launchpad, 5, 37, 78–79

links

navigating to websites via, 193

sending via e-mail, 210–211

using in e-mail signatures, 233

when to send, 211

List view

Finder windows, 28–29

iTunes, 323

local area networks (LANs)

configuring Base Station or Time Capsule, 126–129

defined, 120

expanding range of, 129, 133

installing Base Station or Time Capsule, 126

services provided through, 123

sharing files on, 138–141

sharing screens on, 142–143

logging in, 8–9, 108–111, 114–115

logging out, 22–23

M

MacBook Pro

exterior features of, 4

keyboard layout, 5

monitoring activity, 304–305

ports, 6–7

profiling, 303

restarting, 22

shutting down, 22

Sleep mode, 22

starting up, 8

storage, 16–17

troubleshooting, 316–319

Mail app. *See* e-mail

mailboxes, e-mail, 216, 226–227

mailing labels, printing, 279, 283

Managed with Parental Controls accounts, 110

mapping physical addresses, 279

menu bar, 10–11, 96

menus

application, 73

contextual, 15, 38

Finder, 11

Messages app

accounts, 242–243

audio chat, 246–247

avoiding chat requests, 247

overview, 240–241

sharing Contacts via, 279

sharing documents via Theater feature, 251

sharing screens, 252–253

text chat, 244–245

video chat, 248–250

mice, 21, 154–155

microphones, 246

Microsoft Exchange, 353

MiFi device, 166

Mini DisplayPort adapter, 150

mirroring, AirPlay, 153

Mission Control

browsing closed windows, 47

configuring desktops, 45

Mission Control *(continued)*
    creating desktops, 43
    deleting desktops, 43
    opening, 5
    overview, 36
    switching apps, 83
    switching desktops, 44
    windows management, 36, 46
modems, 144, 166–167
modifier keys, 5, 18
mouse, 21, 154–155
muting sound
    e-mail notifications, 236
    FaceTime sessions, 239
    from keyboard, 5
    Messages audio chat, 240, 247
    Messages video chat, 241, 249
    from System Preferences, 107

N

NAT (network address translation), 130, 165
networking and Internet connections
    AirPort, 121
    audio and video chat, 243
    Ethernet, 121, 134–135
    hubs/routers/access points, 122
    Internet, defined, 120
    Internet accounts, 122, 124–125
    Internet Service Providers, 122
    Internet services and apps, 123
    IP addresses, 123
    local area networks, 120, 123, 126–129
    networks, defined, 120
    security, 123, 130–131
    sharing files, 136–141
    sharing screens, 142–143
    troubleshooting, 144–145
    Wi-Fi, 121, 132–133
No Access permission, 139
notifications
    alerts, 52
    banners, 52
    configuring, 54–55
    disabling, 55
    displaying in Notification Center, 53
    identifying new, 53
    sorting, 53–54
    website, 215

O

optical discs (CDs and DVDs)
    adding audio CD content to iTunes, 334–335
    defined, 17
    erasable, 69
    overview, 17
    storage capacity of, 69
    storing files and folders on, 68–69

P

Pages app, 186–187
parental controls, 112–113
Password Assistant feature, 109
passwords
    AirPort Base Station, 129
    forgotten, 9, 171
    hints, 114
    keeping record of, 319
    logging in with, 9
    PDF file, 266–267
    requiring on restart or wakeup, 172
    resetting with Apple ID, 111
    user account, 108–109, 111
    wireless network, 127
Path bar, 12, 29
PDF (Portable Document Format) files, 259, 266–267
Photo Stream feature, iCloud, 184–185, 358–359
photos. *See* images
Pictures folder, 97
playlists, iTunes, 327, 346–351
pocket address books, 283
podcasts, 342–343
Portable Document Format (PDF) files, 259, 266–267
ports, 4, 6–7
power adapter port, 6–7
Power button, 5, 8
power management
    configuration to minimize power usage, 168
    monitoring battery life, 168–169
    power toolkit, 169
    preferences, setting, 102–103
Preview app, 267
printers
    compatible, 261
    connecting to, 259

inkjet, 258, 263

installing and configuring, 260–263

laser, 258, 263

sharing, 259

printing

calendars, 296–297

contact lists, 282

envelopes, 279, 282

finding Mac drivers, 261

mailing labels, 279, 283

monitoring and controlling, 265

only specific pages, 265

to paper, 264–265

to PDF, 259, 266–267

protocols, 120

Q

Quick Look command, Finder windows, 34

R

Read & Write permission, 139–140, 291

Read Only permission, 139–140, 291

Reading List feature, Safari, 212–213

recent items menu, 65, 95

recovering

deleted e-mail messages, 221

documents after crashes, 85

Recovery HD volume, 306

recovery keys, 170–171

reinstalling removed apps, 79

relative dates, 28

Reminders app, 298–299

restarting MacBook Pro, 22, 316–317

restoring

files with Time Machine, 314–315

previous versions of documents, 86–87

routers, 122, 126

rules, e-mail, 234–235

S

Safari web browser

bookmarks, 200–203

downloading files, 196–197

filling web forms with AutoFill, 209

modes, 188–189

navigating to websites, 190–193

opening multiple web pages, 206–207

preferences for, 214–215

Reading List feature, 212–213

saving web pages, 210

searching web, 194–195

sharing web pages, 210–211

switching web pages, 193

tabbed browsing, 198–199

Top Sites feature, 204–205

viewing movies on web, 208

satellite Internet connections, 122, 124

Saved Searches folder, 65

screen savers, 98–99

Screen Sharing app, 142–143

screenshots, 320

SDXC (Secure Digital eXtended Capacity) card port, 6–7

Search bar

Calendar app, 284

Contacts app, 268

defined, 12

Finder windows, 24, 60

iTunes app, 322, 329

iTunes Store, 337

search engines, 194–195, 214

Secure Digital eXtended Capacity (SDXC) card port, 6–7

security

FileVault data protection, 170–171

firewalls, 131, 173

Internet and network, 123, 129–131

leaving account logged in, 115

logging out, 23

overview, 172

spam, 219, 230–231

web browser, 215

Shared category, Sidebar, 13, 140

sharing

calendars, 290–293

Contact cards, 279

documents, 251

files, 136–141

iTunes content, 344–345

printers, 259

screens, 142–143, 241, 252–253

web pages, 210–211

Sharing & Permissions section, Info window, 67

shutting down MacBook Pro, 22–23

Sidebar, Finder windows

adding apps to, 80

configuring, 33

Sidebar, Finder windows (continued)
    defined, 12
    launching apps from, 80
    overview, 13, 24
    preferences for, 91
signatures, e-mail, 232–233
SIT files, 197
Sleep Indicator light, 4
Sleep mode, 22, 102–103, 169
slideshows, 96, 98
Smart Folders, 64–65
Smart Groups, Contacts, 269, 277, 281
Smart Mailboxes, Mail, 216, 227, 229
Smart Playlists, iTunes, 350–351
sound. See audio
sound effects, 106
spaces. See desktops
spam, 219, 230–231
speakers, external, 107, 158–159
spelling correction, Mail, 223, 237
Spotlight Comments section, Info window, 67
Spotlight feature, 61–63, 229
Spotlight menu, Finder windows, 11
spring-loaded folders and windows, 90
Standard accounts, 9, 108, 110
standard menus, 73
Standard playlists, iTunes, 348–349
starting up MacBook Pro, 8
Status bar, 12
status information, 24
storage. See also iCloud online services
    drives, 16
    of e-mail messages, 219, 226–227, 229
    on external hard drives, 146–149
    of files and folders, 17, 68–69
    on iOS devices, insufficient, 355
    on optical discs, 17, 68–69
    overview, 16
    volumes, 16
streaming music, 179
StuffIt Expander app, 197
SuperDrive, 10
switches, defined, 122
syncing
    audio, 354–355
    bookmarks, 191

    documents, 359
    images, 358–359
    information among multiple devices, 182–183
    to iOS devices, 183, 191, 352, 354–355, 358–359
    overview, 183, 352
    photos via Photo Stream, 358
    via iCloud online services, 182–183, 359
    wirelessly, 355
System Information app, 303, 317
System Preferences app
    Administrator accounts, 93
    displaying panes alphabetically, 93
    opening and using, 92
    searching for panes, 93

T

tabbed browsing, Safari, 188, 198–199
tags, iTunes, 327
text chat, Messages, 240, 243–245
threading e-mail messages, 237
three-finger dragging gesture, 21
Thunderbolt port, 6–7, 147, 150
time
    of received e-mail messages, 217
    setting, 100–101
Time Capsule
    backing up data wirelessly, 312–313
    configuring, 126–127
    duration of backups, 313
    installing, 126
    status lights, 144
    wired connections, 134
time limits, Parental Controls, 113
Time Machine app
    backing up data with, 308–311
    determining when last backup was made, 311
    duration of backups, 311
    restoring files with, 314–315
time zones, 100–101, 295
toolbar
    application windows, 25
    Contacts, 268
    Finder windows, 12, 24, 35
    Mail, 216
Top Sites feature, Safari, 188, 204–205
TOSLINK adapter, 159

trackpad
    configuring, 19
    gestures, 14–15
    overview, 4
tracks, iTunes, 326
Trash, 13, 91
troubleshooting
    determining extent of problem, 317–318
    finding cause of problem, 316–317
    hung app problems, 318–319
    networking and Internet connections, 144–145
    start up problems, 319
TV
    using Apple TV to display on, 152–153
    viewing shows via iTunes, 333
Twitter, 254–255

U

updating software
    App Store, 75, 300–301
    importance of, 301
    on iOS devices using iTunes, 357
    third-party, 302
URLs, navigating to websites via, 190
USB hubs, 160
USB port, 6–7, 147
user accounts, 8–9, 108–111
User List, logging in with, 8–9
usernames, 8–9, 108, 319

V

vCards, 269, 272–273. *See also* Contacts app
versioning documents, 84, 86–87
video
    moving to iOS devices, 354
    podcasts, 342–343
    renting, 339
    usage restrictions, 339
    viewing movies and TV shows via iTunes, 333
    viewing on web, 208
video chat
    FaceTime app, 238–239
    Messages app, 241, 248–251
View menu, 11
viruses, 131

volume
    controlling, 5, 106–107, 208
    external speakers, 159
    Messages audio chat, 240, 246–247
volumes, 16

W

web browsing. *See* Safari web browser
webcam, 4, 110, 248
widgets, 37, 48–51
Wi-Fi, defined, 121, 163. *See also* wireless networks
Window menu, 11
windowed processes, 305
windows
    managing with Mission Control, 36, 46
    overview, 73
    spring-loaded, 90
Windows menu, 89
Windows PCs, 177
wired networks
    connecting to devices, 161
    Ethernet, defined, 121
    multiple active connections, 135
    public, 163
    reasons for using, 135
wireless networks
    cellular broadband wireless modems, 166–167
    connecting Macs through, 133
    connecting to, 162–165
    determining strength of, 133
    expanding range of, 129, 133
    moving iTunes content to iOS devices, 355
    multiple active connections, 135
    public, 125, 162–163
    Wi-Fi, defined, 121, 163
Wish List feature, iTunes Store, 340–341
Write Only (Drop Box) permission, 139

Y

Yahoo! e-mail, 219

Z

zip files, 59, 197